Writing

Words

Reading

Spelling

TEACHER'S GUIDE

Louise Skinner

Dianne Tucker - LaPlount

RED VAN PUBLISHERS, San Diego, CA 92103

WORDS: Writing, Reading, Spelling
Teacher's Guide

ISBN 1-884896-05-7

This book was previously published by Pearson Education, Inc., formerly known as Prentice Hall. Inc. 1993

Red Van Publishers
San Diego, CA 92103

Dedication

To Bette Farnsworth, who introduced us, and whose contributions in time and effort and heart have furthered the cause of literacy for all age groups in the greater San Diego area.

Acknowledgements

We gratefully acknowledge the professional advice and assistance
we received from our friend and colleague, Phyllis J. Gillespie.

We also appreciate the helpful input of our associates,
Lynda J. Balkam and Pat Robison.

We thank the many volunteer literacy tutors and literacy network
coordinators with whom we have been privileged to work
for enthusiastically supporting this program.

We are especially indebted to all of our students.
Over the years, they have given us the opportunity to test
learning theories and develop instructional strategies
that are effective in teaching adults and older adolescents.

Finally we must declare our gratitude to our husbands
for their remarkable understanding and good humor
in bearing with us through this long project.

Contents

SECTION V

SECTION I

Introduction

An incredibly large number of adults and adolescents in our country have not learned to read and write well enough to function effectively as job holders, consumers, or otherwise active members of a complex society. These are yesterday's children who lagged further and further behind during their school years, even though they are of average or above-average intelligence.

Today they belong to, or soon may join, the ranks of the functionally illiterate. These individuals number an estimated 27 million in the United States and, according to the U.S. Department of Education, this number grows by 2.25 million each year.

Almost all functionally illiterate adults can learn to read and write, but their way of acquiring language skills is not the same as that of the average person. Conventional classroom methods did not work for them. They learn differently. *WORDS: Writing, Reading, Spelling* is designed especially for them.

The *WORDS* program was developed by two educators with training in multisensory instructional methods and a combined 34 years of experience in educational therapy, program development, and classroom teaching of adults and older adolescents.

The authors' aim has been to produce an effective, easy-to-use literacy program for adult continuing education instructors as well as volunteer tutors and secondary school teachers. Materials include:

- four Student Books
- a short novel (a supplement to Books Three and Four)
- a Teacher's Guide
- Mastery Reviews (tests) for each of the four levels

There is a general progression in reading difficulty over the four Student Books, beginning at more or less second grade equivalency and increasing gradually to about fifth grade equivalency. This progression is based on language structure, spelling patterns, and letter-sound relationships. No attempt has been made to match each Student Book with a specific grade level.

Material is introduced in carefully ordered steps, with each new lesson building on previous lessons. The tightly structured format helps learners to grasp and remember better. Continual review is provided.

In this program, the writing, reading, and spelling components are integrated. Skill development in word recognition, vocabulary, spelling, sentence writing, and reading comprehension progresses concurrently.

The program provides multisensory teaching techniques—procedures that use, simultaneously, the visual, auditory, and tactile/kinesthetic pathways to the brain. Most literacy students learn better if they see, hear, say, and write at the same time, whenever possible.

The goal is to help learners to understand the nature of their language: the structure of its words and sentences, its letter-sound relationships, its spelling system. They will learn to write well-constructed sentences and to better comprehend reading materials. On this firm foundation, they can continue to build their skills in writing, reading, and spelling.

Format of the Student Books

Each regular lesson in the Student Books follows a similar format. The following lesson parts are explained briefly on the next three pages.

INTRODUCTION OF NEW MATERIAL

PRACTICE EXERCISES

SIGHT WORDS AND EXCEPTIONS

WORD FOCUS (Books One and Two only)

PHONICS REVIEW

AFFIX REVIEW (Books Three and Four only)

SYLLABLE REVIEW (Books Three and Four only)

SENTENCE FOCUS

DICTATION

Four Mastery Review tests, one for each section, are located at the end of each Student Book. They are perforated for easy removal.

INTRODUCTION OF NEW MATERIAL

Each new lesson in Student Books One, Two, Three, and Four builds on previous lessons. New material is introduced by the teacher, who reads aloud all explanations and directions in the lesson itself under the heading *Read with the Teacher.*

Where the Student Book is not self-explanatory, this guide offers suggestions on how to introduce new material.

PRACTICE EXERCISES

Practice exercises vary in each lesson. Their purpose is to reinforce new material; provide review; sharpen visual, auditory, and writing skills; enrich vocabulary, and develop reading comprehension. With a few unavoidable exceptions, no sound or spelling pattern is used in lesson exercises until it has been formally introduced.

Vocabulary enrichment includes exercises using compound words, definitions, synonyms, antonyms, context, crossword puzzles, homophones, prefixes and suffixes, and word origins.

Comprehension skill development comprises activities in following directions, closure, sequencing, categorizing, identifying incorrect words in sentences, and drawing inferences. Proverbs, paragraphs, and longer passages give practice in oral reading and discussion to stimulate critical thinking. A separate reader in novelette form, designed to complement Student Books Three and Four, develops comprehension skills in depth.

SIGHT WORDS AND EXCEPTIONS

Sight words are introduced a few at a time in boxes labeled "Mavericks." These words are not spelled the way they sound; they are not phonetic. (For example, if words such as **was** and **of** were phonetically regular, they would be spelled "wuz" and "uv".) In this program, sight words are not lumped in with the phonetically-regular words but are singled out ahead of time to be memorized as visual wholes. (An easy-to-teach *Sight Word Study Method* is given in this Guide, page 165.)

Some lessons in the Student Books include words in boxes labeled "Exceptions." These words are phonetic but do not follow general spelling rules (e.g., **bus** instead of "buss").

WORD FOCUS (Books One and Two only)

A Word Focus exercise is included in most regular lessons in the first two Student Books. This activity is done orally.

The words in the Word Focus box contain the same patterns as those studied in the current lesson or earlier lessons. The teacher asks students a series of questions about each word. Students learn to respond by "breaking down" a word into parts by sound and letter names (analysis) and "building up" a word in the same way (synthesis). Later the emphasis shifts to syllables, root words, and affixes.

A teacher's script for all Word Focus exercises, including anticipated student responses, begins on page 19 of this Guide.

PHONICS REVIEW

In Books One and Two, Phonics Review follows Word Focus. The Phonics Review page has three parts: decoding, listening, and spelling. These activities use isolated syllables which are spelled the way they sound: **stim**, **traf**, **lect**. Practice with syllables, or "nonsense words," requires learners to decode and spell by sound instead of relying on visual memory.

In Books Three and Four, the Phonics Review exercises use only real words. As new sound and spelling patterns are introduced, emphasis is placed on students' ability to match what they hear with what they see on paper.

AFFIX REVIEW (Books Three and Four only)

In this exercise, toward the end of each regular lesson in Books Three and Four, affixes (prefixes and suffixes) are reviewed. At the same time, students get continual practice using the basic spelling rules they have learned, an important help in building spelling confidence.

Affix Review helps learners maintain and consolidate skills that they have been taught about root (base) words and affixes. They become aware that a long word often is just a root word with affixes added to it.

SYLLABLE REVIEW (Books Three and Four only)

This activity follows Afflix Review in Student Books Three and Four. Syllable Review trains learners to pay close attention to the arrangement of letters in words. The aim is to bring learners to the point where they can automatically divide and pronounce a word.

The syllable Review page is made up of three parts: (1) Both Student Books contain an exercise that requires students to apply the rules of syllable division, mark vowel sounds, and place the accent mark. Familiarity with accent, or stress, helps in pronouncing long words, using a phonetic pronunciation guide, and applying the Double Rule for Two-syllable words. (2) Student Book Three gives practice in dictionary pronunciation; Student Book Four gives practice pronouncing multisyllable words. (3) Both Student Books include two-syllable word diction.

SENTENCE FOCUS

A Sentence Focus exercise is included in each regular lesson of all four Student Books. This activity develops sentence writing skills while strengthening comprehension at the sentence level.

In the first four exercises in Student Book One, an oral question-and-answer procedure introduces to learners the normal order of words that make up a sentence. The grid that appears in Lesson 7 becomes a regular feature for developing sentence writing. The grid shows learners that sentences have "slots" for different types of words and phrases. Question words such as *Who?*, *What?*, and *When?* provide a guide for classifying the parts of a sentence and help learners build their own well-constructed sentences. The grid expands as new headings such as *Where?* and *How?* are added.

In Student Book Four, learners are guided toward independent sentence writing without the grid.

DICTATION

Each regular lesson of the four Student Books ends with Dictation. This activity reinforces spelling and listening skills and provides a model for correct sentence and/or paragraph writing.

The dictations are designed to help learners succeed in the complex task of writing spoken words with few or no errors. Words and word groups are dictated first as a warm-up for sentence dictation. Only words that fit the current or previous lessons are used. Sight words are italicized in Student Book One dictations, alerting the teacher or tutor to remind learners that these are words that do not follow the rules of phonics.

Complete dictations are provided in this Guide (see pages 67-158) along with optional exercises for extra practice.

Questions Asked by Teachers and Tutors

Is WORDS: Writing, Reading, Spelling *for classroom use or for one-to-one tutoring?*

Both. The *WORDS* program is being used successfully with entire classes as well as small groups and in one-to-one tutoring sessions.

What type of learners benefit from this program?

In seven years of field testing, the *WORDS* program has been found to be effective in adult basic education classes, community volunteer tutoring programs, and high school remedial classes. Teachers in advanced ESL (English as a Second Language) adult programs also use *WORDS* with students who speak fluent English, but have difficulty with reading and writing.

Is the program suitable for beginners?

The answer depends on what is meant by "beginners." Very few adults and older adolescents in our society bring a "zero" background to the task of learning to read, write, and spell. What knowledge they do have is often fragmented and disorganized. Learners entering this program at the level of Student Book One generally should be able to:

- accurately match all or most of the consonant sounds of English with the consonant letters;
- write a rudimentary sentence;
- spell at second-through-fourth grade* equivalency on a standardized test of dictated words;
- read at second grade* equivalency or above. For higher-level readers, the spelling (not the reading) score should be the determining factor.

Are tests provided with this program?

Yes. Each Student Book is divided into four parts, with a Mastery Review at the end of each part. You'll find the Mastery Reviews in a perforated section at the back of each Student Book.

Isn't this program too easy for learners who can read but are poor spellers?

Better readers usually zoom through the reading portions of the program; they focus most of their efforts on developing spelling and writing. Decoding syllables, however, captures the immediate interest of adults and older adolescents who read at higher levels. This activity begins in Lesson 2 of Book One.

"Poor spellers," no matter how advanced their reading level, benefit greatly from the systematic training in word structure, phonics, spelling rules, and sentence writing and the intensive dictation practice that *WORDS* provides. Spelling and writing confidence improves, and so does reading rate!

How do I decide where to start a class or learner in the Student Books?

Most learners have gaps to fill at the beginning level and should start with Book One. However, a learner may be ready to start in Book Two if he or she can:

- easily identify and pronounce the short vowel sounds, and
- correctly apply the Silent **e** Spelling Rule (for example, **file** + **ing** = **filing** and **smoke** + **y** = **smoky**).

The reviews at the beginning of Books Two, Three, and Four may also be used as guides for appropriate placement.

---

* "Grade levels" are generally accepted as a standard literacy measurement for adults. However, reading, writing, and spelling skills vary greatly and depend on the adult's life experiences; i.e., environment, interests, occupation, etc.

How much lesson planning is required?

The chore of preparing lesson plans is practically eliminated. The Student Books keep the teacher or tutor going in the right direction. Scripts for the Word Focus exercises, as well as all dictations, are provided in this Guide.

If many learners can't read well, how can they be expected to read the directions in the Student Books?

You're right—we can't assume that learners will be able to read the directions or some of the background information in the Student Books. For this reason, most of the directions in the early Student Books begin with the instruction to *Read with the Teacher* (or sometimes *Work with the Teacher*). This alerts the teacher or tutor to read aloud while students follow along silently, which saves the students embarrassment and frustration.

Is it all right to skip "easy" sections of the Student Books?

Generally speaking, no, because each lesson builds on previous lessons. Also, students may have been taught a particular concept or skill in the past, but cannot apply it successfully. It often happens, too, that individuals are able to recognize and pronounce a word but not spell it.

Is cursive writing taught in this program?

No. That choice is left to the individual learner and teacher or tutor.

If your students opt for training in cursive, we suggest you set aside a regular time during each teaching session for cursive practice. There is a wide variety of published material available to help you structure these lessons. Cambridge Book Company's *Entering the Reader's World* contains a good introduction to both print and cursive writing.

Why does this program attach importance to dividing words into syllables?

Students find reading and spelling longer words less threatening once they learn strategies for dividing words into parts and "sounding them out," one syllable at a time. This procedure forces students to look closely at the arrangement of letters in words. They learn which letter sequences are likely to form a sound unit (**mid** in **middle**) and which are not (**adm** in **admit**).

Research shows that good readers automatically divide longer words into syllables. Learners who are trying to improve their reading need to practice this skill until it becomes automatic for them, too.

When are reading comprehension skills introduced?

Almost immediately. Many literacy students have difficulty comprehending at the sentence level—they don't understand that every sentence has a main idea and that most sentences contain supporting details (extra words, phrases, and/or clauses). The Sentence Focus activity in the Student Books serves two purposes: (1) to help learners write cohesive sentences, and (2) to increase their comprehension skills. As sentence writing skills improve, so does reading comprehension.

Various types of comprehension skill-development exercises are introduced early and are gradually expanded in scope and difficulty as the program progresses. Interpretive and critical thinking skills are emphasized in a high-interest comprehension reader (a short novel), designed to complement Student Books Three and Four.

With 15 to 25 students in an adult education or high school classroom, how can a teacher reach all the students who have special needs in reading, writing, and spelling?

In using *WORDS* to reach all literacy students in a large class, one effective approach is through cooperative learning groups. A group may include as few as two or as many as six learners. This allows the teacher to spend time with one group for direct instruction and demonstration and then move on to another group. For specialized instruction, the teacher can form a large group from three or four smaller groups. Meanwhile, the students within a group work together and help one another. When a new learner joins the class, the teacher introduces him or her to the most appropriate group. (Watch group dynamics take place! Members of the group will take the new member under their wings and become tutors themselves.)

Do the four Student Book levels correspond to grade levels?

The reading material in *WORDS* Student Book One begins at about second grade equivalency. Throughout the series, word length, sentence length, and sentence complexity increase so that students completing Student Book Four are at approximately fifth grade equivalency.

Some learners are in a hurry and want to know just enough about reading and writing to fill out job application forms or pass a driver's license test. Is this program for them?

Unfortunately, no. The *WORDS* program has been carefully designed to help learners become accurate, independent readers and writers. Introduction of material is systematic and cumulative; there are no short cuts, no "quick fixes." Mastery learning is the goal. Perhaps the learners you describe will come back to you later, realizing that they need the basic skills after all.

Does this program offer chronological, page-by-page teaching suggestions?

No, it doesn't. But it does give you all the help you will need. In the *Getting Started* section below, you will find practical suggestions on how to lead students page-by-page through the first three lessons. These three lessons lay the foundation for the entire *WORDS* program.

Getting Started

A Student Book and a pencil are the only materials a learner needs to begin this program. The program is organized in a way that makes it easy to guide students through the lessons.

Most of the directions in the Books begin with the instruction *Read with the Teacher*. This instruction is a signal for you to read out loud while learners follow along silently. Some learners may not be able to read the directions on their own.

If learners are likely to need specific help with an exercise, the instruction will be worded *Work with the Teacher*. Obviously some individuals need much more help than others. Higher-level readers, who are using the program to improve their spelling and writing skills, may zoom through many of the Student Book pages on their own. For this reason, it is important to group your students if you are teaching in a classroom environment.

Where learners are directed to pronounce word lists or read sentences, group reading (reading together out loud) is recommended. In a group situation, unison reading and responses involve all the students—they reinforce each other. Everyone is participating; everyone is learning. And no one is embarrassed by being singled out to read aloud.

One-to-one oral reading practice is recommended, of course, between the student and teacher or tutor whenever possible.

Shortly after you begin Book One, you may want to start using some multisensory teaching techniques. The page-by-page descriptions of the first three lessons suggest when to introduce the first basic multisensory drills; however, this is not mandatory. Give yourself a chance to become familiar with the drills before using them. As you progress through the first book, you will probably rely more and more on these short drills because multisensory teaching can work wonders for many literacy students.

Moderate pacing—neither rushing through nor presenting material too slowly—holds student interest. Research shows that students retain information better if lessons are paced at a moderate rate, allowing time for ample practice and review.

To feel comfortable in teaching this program, you should have a basic knowledge of phonics. You may want to refer to the Phonics Overview section in this Guide from time to time. (See page 176.)

PRESENTING THE FIRST THREE LESSONS

Lessons 1, 2, and 3 of Student Book One lay the foundation for the entire *WORDS* program. Following are page-by-page suggestions for introducing these three lessons.

Lesson 1, page 1

This first page familiarizes learners with the words *consonant* and *vowel*. They need to feel comfortable with the meaning and pronunciation of these terms as they progress through the program.

Lesson 1, page 2

Check to make sure students can write the alphabet without omitting letters, reversing the order of letters, or reversing any letters themselves (for example, **d** for **b** or **p** for **q**). They may refer to page 1 to complete this exercise, if necessary.

Individuals who are not fluent in reciting and writing the alphabet should be drilled on a few letters at a time until they have mastered the entire alphabet.

Even if they can recite and write the alphabet from memory, learners may have difficulty completing the basic closure exercise on the bottom half of this page. Help them to complete this page, and tell them that they may refer to page 1 if they wish.

Lesson 1, page 3

This exercise serves two purposes: to be certain that students can identify letters as vowels and consonants, and to discover possible reversals and inversions that students may make when reciting the letters for you. (With learners who have difficulty with letter reversals or inversions, see the *Visual-Motor Patterning* technique on page 168 of this Guide.)

Lesson 1, page 4

Before starting on page 4, introduce the concept that *letters represent sounds*. Some new learners simply do not realize that each letter of the alphabet is intended to represent a sound and that some letters represent more than one sound.

The procedure that follows helps to establish the concept of letter-sound relationships:

> Writing the letter **a** on the board or sheet of paper, say, "You probably know the name of this letter. Its *NAME* is **a**. The letter **a** has two main *SOUNDS*. These sounds are called the short sound and the long sound. The short sound of the letter **a** is / ă /. Say that sound."
>
> (The student or class repeats / ă /.)
>
> Say, "You can hear this sound at the beginning of words such as **apple**, **accident**, **afternoon**, or **actor**."
>
> (Have the student or class repeat the four words after you, stressing the short sound of **a**.)
>
> Say, "The other main sound of the letter **a** is the long sound. The long sound is the same as the name of the letter in the alphabet. The *NAME* of the letter is **a** and the long *SOUND* is / ā /. You can hear this sound at the beginning of words such as **April**, **ape**, **apron**, or **acorn**."
>
> (Have the student or class repeat the four words, stressing the long sound of **a**.)
>
> Point to the letter on the board or sheet of paper. "The name of this letter is **a**. It has two main sounds, / ă / and / ā /."
>
> Next, write the letter **b** on the board or paper. Ask, "What sound does this letter represent?"
>
> The student or class may at first give the letter's name rather than its sound. If so, say: "The *name* of the letter is **b**. Can you tell me the *sound* it represents?"
>
> (Student or class responds: / b /.)
>
> "Right! The letter **a** has two main sounds — / ă / and / ā /. The letter **b** has only one sound — / b /. You can hear this sound at the beginning of **boss** or **budget** and at the end of **rib** or **grab**."

If the concept is clear to the student or class, go on to *Read with the Teacher* on page 4. Say the *SOUNDS* of these 16 consonant letters:

1. / d /	5. / n /	9. / h /	13. / r /
2. / z /	6. / k /	10. / v /	14. / s /
3. / b /	7. / m /	11. / f /	15. / p /
4. / j /	8. / t /	12. / l /	16. / w /

Learners must be able to write the correct letter for each of these consonant sounds automatically. Make a note of any sound a learner is unsure of. You can teach any consonant sound at the same time that you introduce the multisensory technique, *Short Vowel Drill*, page 162 of this Guide.

Next, guide students through the activity on the bottom half of page 4.

Lesson 2, page 5

Before starting Lesson 2, introduce the concept that *vowels give voice to words*.

Identifying the vowel sound is the key to success in sounding out and spelling phonetically-regular words. Learners need to be made aware of the special function of the vowel.

Begin by reminding them that 21 of the alphabet's 26 letters are consonants. Only five letters—and sometimes six, when we include the **y**—are vowels. The following procedure introduces the teaching point that vowels give "voice" to words:

Ask, "Why do we need vowels? Let me demonstrate."

Write the following sentence on the chalkboard:

A fat cat sat on my foot.

Ask for a volunteer to read the sentence out loud. After a student reads the sentence, say, "Now I'll take away the vowels. Listen to how this sentence sounds without them."

Erase or cross out the vowels and read:

ft ct st n m ft.

The result is a series of sputters, hums, and hisses. Ask students why vowels are needed. They will be able to answer, in their own words, that without vowels there is almost no sound to words—vowels give "voice" to words.

Guide students through page 5. Pronounce the short vowels and have students repeat after you. Encourage them to start memorizing the key words. Key words help them to remember the sounds of the short vowels.

Lesson 2, page 6

Guide students through the activity at the top of the page.

Before starting the bottom half of this page, introduce the concept that *longer words can be broken into syllables*.

Try this age-old method of introducing the idea of syllables:

Say, "A syllable is a word or part of a word that has one vowel sound. How many syllables does each of you have in your own name? For example, the name **Jill** has one syllable; the name **Tony** has two syllables, or parts: **To - ny**. **Alexander** has four syllables: **Al - ex - an - der**." Pronounce each student's name in turn and ask the student how many syllables his or her name contains.

Tell learners that longer words can always be divided into parts for easier reading and spelling. Use examples such as **September: Sep - tem - ber** and **organize: or - gan - ize**. (Rules for dividing words into syllables are introduced in Student Book Two, when learners will be working with two-syllable words.)

Guide students through this page.

Lesson 2, pages 7 – 9

Guide students through these pages.

Lesson 2, page 10

Guide students in filling in the squares.

At the bottom of this page, say the sounds of these vowels; students write the corresponding letter:

1. /ă/ 2. /ĭ/ 3. /ŏ/ 4. /ă/ 5. /ĕ/ 6. /ŭ/ 7. /ŏ/ 8. /ĭ/

Lesson 2, page 11

The sight words in the *maverick(s)* box are commonly used English words that are not spelled the way they sound. The word that sounds like / ŭv /, for example, is spelled **of**. Awareness of the difference between sight words and phonetically-regular words relieves a lot of confusion for the new learner. It is important not to lump the two types of words together without warning or explanation.

(*Note:* The word **a** is listed as a sight word because of its pronunciation. In American speech, it is generally pronounced as a weak short **u**: / ŭ /. New readers tend to pronounce it with the sound of long **a**. If learners are reminded to pronounce it naturally as we do in speech, they will get into the habit of reading it that way. Also, it helps them to pick up on this sound in dictation.)

Introduce the idea of sight words by saying, "Some common English words are not spelled the way they sound. For example, the word that sounds like / lăf / is spelled **laugh**. Why? A few hundred years ago, the word **laugh** was pronounced differently than it is today. The old spelling has been kept. Today, we call it a *nonphonetic* spelling, or *sight word*. In this program, sight words in the *maverick(s)* boxes are words with nonphonetic spellings. You must memorize these spellings."

The *Sight Word Study Method* is on page 165 of this Guide. You may choose to introduce it now or wait until one of the following lessons.

Guide students through the activity on the bottom half of this page.

Lesson 2, page 12

Pronounce the words in the first five lines. Students should repeat after you. Then go back to number 1 and pronounce any word you wish. Give the students time to find and circle it. Continue pronouncing one word in each line through number 5. At this point, go back to number 1 again and, line by line, give the correct answer. In this way, students get quick feedback on their answers. Follow the same routine for numbers 6 – 10.

Guide students through the activity on the bottom half of this page.

Lesson 2, page 13

The exercise at the top of the page helps to develop visual awareness of letter shapes. Students should circle the words, tracking from left to right in reading style.

Say the sounds of these vowels; students write the key word for each sound:

1. /ă/   2. /ĕ/   3. /ĭ/   4. /ŏ/   5. /ŭ/

See the teacher's script for Word Focus, with the expected student responses, beginning on page 19 of this Guide.

Lesson 2, page 14

(Before starting this page, you may choose to introduce the *Short Vowel Drill* on page 162 of this Guide, or you may prefer to wait until one of the following lessons to introduce that drill.)

The Phonics Review page in this lesson and in each regular lesson throughout Student Book One has three sections: top (decoding), middle (listening), and bottom (spelling).

Isolated syllables which are spelled the way they sound are used on this page. In working with these syllables, learners are forced to pay attention to each letter and its sound, instead of relying on visual memory alone.

Explain to students that the syllables on this page may not be real words but could be *parts* of long words; for example, **tem** in the word **temper** or **September**.

1. Guide students through the top section of Phonics Review, which gives practice in decoding, or "reading" syllables. First, read out loud the instructions under *Work with the Teacher*. Then say, "I'm going to lead you through this activity."

Write the letters **L S S** vertically on the chalkboard or a sheet of paper:

L
S
S

Say, "This is a formula we're going to follow. The **L** stands for **Letter** (the *vowel* letter); the first **S** stands for **Sound**, and the second **S** stands for **Syllable**." Tell them again that you will lead them and they are to respond to your cue. (If you are working with more than one student, have a group or the class respond in unison to your cues.) Remind them to point to the vowel as they answer your questions.

Script for the Phonics Review decoding activity:

TEACHER:	Look at Number 1 on page 14. Say the name of the vowel letter and point to it.
RESPONSE:	**a**
TEACHER:	Say the sound of the vowel.
RESPONSE:	/ ă /
TEACHER:	Say the syllable.
RESPONSE:	/ băf /

Learners will become used to the routine after several syllables have been reviewed. In a one-to-one tutoring situation, the learner will soon be able to do this without any cues from you. If working with a group, cue words (Letter? Sound? Syllable?) will still be necessary to keep students responding together.

2. The middle section of Phonics Review involves listening (auditory discrimination). First pronounce all of the syllables in a row. Students should repeat after you. Then say one syllable for them to circle. Give the correct answer for immediate feedback before going on to the next row.

3. The bottom section of Phonics Review gives students a chance to practice phonetic spelling. Choose any three syllables on this page and dictate them. Give immediate feedback by writing the syllable on the chalkboard or a sheet of paper as soon as learners have written their own.*

Lesson 2, pages 15 – 16

Guide the students through the Sentence Focus exercise orally. First, read the sentence out loud; then, ask students a series of questions about it. Liven up the exercise by stressing the question words.

Train students to respond in a complete sentence and to emphasize the specific word or words that answer the question. (Groups of students may respond in unison.)

Tell them that this type of exercise will help in several ways:
- It builds sentence writing and comprehension skills.
- It gives practice in short-term recall (remembering).
- It helps to improve oral expression at the sentence level (speaking in complete sentences).

---

* With learners who have difficulty with this phonetic spelling exercise, use the *Letter-Card Spelling* technique on page 165 of this Guide.

Remember to exaggerate the question word and to coax students to exaggerate the specific word or words that answer the question. Each time students must respond in a complete sentence.

Script for the Sentence Focus activity:

TEACHER:	"Jeff had a map in his van." (Pause.)
	"*Who* had a map in his van?" (Stress the word "who.")
RESPONSE:	"*Jeff* had a map in his van." (Stress the word "Jeff.")
TEACHER:	"*Where* did Jeff have a map?"
RESPONSE:	"Jeff had a map *in his van*."
TEACHER:	"Jeff had *what* in his van?"
RESPONSE:	"Jeff had *a map* in his van."

This exercise develops into a humorous, chant-like routine when both teacher and students heavily accent the stressed word or words while saying the rest of the sentence in a normal voice. (In later lessons, when a Sentence Focus grid is introduced, encourage students to continue on their own this question-and-answer procedure for each part of the sentence.)

Lesson 2, page 17

Dictation. (See pages 65 – 67 of this Guide.)

Lesson 3, page 18

Guide students through this page. Pronounce the long vowels; have students repeat after you. Encourage them to start memorizing the key words.

Lesson 3, page 19

Guide students through this page.

Lesson 3, page 20

Dictate:

1. kit	4. rob	7. tap	10. not	13. mat	16. bit
2. mad	5. pin	8. rip	11. at	14. rod	17. mop
3. hop	6. tub	9. dim	12. fin	15. win	18. nap

Read the sight words in the box; have students repeat after you. Review *Sight Word Study Method*, page 165 of this Guide.

Lesson 3, page 21

Guide students through this page. The answers to the first group of words are **bake, fake, lake, make, rake, take, wake.**

Lesson 3, page 22

Guide students through this page. To be correct, each word should end with silent **e**, both horizontally and vertically.

Lesson 3, page 23

Guide students through this page. Read the sight words in the box; have students repeat after you. These three words, which will be reviewed repeatedly in the program, are difficult for most learners. If necessary, go over the *Sight Word Study Method* again. This multisensory technique is becoming very important at this point.

Lesson 3, pages 24 – 25

Guide students through these pages.

For the teacher's script to *Word Focus*, with expected student responses, see pages 20 – 21 of this Guide.

Lesson 3, page 26

(Before starting this page, you may choose to introduce the *Long Vowel Drill* on page 163 of this Guide, or you may prefer to wait until one of the following lessons to introduce that drill.)

Refer to the **LSS** procedure on pages 14 (bottom) and 15 of this Guide. Substitute this script for the top section of the Phonics Review decoding activity:

TEACHER:	Look at number 1. Say the name of the *vowel pattern* and point to it.
RESPONSE:	**a** with an **e** at the end.
TEACHER:	Say the sound of the vowel.
RESPONSE:	/ ā /
TEACHER:	Say the syllable.
RESPONSE:	/ nāt /

Follow the same routine for the middle section (listening) and bottom section (spelling) given in Lesson 2 on page 15 of this Guide.

Lesson 3, page 27

Follow the Sentence Focus procedure introduced in Lesson 2 on pages 15 and 16 of this Guide.

Lesson 3, page 28

Dictation. See page 71 of this Guide.

Word Focus

A Word Focus exercise appears in each regular lesson of Student Books One and Two. (For example, see page 13 of Lesson 2 in Book One.)

This activity is done orally. The teacher's script and anticipated student responses for all Word Focus exercises are provided on pages 19–64 of this Guide.

Word Focus exercises give learners in-depth practice taking apart and rebuilding words in four ways, through

- letters and sounds in a word;

- letter pairs and letter groups (blends and sound "families");

- syllables; and

- roots and endings (meaningful word parts).

(*Note:* If a letter appears in boldface, say the letter name: **m** — say "em."
If a letter is enclosed by slashes, say the letter sound: / m / — say "mmm.")

Word Focus strengthens word recognition and oral spelling skills. It also develops vocabulary through oral discussion of target-word meanings. Some uncommon words have been included to challenge learners to "discover" the pronunciation through phonetic decoding.

In a group or class situation, have students respond in unison. It may take some individuals longer to respond than others, but they learn by listening; eventually, they will be able to keep up with the group.

TEACHER SAYS:	*STUDENT RESPONDS:*
The first word is *sod*.	**sod**
Name the letter that stands for / s /.	**s**
Name the letter that stands for / ŏ /.	**o**
Name the letter that stands for / d /.	**d**
Spell the word **sod**.	(Names each letter while forming the word with fingertips on desktop)
Give the sound for the letter **o**.	/ ŏ /
Give the sound for the letter **d**.	/ d /
Give the sound for the letter **s**.	/ s /
Give the sound for the letters **o - d**.	/ ŏd /
Say the word.	/ sŏd /
(Discuss the meaning.)	
The second word is *hem*.	**hem**
Name the letter that stands for / h /.	**h**
Name the letter that stands for / ĕ /.	**e**
Name the letter that stands for / m /.	**m**
Spell the word **hem**.	(Names each letter while forming the word with fingertips on desktop)
Give the sound for the letter **e**.	/ ĕ /
Give the sound for the letter **m**.	/ˌm /
Give the sound for the letters **e - m**.	/ ĕm /
Give the sound for the letter **h**.	/ h /
Say the word.	/ hĕm /
(Discuss the meaning.)	
The third word is *vat*.	**vat**
Name the letter that stands for / v /.	**v**
Name the letter that stands for / ă /.	**a**
Name the letter that stands for / t /.	**t**
Name the letters that stand for / ăt /.	**a - t**
Spell the word **vat**.	(Names each letter while forming the word with fingertips on desktop)
Give the sound for the letter **a**.	/ ă /
Give the sound for the letter **t**.	/ t /
Give the sound for the letters **a - t**.	/ ăt /
Give the sound for the letter **v**.	/ v /
Say the word.	/ văt /
(Discuss the meaning.)	

The fourth word is *lip*.

lip

Name the letter that stands for / ĭ /.

i

Name the letter that stands for / l /.

l

Name the letters that stand for / ĭp /.

i - p

Spell the word **lip**.

(Names each letter while forming the word with fingertips on desktop)

Give the sound for the letter **i**.

/ ĭ /

Give the sound for the letter **l**.

/ l /

Give the sound for the letters **i - p**.

/ ĭp /

Say the word.

/ lĭp /

(Discuss the meaning.)

The last word is *buff*.

buff

Name the letter that stands for / ŭ /.

u

Name the letter that stands for / b /.

b

Name the letters that stand for / f /.

f - f

Name the letters that stand for / ŭf /.

u - f - f

Spell the word **buff**.

(Names each letter while forming the word with fingertips on desktop)

*(Reminder: When a word with one vowel ends in **f**, **l**, **s**, or **z**, the last letter usually doubles.*

Give the sound for the letter **b**.

/ b /

Give the sound for the letter **u**.

/ ŭ /

Give the sound for the letters **f - f**.

/ f /

Say the word.

/ bŭf /

(Discuss the meaning.)

WORD FOCUS   **Book One: Lesson 3**

The first word is *lop*.

lop

Name the letter that stands for / ŏ /.

o

Name the letter that stands for / l /.

l

Name the letters that stand for / ŏp /.

o - p

Spell the word **lop**.

(Names each letter while forming the word with fingertips on desktop)

Give the sound for the letter **o**.

/ ŏ /

Give the sound for the letters **o - p**.

/ ŏp /

Give the sound for the letter **l**.

/ l /

Say the word.

/ lŏp /

(Discuss the meaning.)

The second word is *lope*.

                                         lope

Name the letter pattern that stands for / ō /.   (Wording will vary.)
*(Reminder: **o** with an **e** at the end of the word)*

Name the letter that stands for / l /.   **l**

Name the letters that stand for / ōp /.   **o - p - e**

Spell the word **lope**.   (Names each letter while forming the
                                       word with fingertips on desktop)

Give the sound for the letter **o**.   / ō /

Give the sound for the letter **e**.   No sound

Give the sound for the letters **o - p - e**.   / ōp /

Give the sound for the letter **l**.   / l /

Say the word.   / lōp /

If we take away the **e**, what is the sound?   / lŏp /
(Explain, or have student respond.)

(Discuss the meaning.)

The next word is *fame*.

                                         fame

Name the letter pattern that stands for / ā /.   (Wording will vary.)
*(Reminder: **a** with an **e** at the end of the word)*

Name the letter that stands for / m /.   **m**

Name the letter that stands for / f /.   **f**

Name the letters that stand for / ām /.   **a - m - e**

Spell the word **fame**.   (Names while forming letters)

Give the sound for the letter **a**.   / ā /

Give the sound for the letter **e**.   No sound

Give the sound for the letter **f**.   / f /

Give the sound for the letters **a - m - e**.   / ām /

Say the word.   / fām /

(Discuss the meaning.)

The last word is *jute*.

                                         jute

Name the letter pattern that stands for / ōō /.   (Wording will vary.)
*(Reminder: **u** with an **e** at the end of the word)*

Name the letter that stands for / j /.   **j**

Name the letters that stand for / ōōt /.   **u - t - e**

Spell the word **jute**.   (Names while forming letters)

Give the sound for the letter **j**.   / j /

Give the sound for the letters **u - t - e**.   / ōōt /

Say the word.   / jōōt /

If we take away the **e**, what is the sound?   / jŭt /

(Discuss the meaning.)

TEACHER SAYS:	*STUDENT RESPONDS:*

The first word is *fuss*.   **fuss**

Name the letter that stands for / ŭ /.   **u**

Name the letter that stands for / f /.   **f**

Name the letters that stand for / s /.   **s - s**
*(Reminder: When a word with one vowel ends
in **f**, **l**, **s**, or **z**, the last letter usually doubles.)*

Name the letters that stand for / ŭs /.   **u - s - s**

Spell the word **fuss**.   (Names while forming letters)

Give the sound for the letter **f**.   / f /

Give the sound for the letter **u**.   / ŭ /

Give the sound for the letters **s - s**.   / s /

Say the word.   / fŭs /

(Discuss the meaning.)

The next word is *fuse*.   **fuse**

Name the letter pattern that stands for / ū /.   **u** with an **e**
                                                          at the end of the word

Name the letter that stands for / z /.   **s**

Name the letters that stand for / ūz /.   **u - s - e**

Name the letter that stands for / f /.   **f**

Spell the word **fuse**.   (Names while forming letters)

Give the sound for the letter **s**.   / z /

Give the sound for the letter **u**.   / ū /

Give the sound for the letters **u - s - e**.   / ūz /

Give the sound for the letter **f**.   / f /

Say the word.   / fūz /

(Discuss the meaning.)

The third word is *sip*.   **sip**

Name the letter that stands for / s /.   **s**

Name the letter that stands for / ĭ /.   **i**

Name the letter that stands for / p /.   **p**

Spell the word **sip**.   (Names while forming letters)

Give the sound for the letter **i**.   / ĭ /

Give the sound for the letter **p**.   / p /

Give the sound for the letters **i - p**.   / ĭp /

Give the sound for the letter **s**.   / s /

Say the word.   / sĭp /

(Discuss the meaning.)

TEACHER SAYS:	STUDENT RESPONDS:
The last word is _site_.	site
Name the letter pattern that stands for / ī /.	i with an e at the end of the word
Name the letter that stands for / īt /.	i - t - e
Name the letter that stands for / s /.	s
Spell the word **site**.	(Names while forming letters)
Give the sound for the letter **s**.	/ s /
Give the sound for the letter **i**.	/ ī /
Give the sound for the letter **e**.	No sound
Give the sound for the letters **i - t - e**.	/ īt /
Say the word.	/ sīt /
(Discuss the meaning.)	

WORD FOCUS   Book One: Lesson 6

TEACHER SAYS:	STUDENT RESPONDS:
The first word is _yon_.	yon
Name the letter that stands for / ŏ /.	o
Name the letter that stands for / n /.	n
Name the letters that stand for / ŏn /.	o - n
Name the letter that stands for / y /.	y
Spell the word **yon**.	(Names while forming letters)
In this word, is the **y** letter a vowel or a consonant?	Consonant
Explain. _(Reminder: If **y** is the first letter of a word, it is a consonant.)_	(Wording will vary.)
Give the sound for the letter **y**.	/ y /
Give the sound for the letter **o**.	/ ŏ /
Give the sound for the letter **n**.	/ n /
Say the word.	/ yŏn /
(Discuss the meaning.)	

The next word is *lye*.   lye

Name the letter pattern that stands for / ī /.   **y - e**

Name the letter that stands for / l /.   **l**

Spell the word **lye**.   (Names while forming letters)

In this word, is the **y** letter a vowel
or a consonant?   Vowel

Explain.   (Wording will vary.)
*(Reminder: If y takes the place of an i
within a word, it is a vowel.)*

Give the sound for the letter **l**.   / l /

Give the sound for the letter **y**.   / ī /

Give the sound for the letter **e**.   No sound

Say the word.   / lī /

(Discuss the meaning.)

WORD FOCUS   **Book One: Lesson 7**

The first word is *quite*.   quite

Name the letters that stand for / kw /.   **q - u**

Name the letter pattern that stands for / ī /.   **i** with an **e**
                                                                                                                  at the end of the word

Name the letter that stands for / t /.   **t**

Name the letters that stand for / īt /.   **i - t - e**

Spell the word **quite**.   (Names while forming letters)

Give the sound for the letter **i**.   / ī /

Give the sound for the letter **e**.   No sound

Give the sound for the letters **q - u**.   / kw /

Say the word.   / kwīt /

If you take away the **e**, what is the sound?   / kwĭt /

(Discuss the meaning.)

The second word is *quit*.   quit

Name the letters that stand for / kw /.   **q - u**

Name the letter that stands for / ĭ /.   **i**

Name the letter that stands for / t /.   **t**

Spell the word **quit**.   (Names while forming letters)

Give the sound for the letters **q - u**.   / kw /

Give the sound for the letters **i - t**.   / ĭt /

Say the word.   / kwĭt /

(Discuss the meaning.)

TEACHER SAYS:	STUDENT RESPONDS:
The last word is *lox*.	lox
Name the letter that stands for / ŏ /.	o
Name the letter that stands for / ks /.	x
Name the letter that stands for / l /.	l
Name the letters that stand for / ŏks /.	o - x
Spell the word **lox**.	(Names while forming letters)
Give the sound for the letter **l**.	/ l /
Give the sound for the letter **o**.	/ ŏ /
Give the sound for the letter **x**.	/ ks /
Say the word.	/ lŏks /
(Discuss the meaning.)	

WORD FOCUS Book One: Lesson 8

The first word is *cod*.	cod
Name the letter that stands for / ŏ /.	o
Name the letter that stands for / d /.	d
Name the letter that stands for / k /.	c
Name the letters that stand for / ŏd /.	o - d
Spell the word **cod**.	(Names while forming letters)
In this word, is the **c** hard or soft?	Hard
Explain.	(Wording will vary.)
*(Reminder: The **c** does not have **e**, **i**, or **y** after it, so the sound of **c** is hard.)*	
Give the sound for the letter **o**.	/ ŏ /
Give the sound for the letters **o - d**.	/ ŏd /
Give the sound for the letter **c**.	/ k /
Say the word.	/ kŏd /
(Discuss the meaning.)	

TEACHER SAYS:	STUDENT RESPONDS:
The second word is *code.*	code
Name the letter pattern that stands for / ō /.	**o** with an **e** at the end of the word
Name the letter that stands for / d /.	**d**
Name the letters that stand for / ōd /.	**o - d - e**
Name the letter that stands for / k /.	**c**
Spell the word **code.**	(Names while forming letters)
In this word, is the **c** hard or soft?	Hard
Explain.	(Wording will vary.)
*(Reminder: The **c** does not have **e**, **i**, or **y** after it, so the sound of **c** is hard.)*	
Give the sound for the letter **e.**	No sound
Give the sound for the letter **c.**	/ k /
Give the sound for the letters **o - d - e.**	/ ōd /
Say the word.	/ kōd /
If we take away the **e**, what is the sound?	/ kŏd /
(Discuss the meaning.)	

The next word is *cyme.*	cyme
Name the letter pattern that stands for / ī /.	**y** with an **e** at the end of the word
Name the letter that stands for / s /.	**c**
Name the letters that stand for / īm /.	**y - m - e**
Spell the word **cyme.**	(Names while forming letters)
In this word, is the **c** hard or soft?	Soft
Explain.	(Wording will vary.)
*(Reminder: When **c** has **e**, **i**, or **y** after it, the sound of the **c** is usually soft.)*	
Give the sound for the letter **y.**	/ ī /
Give the sound for the letter **e.**	No sound
Give the sound for the letter **c.**	/ s /
Give the sound for the letters **y - m - e.**	/ īm /
Say the word.	/ sīm /
(Discuss the meaning.)	

TEACHER SAYS:	STUDENT RESPONDS:

The last word is *lice*.

Name the letter pattern that stands for / ī /.

Name the letter that stands for / s /.

Name the letter that stands for / l /.

Name the letters that stand for / īs /.

Spell the word **lice**.
(*Explain: In this word, the letter* **e** *has two functions: It makes the* **i** *long, and it makes the* **c** *soft.*)

Give the sound for the letter **l**.

Give the sound for the letter **i**.

Give the sound for the letter **c**.

Give the sound for the letter **e**.

Say the word.

If we take away the **l**, what is the sound?

(Discuss the meaning.)

lice

i with an **e**
at the end of the word

c

l

i - c - e

(Names while forming letters)

/ l /

/ ī /

/ s /

No sound

/ līs /

/ īs /

WORD FOCUS

The first word is *fig*.

Name the letter that stands for / ĭ /.

Name the letter that stands for / g /.

Name the letters that stand for / ĭg /.

Spell the word **fig**.

In this word, is the **g** hard or soft?

Tell me why.
(*Reminder: The* **g** *does not have* **e**, **i**, *or* **y** *after it, so the sound of* **g** *is hard.*)

Give the sound for the letter **f**.

Give the sound for the letter **i**.

Give the sound for the letter **g**.

Say the word.

(Discuss the meaning.)

fig

i

g

i - g

(Names while forming letters)

Hard

(Wording will vary.)

/ f /

/ ĭ /

/ g /

/ fĭg /

TEACHER SAYS:	STUDENT RESPONDS:

The second word is *sage*. · sage

Name the letter pattern that stands for / ā /. · **a** with an **e** at the end of the word

Name the letter that stands for / j /. · **g**

Name the letters that stand for / āj /. · **a - g - e**

Name the letter that stands for / s /. · **s**

Spell the word **sage**. · (Names while forming letters)

In this word, is the **g** hard or soft? · Soft

Tell me why. · (Wording will vary.)
(Reminder: When g has an e, i, or y after it, the sound of g is usually soft.)

Give the sound for the letter **s**. · / s /

Give the sound for the letter **a**. · / ā /

Give the sound for the letter **g**. · / j /
(Explain: In this word, the letter e has two functions:
It makes the a long, and it makes the g soft.)

Say the word. · / sāj /

(Discuss the meaning.)

The third word is *gap*. · **gap**

Name the letter that stands for / g /. · **g**

Name the letters that stand for / ăp /. · **a - p**

Spell the word **gap**. · (Names while forming letters)

Give the sound for the letter **a**. · / ă /

Give the sound for the letter **p**. · / p /

Give the sound for the letter **g**. · / g /

In this word, is the **g** hard or soft? · Hard

Tell me why. (Offer help.) · The **g** does not have **e, i,** or **y** after it, so the sound of **g** is hard.

Say the word. · / găp /

(Discuss the meaning.)

The last word is *gibe*. · **gibe**

Name the letter pattern that stands for / ī /. · **i** with an **e** at the end of the word

Name the letter that stands for / j /. · **g**

Name the letters that stand for / īb /. · **i - b - e**

Spell the word **gibe**. · (Names while forming letters)

In this word, is the **g** hard or soft? · Soft

Tell me why. (Offer help.) · When **g** has **e, i,** or **y** after it, the sound of **g** is usually soft.

Give the sound for the letter **g**. · / j /

Give the sound for the letter **i**. · / ī /

Give the sound for the letter **b**. · / b /

Give the sound for the letter **e**. · No sound

Say the word. · / jīb /

(Discuss the meaning.)

TEACHER SAYS:	_STUDENT RESPONDS:_
The first word is _clot_.	clot
Name the letter that stands for / k /.	c
Name the letter that stands for / l /.	l
Name the letter that stands for / ŏ /.	o
Name the letter that stands for / t /.	t
Spell the word **clot**.	(Names while forming letters)
Give the sound for the letter **o**.	/ ŏ /
Give the sound for the letter **c**.	/ k /
Give the sound for the letter **l**.	/ l /
Give the sound for the letters **c - l**.	/ kl /
Give the sound for the letters **o - t**.	/ ŏt /
Say the word.	/ klŏt /
(Discuss the meaning.)	

The next word is _twinge_.	twinge
Name the letter that stands for / ĭ /.	i
Name the letter that stands for / t /.	t
Name the letter that stands for / w /.	w
Name the letters that stand for / tw /.	t - w
Name the letters that stand for / ĭn /.	i - n
Name the letters that stand for / wĭn /.	w - i - n
Name the letters that stand for / twĭn /.	t - w - i - n
Name the letter that stands for / j /.	g
Spell the word **twinge**.	(Names while forming letters)
(_Explain: In this word, the letter **e** has one important function: It makes the **g** soft._)	
Give the sound for the letters **t - w**.	/ tw /
Give the sound for the letter **i**.	/ ĭ /
Give the sound for the letters **t - w - i - n**.	/ twĭn /
Give the sound for the letter **g**.	/ j /
Say the word.	/ twĭnj /
(Discuss the meaning.)	

The third word is *frame.*

Name the letter pattern that stands for / ā /.

Name the letter that stands for / f /.

Name the letter that stands for / r /.

Name the letters that stand for / fr /.

Name the letters that stand for / ām /.

Spell the word **frame.**

Give the sound for the letter **a.**

Give the sound for the letter **e.**

Give the sound for the letters **f - r.**

Give the sound for the letters **a - m - e.**

Say the word.

If we take away the **e,** what is the sound?

(Discuss the meaning.)

frame

a with an **e**
at the end of the word

f

r

f - r

a - m - e
(Names while forming letters)

/ ā /

No sound

/ fr /

/ ām /

/ frām /

/ frăm /

The last word is *scrod.*

Name the letter that stands for / s /.

Name the letter that stands for / k /.

Name the letters that stand for / sk /.

Name the letter that stands for / r /.

Name the letters that stand for / skr /.

Name the letter that stands for / ŏ /.

Name the letters that stand for / ŏd /.

Spell the word **scrod.**

Give the sound for the letter **o.**

Give the sound for the letter **c.**

Is that **c** hard or soft?

Tell me why. (Offer help.)

Give the sound for the letters **s - c.**

Give the sound for the letters **o - d.**

Say the word.

(Discuss the meaning.)

scrod

s

c

s - c

r

s - c - r

o

o - d
(Names while forming letters)

/ ŏ /

/ k /

Hard

The **c** does not have **e, i,** or **y**
after it, so the sound of **c** is hard.

/ sk /

/ ŏd /

/ skrŏd /

TEACHER SAYS:	STUDENT RESPONDS:

The first word is *vend*.   vend

Name the letter that stands for / ĕ /.   **e**

Name the letter that stands for / n /.   **n**

Name the letter that stands for / d /.   **d**

Name the letters that stand for / nd /.   **n - d**

Name the letter that stands for / v /.   **v**

Spell the word **vend**.   (Names while forming letters)

Give the sound for the letter **v**.   / v /

Give the sound for the letter **e**.   / ĕ /

Give the sound for the letters **n - d**.   / nd /

Give the sound for the letters **e - n - d**.   / ĕnd /

Say the word.   / vĕnd /

(Discuss the meaning.)

The next word is *cyst*.   cyst

Name the letter that stands for the first / s /.   **c**

Name the letter that stands for the second / s /.   **s**

Name the letter that stands for / ĭ /.   **y**

Name the letters that stand for / st /.   **s - t**

Name the letters that stand for / ĭst /.   **y - s - t**

Spell the word **cyst**.   (Names while forming letters)

In this word, is the **c** hard or soft?   Soft

Tell me why.   When **c** has **e**, **i**, or **y** after it, the sound of **c** is usually soft.

Give the sound for the letter **c**.   / s /

Give the sound for the letter **y**.   / ĭ /

Give the sound for the letter **s**.   / s /

Give the sound for the letter **t**.   / t /

Say the word.   / sĭst /

(Discuss the meaning.)

TEACHER SAYS:	*STUDENT RESPONDS:*
The third word is *blond*.	blond
Name the letter that stands for / b /.	**b**
Name the letter that stands for / l /.	**l**
Name the letters that stand for / bl /.	**b - l**
Name the letter that stands for / ŏ /.	**o**
Name the letter that stands for / n /.	**n**
Name the letter that stands for / d /.	**d**
Name the letters that stand for / nd /.	**n - d**
Spell the word **blond**.	(Names while forming letters)
Give the sound for the letter **o**.	/ ŏ /
Give the sound for the letters **n - d**.	/ nd /
Give the sound for the letters **o - n - d**.	/ ŏnd /
Give the sound for the letters **b - l**.	/ bl /
Say the word.	/ blŏnd /
(Discuss the meaning.)	
The last word is *sprint*.	sprint
Name the letter that stands for / s /.	**s**
Name the letter that stands for / p /.	**p**
Name the letter that stands for / r /.	**r**
Name the letters that stand for / spr /.	**s - p - r**
Name the letter that stands for / ĭ /.	**i**
Name the letter that stands for / n /.	**n**
Name the letters that stand for / nt /.	**n - t**
Spell the word **sprint**.	(Names while forming letters)
Give the sound for the letter **i**.	/ ĭ /
Give the sound for the letters **s - p**.	/ sp /
Give the sound for the letters **s - p - r**.	/ spr /
Give the sound for the letters **i - n - t**.	/ ĭnt /
Say the word.	/ sprĭnt /
If we take away the **s**, what is the sound?	/ prĭnt /
(Discuss the meaning.)	

TEACHER SAYS:	*STUDENT RESPONDS:*
The next word is *wind* (/ wīnd /).	**wind**
Name the letter that stands for / ī /.	**i**
Name the letter that stands for / w /.	**w**
Name the letter that stands for / n /.	**n**
Name the letters that stand for / nd /.	**n - d**
Spell the word **wind.**	(Names while forming letters)
(Explain: A vowel in a closed syllable usually is short, but this word belongs to the / īnd / family, so the i is long.)	
Give the sound for the letter **w.**	/ w /
Give the sound for the letter **i.**	/ ī /
Give the sound for the letter **n.**	/ n /
Give the sound for the letter **d.**	/ d /
Give the sound for the letters **n - d.**	/ nd /
Say the word.	/ wīnd /
(Discuss the meaning.)	
What is the meaning if **w - i - n - d** is pronounced with a short vowel sound — / wĭnd /?	(Answers will vary.)

The second word is *host*.	**host**
Name the letter that stands for / ō /.	**o**
Name the letters that stand for / st /.	**s - t**
Name the letters that stand for / ōst /.	**o - s - t**
Name the letter that stands for / h /.	**h**
Spell the word **host.**	(Names while forming letters)
(Explain: A vowel in a closed syllable usually is short, but this word belongs to the / ōst / family, so the o is long.)	
Give the sound for the letters **s - t.**	/ st /
Give the sound for the letters **o - s - t.**	/ ōst /
Say the word.	/ hōst /
(Discuss the meaning.)	

TEACHER SAYS:	STUDENT RESPONDS:

The third word is *scold*. · scold

Name the letter that stands for / s /. · **s**

Name the letter that stands for / k /. · **c**

Name the letters that stand for / sk /. · **s - c**

Name the letter that stands for / l /. · **l**

Name the letter that stands for / d /. · **d**

Name the letters that stand for / ld /. · **l - d**

Name the letter that stands for / ō /. · **o**

Spell the word **scold**. · (Names while forming letters)

Why does the **o** have a long sound? · A vowel in a closed syllable usually
(Offer help.) · is short, but this word belongs
to the / ōld / family, so the **o** is long.

Give the sound for the letters **s - c**. · / sk /

Give the sound for the letters **o - l - d**. · / ōld /

Say the word. · / skōld /

(Discuss the meaning.)

The last word is *mild*. · **mild**

Name the letter that stands for / ī /. · **i**

Name the letters that stand for / īld /. · **i - l - d**

Name the letter that stands for / m /. · **m**

Spell the word **mild**. · (Names while forming letters)

(*Explain: A vowel in a closed syllable usually is short,
but this word belongs to the / īld / family, so the **i** is long.*)

Give the sound for the letter **m**. · / m /

Give the sound for the letter **i**. · / ī /

Give the sound for the letter **l**. · / l /

Give the sound for the letter **d**. · / d /

Say the word. · / mīld /

(Discuss the meaning.)

WORD FOCUS

The first word is *snarl*. · snarl

Name the letters that stand for / sn /. · **s - n**

Name the letters that stand for / är /. · **a - r**

Name the letters that stand for / ärl /. · **a - r - l**

Spell the word **snarl**. · (Names while forming letters)

Give the sound for the letters **s - n**. · / sn /

Give the sound for the letters **a - r**. · / är /

Give the sound for the letter **l**. · / l /

Say the word. · / snärl /

(Discuss the meaning.)

TEACHER SAYS:	STUDENT RESPONDS:

The next word is *gall*. gall

Name the letter that stands for / ȯ / ("aw"). **a**

Name the letter that stands for / g /. **g**

In this word, is the **g** hard or soft? Hard

Tell me why. (Offer help if needed.) The **g** does not have **e**, **i**, or **y** after it, so the sound of **g** is hard.

Name the letters that stand for / l /. **l - l**
(Reminder: When a word with one vowel ends in f, l, s, or z, the last letter usually doubles.)

Spell the word **gall**. (Names while forming letters)

If we take away the **g**, what is the sound? / ȯl /

Give the sound for the letter **g**. / g /

Give the sound for the letter **a**. / ȯ / ("aw")

Give the sound for the letters **l - l**. / l /

Say the word. / gȯl /

(Discuss the meaning.)

The third word is *balk* (/ bȯk /). balk

Name the letter that stands for / ȯ /. **a**

Name the letter that stands for / b /. **b**

Name the letters that stand for / ȯk /. **a - k**

Name the letter that is silent. **l**

Spell the word **balk**. (Names while forming letters)

Give the sound for the letter **b**. / b /

Give the sound for the letter **a**. / ȯ /

Give the sound for the letter **l**. No sound

Give the sound for the letter **k**. / k /

Say the word. / bȯk /

(Discuss the meaning.)

The last word is *halt*. halt

Name the letter that stands for / h /. **h**

Name the letter that stands for / ȯ /. **a**

Name the letter that stands for / l /. **l**

Name the letters that stand for / ȯlt /. **a - l - t**

Spell the word **halt**. (Names while forming letters)

Give the sound for the letter **h**. / h /

Give the sound for the letter **a**. / ȯ /

Give the sound for the letter **l**. / l /

Give the sound for the letter **t**. / t /

Say the word. / hȯlt /

(Discuss the meaning.)

TEACHER SAYS:	*STUDENT RESPONDS:*
The first word is *bonded*.	**bonded**
Name the letter that stands for / ŏ /.	**o**
Name the letters that stand for / bŏn /.	**b - o - n**
Name the letters that stand for / ŏnd /.	**o - n - d**
Name the letters that stand for / əd /.	**e - d**
Spell the word **bonded**.	(Names while forming letters)

*(Reminder: When the root word ends in the sound of **d** or **t**,
the affix **ed** is a separate syllable and has the sound of / əd /.)*

Give the sound for the letter **b**.	/ b /
Give the sound for the letters **o - n - d**.	/ ŏnd /
Give the sound for the letters **e - d**.	/ əd /
What does the affix **ed** mean?	"In the past"
Say the word.	/ bŏndəd /

(Discuss the meaning, using the past tense.)

The second word is *filmed*.	**filmed**
Name the letter that stands for / ĭ /.	**i**
Name the letters that stand for / fĭl /.	**f - i - l**
Name the letter that stands for / m /.	**m**
Name the letters that stand for / d /.	**e - d**
Spell the word **filmed**.	(Names while forming letters)

*(Reminder: When the root word ends in a voiced sound,
such as / m /, the affix **ed** is pronounced / d /.)*

Give the sound for the letter **f**.	/ f /
Give the sound for the letters **i - l - m**.	/ ĭlm /
Give the sound for the letters **e - d**.	/ d /
Say the word.	/ fĭlmd /

(Discuss the meaning.)

The last word is *talked*.	**talked**
Name the letter that stands for the first / t /.	**t**
Name the letter that stands for / ȯ /.	**a**
Name the letter that is silent.	**l**
Name the letter that stands for / k /.	**k**
Name the letter that stands for the *second* / t /.	**e - d**

*(Reminder: When the root word ends in a voiceless sound,
such as / k /, the affix **ed** is pronounced / t /.)*

Spell the word **talked**.	(Names while forming letters)
Give the sound for the letter **a**.	/ ȯ /
Give the sound for the letters **a - l - k**.	/ ȯk /
Give the sound for the letters **t - a - l - k**.	/ tȯk /
Give the sound for the letters **e - d**.	/ t /
Say the word.	/ tȯkt /
What does the affix **ed** mean?	"In the past"

(Discuss the meaning, using the past tense.)

TEACHER SAYS:	*STUDENT RESPONDS:*
The first word is *sulking*.	sulking
Name the letter that stands for / ŭ /.	**u**
Name the letters that stand for / ĭng /.	**i - n - g**
Name the letter that stands for / l /.	**l**
Name the letter that stands for / k /.	**k**
Name the letters that stand for / lk /.	**l - k**
Name the letters that stand for / ŭlk /.	**u - l - k**
Name the letters that stand for / sŭlk /.	**s - u - l - k**
Spell the word **sulking**.	(Names while forming letters)
Give the sound for the letter **u**.	/ ŭ /
Give the sound for the letters **u - l**.	/ ŭl /
Give the sound for the letters **u - l - k**.	/ ŭlk /
Give the sound for the letters **s - u - l - k**.	/ sŭlk /
Give the sound for the letters **i - n - g**.	/ ĭng /
Say the word.	/ sŭlkĭng /
(Discuss the meaning.)	

TEACHER SAYS:	*STUDENT RESPONDS:*
The second word is *grasping*.	grasping
Name the letter that stands for / g /.	**g**
In this word, is the **g** hard or soft?	Hard
Tell me why.	The **g** does not have **e**, **i**, or **y** after it, so the sound of **g** is hard.
Name the letters that stand for / gr /.	**g - r**
Name the letter that stands for / ă /.	**a**
Name the letters that stand for / ăsp /.	**a - s - p**
Name the letters that stand for / ĭng /.	**i - n - g**
Spell the word **grasping**.	(Names while forming letters)
Give the sound for the letter **a**.	/ ă /
Give the sound for the letters **a - s - p**.	/ ăsp /
Give the sound for the letters **r - a - s - p**.	/ răsp /
Give the sound for the letters **g - r - a - s - p**.	/ grăsp /
Give the sound for the letters **i - n - g**.	/ ĭng /
Say the word.	/ grăspĭng /
(Discuss the meaning.)	

TEACHER SAYS:	*STUDENT RESPONDS:*

The first word is *voted*.

         voted

Name the letter that stands for / v /.

         v

Name the letter that stands for / ō /.

         o

Name the letter that stands for / t /.

         t

Name the letters that stand for / əd /.

         e - d

Spell the word **voted**.

      (Names while forming letters)

What is the root word?

         vote

What happens to the silent **e** in the
root word when the affix **ed** is added?
*(Reminder: When a word ends in silent e,
drop the e before adding the affix **ed**.)*

      The **e** is dropped.

What does the affix **ed** mean?

       "In the past"

Give the sound for the letter **o**.

         / ō /

Give the sound for the letters **e - d**.

         / əd /

Say the word.

       / vōtəd /

(Discuss the meaning.)

The second word is *slicing*.

       slicing

What is the root word?

         slice

Name the letters that stand for / sl /.

         s - l

Name the letter that stands for / ī /.

         i

Name the letter that stands for the second / s /.

         c

Name the letters that stand for / ĭng /.

         i - n - g

Spell the word **slicing**.

      (Names while forming letters)

What happens to the silent **e** in the
root word when the affix **ing** is added?

      The **e** is dropped.

In this word, is the **c** hard or soft?

        Soft

How do you know?

     When **c** has **e**, **i**, or **y** after it,
     the sound of **c** is usually soft.

Give the sound for the letter **i**.

         / ī /

Give the sound for the letters **s - l - i**.

         / slī /

Give the sound for the letter **c**.

         / s /

Say the word.

       / slīsĭng /

(Discuss the meaning.)

TEACHER SAYS:	STUDENT RESPONDS:

The third word is *closed*. — closed

Name the letter that stands for / k /. — c

Name the letters that stand for / kl /. — c - l

Name the letter that stands for / ō /. — o

Name the letter that stands for / z /. — s

Name the letters that stand for / d /. — e - d

Spell the word **closed**. — (Names while forming letters)

What is the root word? — **close**

What happens to the silent **e** when the affix **ed** is added? — The **e** is dropped.

Give the sound for the letter **c**. — / k /

Give the sound for the letter **s**. — / z /

Give the sound for the letter **o**. — / ō /

Give the sound for the letters **e - d**. — / d /

Say the word. — / klōzd /

(Discuss the meaning.)

The last word is *typing*. — typing

What is the root word? — **type**

What happens to the silent **e** when the affix **ing** is added? — The **e** is dropped.

Name the letter that stands for / t /. — t

Name the letter that stands for / ī /. — y

Name the letter that stands for / p /. — p

Name the letters that stand for / ıng /. — i - n - g

Spell the word **typing**. — (Names while forming letters)

Give the sound for the letter **y**. — / ī /

Give the sound for the letters **t - y**. — / tī /

Give the sound for the letters **p - i - n - g**. — / pĭng /

Say the word. — / tīpĭng /

(Discuss the meaning.)

TEACHER SAYS:	*STUDENT RESPONDS:*
The first word is *flossed*.	**flossed**
Name the letters that stand for / fl /.	**f - l**
Name the letter that stands for / ȯ /.	**o**
Name the letters that stand for / s /.	**s - s**
Name the letters that stand for / t /.	**e - d**
Spell the word **flossed**.	(Names while forming letters)
What is the root word?	**floss**
Give the sound for the letter **o**.	/ ȯ /
Give the sound for the letters **o - s - s**.	/ ȯs /
Give the sound for the letters **f - l - o - s - s**.	/ flȯs /
What does the affix **ed** mean?	"In the past"
Give the sound for the affix **ed**.	/ t /
Say the word.	/ flȯst /
(Discuss the meaning.)	
The second word is *pulling*.	**pulling**
Name the letter that stands for / p /.	**p**
Name the letter that stands for / o͝o /.	**u**
Name the letters that stand for / l /.	**l - l**
Name the letters that stand for / ĭng /.	**i - n - g**
Spell the word **pulling**.	(Names while forming letters)
What is the root word?	**pull**
Give the sound for the letter **u**.	/ o͝o /
Give the sound for the letter **p**.	/ p /
Give the sound for the letters **l - l**.	/ l /
Give the sound for the letter **i**.	/ ĭ /
Give the sound for the affix **ing**.	/ ĭng /
Say the word.	/ po͝olĭng /
(Discuss the meaning.)	

TEACHER SAYS:	*STUDENT RESPONDS:*

The first word is *mishap*.   **mishap**

How many syllables?   Two

Where should you divide this word?   Between the **s** and **h** *or*
                                                            Between the consonants **s** and **h**

Give the sound for the letter **i**.   / ĭ /

Give the sound for the letter **a**.   / ă /

Give the sound for the letters **h - a - p**.   / hăp /

Give the sound for the letters **m - i - s**.   / mĭs /

Say the word, then spell it.   (Names while forming letters)

(Discuss the meaning.)

The second word is *entice*.   **entice**

How many syllables?   Two

Where should you divide this word?   Between the **n** and **t** *or*
                                                            Between the consonants **n** and **t**

Give the sound for the first letter **e**.   / ĕ /

Give the sound for the letter **i**.   / ī /

Give the sound for the last letter **e**.   No sound

The silent **e** at the end has two functions —

tell me one function.   The **e** at the end makes the **c** soft.

What's the other function?   The **e** at the end makes the **i** sound long.

Give the sound for the letter **c**.   / s /

Say the word, then spell it.   (Names while forming letters)

(Discuss the meaning.)

The third word is *fulfill*.   **fulfill**

How many syllables?   Two

Where should you divide this word?   Between **l** and **f**

Give the sound for the letter **i**.   / ĭ /

Give the sound for the letter **u**.   / o͝o /

Give the sound for the letters **f - u - l**.   / fo͝ol /

Give the sound for the letters **f - i - l - l**.   / fĭl /

What sound comes *after* the letter **u**?   / l /

What sound comes *after* the first letter **f**?   / o͝o /

Say the word, then spell it.   (Names while forming letters)

(Discuss the meaning.)

TEACHER SAYS:	STUDENT RESPONDS:
The last word is *splendid.*	**splendid**
How many syllables?	Two
Where should you divide this word?	Between **n** and **d**
Give the sound for the letters **s** - **p**.	/ sp /
Give the sound for the letter **e**.	/ ĕ /
Give the sound for the letter **i**.	/ ĭ /
What sound comes *after* the letter **e**?	/ n /
What sound comes *after* the letter **p**?	/ l /
What sound comes *after* the letter **n**?	/ d /
What sound comes *after* the first letter **d**?	/ ĭ /
Give the sound for the letters **l** - **e** - **n**.	/ lĕn /
Give the sound for the letters **p** - **l** - **e** - **n**.	/ plĕn /
Give the sound for the letters **s** - **p** - **l** - **e** - **n**.	/ splĕn /
Give the sound for the letters **d** - **i** - **d**.	/ dĭd /
Say the word, then spell it.	(Names while forming letters)
(Discuss the meaning.)	

WORD FOCUS

The first word is *symbol.*	**symbol**
How many syllables?	Two
Where should you divide this word?	Between **m** and **b**
Listen to the word again: SYM bol (sĭm' bəl).	
Which syllable is the *strong* syllable?	The first syllable
Which syllable is the weak syllable?	The second syllable
Give the sound for the letter **y**.	/ ĭ /
Give the sound for the letter **o**. (Offer help.) *(Reminder: The letter **o** is in the weak syllable, and the sound is a weak / ŭ /.)*	/ ə /
What is this sound called?	Schwa
Give the sound for the letters **s** - **y** - **m**.	/ sĭm /
Give the sound for the letters **b** - **o** - **l**.	/ bəl /
Say the word, then spell it.	(Names while forming letters)
(Discuss the meaning.)	

TEACHER SAYS:	STUDENT RESPONDS:

The second word is *nimbus*. nimbus

How many syllables? Two

Where should you divide this word? Between **m** and **b**

Listen to the word again: NIM bus (nĭm' bəs).

Which syllable is the *strong* syllable? The first syllable

Which syllable is the weak syllable? The second syllable

Give the sound for the letters **n - i - m**. / nĭm /

Give the sound for the letters **b - u - s**. / bəs /

Give the sound for the letter **i** in the first syllable. / ĭ /

Give the sound for the letter **u** in the second syllable. / ə /

Say the word, then spell it. (Names while forming letters)

(Discuss the meaning.)

The last word is *pendant*. pendant

How many syllables? Two

Where should you divide this word? Between **n** and **d**

Listen to the word again: PEN dant (pĕn' dənt).

Which syllable is the *strong* syllable? The first syllable

Which syllable is the weak syllable? The second syllable

Give the sound of the letter **e** in the strong syllable. / ĕ /

Give the sound of the letter **a** in the weak syllable. / ə /

Yes, the letter **a** is in the weak syllable, and the
sound is a weak / ŭ /. What is this sound called? Schwa

What sound comes after the letter **p**? / ĕ /

What sound comes after the first **n**? / d /

What sound comes after the second **n**? / t /

What sound comes after the letter **d**? / ə /

Right! The weak / ŭ /, the schwa sound.

Give the sound for the letters **p - e - n**. / pĕn /

Give the sound for the letters **d - a - n - t**. / dənt /

Say the word, then spell it. (Names while forming letters)

(Discuss the meaning.)

TEACHER SAYS:	*STUDENT RESPONDS:*
The first word is *slush*.	slush
How many syllables?	One
Give the sound for the letter **u**.	/ ŭ /
Give the sound for the letters **s - h**.	/ sh /
Give the sound for the letters **s - l**.	/ sl /
What sound comes after the letter **l**?	/ ŭ /
What sound comes after the letter **u**?	/ sh /
Give the sound for the letters **u - s - h**.	/ ŭsh /
Say the word, then spell it.	(Names while forming letters)
(Discuss the meaning.)	

The second word is *quench*.	quench
How many syllables?	One
Give the sound for the letter **e**.	/ ĕ /
Give the sound for the letters **q - u**.	/ kw /
Give the sound for the letters **c - h**.	/ ch /
Give the sound for the letters **q - u - e - n**.	/ kwĕn /
What sound comes after the letter **e**?	/ n /
What sound comes after the letter **n**?	/ ch /
What sound comes *before* the letter **n**?	/ ĕ /
What sound comes *before* the letter **e**?	/ kw /
Say the word, then spell it.	(Names while forming letters)
(Discuss the meaning.)	

The third word is *shallop*.	shallop
How many syllables?	Two
Where should you divide this word?	Between the two **l**'s
Listen to the word again: SHAL lop (shăl' əp).	
Which syllable is the *strong* syllable?	The first syllable
Which syllable is the weak syllable?	The second syllable
Give the sound for the letter **o** (weak syllable).	/ ə /
What is this sound called?	Schwa
Give the sound for the letter **a** (strong syllable).	/ ă /
Give the sound for the letters **s - h**.	/ sh /
What sound comes after the letters **s - h**?	/ ă /
What sound comes after the letter **o**?	/ p /
What sound comes *before* the letter **o**?	/ l /
What sound comes before the letter **a**?	/ sh /
Give the sound for the letters **s - h - a - l**.	/ shăl /
Give the sound for the letters **l - o - p**.	/ ləp /
Say the word, then spell it.	(Names while forming letters)
(Discuss the meaning.)	

TEACHER SAYS:	STUDENT RESPONDS:

The last word is *chastise*. — chastise

How many syllables? — Two

Where should you divide this word? — Between **s** and **t**

Listen to the word again: CHAS TISE (chăs tīz').

Do we hear a really weak syllable in this word? — No.
*(No. We can hear two strong syllables, even though the
first syllable is just a little weaker than the second.
But we do hear strong vowel sounds in both syllables.
There is no schwa sound in this word.)*

Give the sound for the letter **a**. — / ă /

Give the sound for the letter **i**. — / ī /

Give the sound for the letter **e**. — No sound

Give the sound for the second letter **s**. — / z /

Give the sound for the letters **c - h**. — / ch /

Give the sound for the letters **i - s - e**. — / īz /

Say the word, then spell it. — (Names while forming letters)

(Discuss the meaning.)

WORD FOCUS   Book Two: Lesson 4

The first word is *hutch*. — hutch

How many syllables? — One

Give the sound for the letters **t - c - h**. — / ch /

Give the sound for the letter **u**. — / ŭ /

What sound comes *after* the letter **h**? — / ŭ /

What sound comes *before* the letter **u**? — / h /

What sound comes *before* the letter **t**? — / ŭ /

Say the word, then spell it. — (Names while forming letters)

(Discuss the meaning.)

The next word is *ratchet*. — ratchet

How many syllables? — Two

Where should you divide this word? — Between **h** and **e**

Which syllable is the *strong* syllable? — The first syllable

Which syllable is the weak syllable? — The second syllable

Give the sound for the letter **a**. — / ă /

Give the sound for the letter **e**. — / ə /

Give the sound for the letters **e - t**. — / ət /

Give the sound for the letters **t - c - h**. — / ch /

What sound comes *before* the letter **a**? — / r /

What sound comes *after* the letter **e**? — / t /

Say the word, then spell it. — (Names while forming letters)

(Discuss the meaning.)

TEACHER SAYS:	STUDENT RESPONDS:

The third word is *blotch*.   blotch

How many syllables?	One
What sound comes *after* the letter **l**?	/ ŏ /
What sound comes *before* the letter **l**?	/ b /
What sound comes *before* the letter **t**?	/ ŏ /
Give the sound for the letters **t - c - h**.	/ ch /
If you take away the **c - h**, what is the sound?	/ blŏt /
Say the word, then spell it.	(Names while forming letters)
(Discuss the meaning.)	

The last word is *dispatch*.   dispatch

How many syllables?	Two
Where should you divide this word?	Between s and **p**
Give the sound for the letter **a**.	/ ă /
What sound comes *before* the letters **t - c - h**?	/ ă /
What sound comes *after* the letter **p**?	/ ă /
Give the sound for the letters **p - a - t - c - h**.	/ pătch /
If you take away the **c - h** in the second syllable, what sound is left?	/ păt /
Give the sound for the letters **d - i - s**.	/ dĭs /
Say the word, then spell it.	(Names while forming letters)
(Discuss the meaning.)	

WORD FOCUS   Book Two: Lesson 6

The first word is *toxic*.   toxic

How many syllables?	Two
Where should you divide this word?	Between the **x** and **i**
Give the sound for the letter **o**.	/ ŏ /
Is the first syllable an open or closed syllable? *(Reminder: The sound of **o** is short, so the **x** stays in the first syllable. A closed syllable ends with a consonant.)*	A closed syllable
What sound comes *before* the letter **c**?	/ ĭ /
What sound is *in front of* the letter **c**?	/ ĭ /
What sound is *in front of* the letter **x**?	/ ŏ /
What sound comes *after* the letter **x**?	/ ĭ /
What sound comes *before* the letter **o**?	/ t /
Give the sound for the letters **t - o - x**.	/ tŏx /
Give the sound for the letters **i - c**.	/ ĭc /
Say the word, then spell it.	(Names while forming letters)
(Discuss the meaning.)	

TEACHER SAYS:	STUDENT RESPONDS:

The second word is *equal*. equal

How many syllables?	Two
Where should you divide this word?	Between the **e** and **q**
Give the sound for the letter **e**.	/ ē /
Is the first syllable open or closed? *(Reminder: The **e** is long, so there is no consonant after it. An open syllable ends with a vowel.)*	Open
Which syllable is the *strong* syllable?	The first syllable
Can a vowel be alone in a syllable?	Yes
Can a consonant be alone in a syllable?	No
Which syllable is the *weak* syllable?	The second syllable
Give the sound for the letters **q - u**.	/ kw /
Give the sound for the letter **a** in the weak syllable.	/ ə /
What is that sound called?	Schwa
What sound comes *before* the letter **q**?	/ ē /
What sound is *in front of* the letter **q**?	/ ē /
Say the word, then spell it.	(Names while forming letters)
(Discuss the meaning.)	

The third word is *slogan*. slogan

How many syllables?	Two
Which syllable is the *strong* syllable?	The first syllable
Is the first syllable open or closed?	Open
Which syllable is the weak syllable?	The second syllable
Give the sound for the letter **a**.	/ ə /
What sound is *in front of* the letter **a**?	/ g /
Is that **g** hard or soft?	Hard
Why?	The **g** does not have an **e**, **i**, or **y** after it, so the **g** is hard.
What sound comes *after* the letter **a**?	/ n /
Give the sound for the letters **g - a - n**.	/ gən /
What sound is *in front of* the letter **l**?	/ s /
What sound is *in front of* the letter **o**?	/ l /
Give the sound for the letters **s - l**.	/ sl /
Give the sound for the letter **o**.	/ ō /
Give the sound for the letters **s - l - o**.	/ slō /
Say the word, then spell it.	(Names while forming letters)
(Discuss the meaning.)	

TEACHER SAYS:	*STUDENT RESPONDS:*
The last word is *tepid.*	**tepid**
How many syllables?	Two
Is the first syllable open or closed?	Closed
How do you know?	(Wording will vary.)
Is the vowel in the first syllable long or short?	Short
What sound comes *after* the letter **t**?	/ ĕ /
What sound comes *before* the letter **p**?	/ ĕ /
What sound is *in front of* the letter **p**?	/ ĕ /
Give the sound for the letters **t - e - p**.	/ tĕp /
Is the first syllable the strong syllable?	Yes
(Yes, and the second syllable is the weak syllable. But in this word, the **i** *in the second syllable does not have a schwa sound. It has a short* **i** *sound. This sometimes happens with the letter* **i** *in weak syllables. So. . . .)*	
Give the sound for the letter **i**.	/ ĭ /
Give the sound for the letters **i - d**.	/ ĭd /
Say the word, then spell it.	(Names while forming letters)
(Discuss the meaning.)	

WORD FOCUS   Book Two: Lesson 7

The first word is *grotto.*	**grotto**
How many syllables?	Two
Where should you divide this word?	Between the two **t**'s
Is the first syllable open or closed?	Closed
Is the second syllable open or closed?	Open
Give the sound for the letter **o** in the first syllable.	/ ŏ /
Give the sound for the letter **o** in the second syllable.	/ ō /
What sound comes *before* the last letter **o**?	/ t /
What sound is *in front of* the letter **r**?	/ g /
What sound comes *after* the letter **g**?	/ r /
Give the sound for the letters **g - r - o - t**.	/ grŏt /
Give the sound for the letters **t - o**.	/ tō /
Say the word, then spell it.	(Names while forming letters)
(Discuss the meaning.)	

TEACHER SAYS:	STUDENT RESPONDS:

The second word is *zany*.

zany

How many syllables?	Two
Where should you divide this word?	Between the **a** and **n**
Is the first syllable open or closed?	Open
Is the second syllable open or closed?	Open
What sound is *in front of* the letter **n**?	/ ā /
What sound comes *after* the letter **n**?	/ ē /
(Reminder: *The letter **y** at the end of a two-syllable word almost always sounds like the long **e**.*)	
Give the sound for the letters **z - a**.	/ zā /
Give the sound for the letters **n - y**.	/ nē /
Say the word, then spell it.	(Names while forming letters)
(Discuss the meaning.)	

The third word is *matron*.

matron

How many syllables?	Two
Where should you divide this word?	Between the **a** and **t**
Which syllable is the strong syllable?	The first syllable
Is the first syllable open or closed?	Open
Give the sound for the letter **a**.	/ ā /
Which syllable is the weak syllable?	The second syllable
Is the second syllable open or closed?	Closed
Give the sound for the letter **o**.	/ ə /
What is that sound called?	Schwa
Give the sound for the letters **t - r - o - n**.	/ trən /
Say the word, then spell it.	(Names while forming letters)
(Discuss the meaning.)	

The fourth word is *solo*.

solo

How many syllables?	Two
Is the first syllable open or closed?	Open
Is the second syllable open or closed?	Open
What sound comes after the letter **s**?	/ ō /
What sound is in front of the letter **l**?	/ ō /
What sound comes after the letter **l**?	/ ō /
What sound comes *between* the two **o**'s?	/ l /
What sound comes *between* the **s** and **l**?	/ ō /
Say the word, then spell it.	(Names while forming letters)
(Discuss the meaning.)	

TEACHER SAYS:	*STUDENT RESPONDS:*
The fifth word is *nobody*.	**nobody**
How many syllables?	Three
Where should the first division be?	Between **o** and **b**
Where should the second division be?	Between **d** and **y**
Is the first syllable open or closed?	Open
Give the sound for the letter **o** in the first syllable.	/ ō /
Give the sound for the letters **n - o**.	/ nō /
Is the second syllable open or closed?	Closed
Give the sound for the letter **o** in the second syllable.	/ ŏ /
Give the sound for the letters **b - o - d**.	/ bŏd /
Is the third syllable open or closed?	Open
Give the sound for the letter **y** in the third syllable.	/ ē /
Can a vowel be alone in a syllable?	Yes
Can a consonant be alone in a syllable?	No
Say the word, then spell it.	(Names while forming letters)
(Discuss the meaning.)	

WORD FOCUS   Book Two: Lesson 8

The first word is *thrash*.	**thrash**
How many syllables?	Two
Is this an open or a closed syllable?	Closed
Give the sound for the letters **t - h**.	/ th /
Give the sound for the letters **t - h - r**.	/ thr /
Give the sound for the letters **s - h**.	/ sh /
What sound comes between **r** and **s**?	/ ă /
Say the word, then spell it.	(Names while forming letters)
(Discuss the meaning.)	
The next word is *pithy*.	**pithy**
How many syllables?	Two
Where should you divide this word?	Between **h** and **y**
Is the first syllable open or closed?	Closed
Give the sound for the letter **i**.	/ ĭ /
What sound comes after the letter **i**?	/ th /
Is the second syllable open or closed?	Open
Give the sound for the letter **y**.	/ ē /
Is the letter **y** a vowel or a consonant?	Vowel
What sound comes between the **i** and **y**?	/ th /
Say the word, then spell it.	(Names while forming letters)
(Discuss the meaning.)	

TEACHER SAYS:	STUDENT RESPONDS:
The last word is *fathom*.*	**fathom**
How many syllables?	Two
Where should you divide this word?	Between **h** and **o**
Is the first syllable open or closed?	Closed
Is the second syllable open or closed?	Closed
Which syllable is the strong syllable?	The first syllable
Give the sound for the letter **a**.	/ ă /
Which syllable is the weak syllable?	The second syllable
Give the sound for the letter **o**.	/ ə /
What is this sound called?	Schwa
Listen to the word again: FATH om (fă~~th~~' əm)	
Give the sound for the letters **t - h**.	/ ~~th~~ /
Pronounce the first syllable.	/ fa~~th~~ /
Pronounce the second syllable.	/ əm /
Say the word, then spell it.	(Names while forming letters)
(Discuss the meaning.)	

WORD FOCUS

Book Two: Lesson 9

The first word is *whet*.	**whet**
Give the sound for the letters **w - h**.	/ hw /
What sound is in front of the letter **t**?	/ ě /
Give the sound for the letters **e - t**.	/ ět /
If we take away the **h**, what is the sound?	/ wět /
Say the word **wet** again.	/ wět /
Now say **whet**.	/ hwět /
Can you hear the difference?	
(If the answer is "no," compare the words again.	
Demonstrate holding the hand in front of the mouth;	
*the breath can be felt when pronouncing **whet**.)*	
Say the word, then spell it.	(Names while forming letters)
(Discuss the meaning.)	

---

* **th** is voiced.

TEACHER SAYS:	*STUDENT RESPONDS:*

The second word is *phantom*.

<table>
<tr><td></td><td>phantom</td></tr>
<tr><td>How many syllables are in this word?</td><td>Two</td></tr>
<tr><td>Where should you divide this word?</td><td>Between n and t</td></tr>
<tr><td>Which syllable is the strong syllable?</td><td>The first syllable</td></tr>
<tr><td>Is the first syllable open or closed?</td><td>Closed</td></tr>
<tr><td>What sound does the letter a make?</td><td>/ ă /</td></tr>
<tr><td>What sound do the letters p - h make?</td><td>/ f /</td></tr>
<tr><td>Which syllable is the weak syllable?</td><td>The second syllable</td></tr>
<tr><td>Give the sound for the letter o.</td><td>/ ə /</td></tr>
<tr><td>Pronounce the first syllable.</td><td>/ făn /</td></tr>
<tr><td>Pronounce the second syllable.</td><td>/ təm /</td></tr>
<tr><td>Say the word, then spell it.</td><td>(Names while forming letters)</td></tr>
<tr><td>(Discuss the meaning.)</td><td></td></tr>
</table>

The last word is *whimsy*.

<table>
<tr><td></td><td>whimsy</td></tr>
<tr><td>How many syllables?</td><td>Two</td></tr>
<tr><td>Where should you divide this word?</td><td>Between m and s</td></tr>
<tr><td>Which syllable is the strong syllable?</td><td>The first syllable</td></tr>
<tr><td>Give the sound for the letter i.</td><td>/ ĭ /</td></tr>
<tr><td>Give the sound for the letters w - h.</td><td>/ hw /</td></tr>
<tr><td>Pronounce the first syllable.</td><td>/ hwĭm /</td></tr>
<tr><td>Give the sound for the letter s.</td><td>/ z /</td></tr>
<tr><td>Give the sound for the letter y.</td><td>/ ē /</td></tr>
<tr><td>Is the letter y a vowel or a consonant?</td><td>Vowel</td></tr>
<tr><td>Pronounce the second syllable.</td><td>/ zē /</td></tr>
<tr><td>Say the word, then spell it.</td><td>(Names while forming letters)</td></tr>
<tr><td>(Discuss the meaning.)</td><td></td></tr>
</table>

WORD FOCUS

Book Two: Lesson 11

The first word is *bobble*.

<table>
<tr><td></td><td>bobble</td></tr>
<tr><td>How many syllables?</td><td>Two</td></tr>
<tr><td>Where should you divide this word?</td><td>Between the two b's</td></tr>
<tr><td>(Reminder: If a word ends in Consonant-le, you can count back three letters, starting at the end of the word. The word will automatically be divided for you. Or, you can use the regular rule.)</td><td></td></tr>
<tr><td>Which syllable is the strong syllable?</td><td>The first syllable</td></tr>
<tr><td>Is the first syllable open or closed?</td><td>Closed</td></tr>
<tr><td>What sound comes after the first letter b?</td><td>/ ŏ /</td></tr>
<tr><td>Pronounce the first syllable.</td><td>/ bŏb /</td></tr>
<tr><td>Pronounce the second syllable.</td><td>/ bəl /</td></tr>
<tr><td>Say the word, then spell it.</td><td>(Names while forming letters)</td></tr>
<tr><td>(Discuss the meaning.)</td><td></td></tr>
</table>

TEACHER SAYS:	*STUDENT RESPONDS:*

The second word is *dwindle*. dwindle

How many syllables? Two

Where should you divide this word? Between **n** and **d**

Is the first syllable open or closed? Closed

What sound comes between the **w** and **n**? / ĭ /

Give the sound for the letters **d - w**. / dw /

Give the sound for the letters **d - w - i - n**. / dwĭn /

In the first syllable, if you take away the **d**, what sound is left? / wĭn /

Pronounce the second syllable. / dəl /

In the second syllable, what sound comes before the letter **l**? / d /

In the second syllable, what sound comes after the letter **d**? / l /

Say the word, then spell it. (Names while forming letters)

(Discuss the meaning.)

The last word is *trifle*. trifle

How many syllables? Two

Where should you divide this word? Between **i** and **f**

How do you know where to divide this word? (Answers will vary.)

How do you know not to divide it between **f** and **l**?
*(There are two correct answers: Count back three letters, starting at the end of the word, and it will automatically be divided; or, the word should be divided after the open syllable / trī /. Some students may confuse this word with **triple**.)*

Is the first syllable open or closed? Open

What sound comes before the letter **f**? / ī /

Pronounce the first syllable. / trī /

Pronounce the second syllable. / fəl /

Say the word, then spell it. (Names while forming letters)

(Discuss the meaning.)

WORD FOCUS   Book Two: Lesson 12

The first word is *throng*. throng

Give the sound for the letter **o**. / ŏ /

Give the sound for the letters **o - n - g**. / ŏng /

What sound comes between **h** and **o**? / r /

Give the sound for the letters **t - h**. / th /

Say the word, then spell it. (Names while forming letters)

(Discuss the meaning.)

TEACHER SAYS:	*STUDENT RESPONDS:*

The next word is *clink*. clink

Give the sound for the letters **c - l**.	/ kl /
What sound comes between **l** and **n**?	/ ĭ /
What sound comes before the letter **i**?	/ l /
What sound comes after the letter **c**?	/ l /
What sound is in front of the letter **l**?	/ k /
Give the sound for the letters **n - k**.	/ nk /
Give the sound for the letters **i - n - k**.	/ ĭnk /
If you take away the **c** in this word, what is the sound?	/ lĭnk /
Say the word, then spell it.	(Names while forming letters)
(Discuss the meaning.)	

The last word is *shantung*. shantung

How many syllables?	Two
Where should you divide this word?	Between **n** and **t**
Is the first syllable open or closed?	Closed
Is the second syllable open or closed?	Closed
Give the sound for the letter **u**.	/ ŭ /
Give the sound for the letter **a**.	/ ă /
Give the sound for the letters **s - h**.	/ sh /
If we take away the **sh** in the first syllable, what is the sound?	/ ăn /
If we take away the **g** in the second syllable, what is the sound?	/ tŭn /
Pronounce the first syllable.	/ shăn /
Pronounce the second syllable.	/ tŭng /
Say the word, then spell it.	(Names while forming letters)
(Discuss the meaning.)	

WORD FOCUS Book Two: Lesson 13

The first word is *chuckle*. chuckle

How many syllables?	Two
Where should you divide this word?	Between **k** and **l**
*(Reminder: If a word has the **ck** digraph, you cannot divide the **c** and **k**. Demonstrate: **chuck le**.)*	
What sound comes between **ch** and **ck**?	/ ŭ /
Give the sound for the letters **c - h**.	/ ch /
Give the sound for the letters **c - k**.	/ k /
Pronounce the first syllable.	/ chŭk /
Pronounce the second syllable.	/ əl /
Which syllable is the strong syllable?	The first syllable
Say the word, then spell it.	(Names while forming letters)
(Discuss the meaning.)	

TEACHER SAYS:	STUDENT RESPONDS:

The second word is *brackish*.　　　　　　　　brackish

How many syllables?	Two
Which syllable is the strong syllable?	The first syllable
Which syllable is the weak syllable?	The second syllable
Pronounce the first syllable.	/ brăk /
Pronounce the second syllable.	/ ĭsh /
Where should you divide this word?	Between **k** and **i**
Say the word, then spell it.	(Names while forming letters)
(Discuss the meaning.)	

The last word is *fetlock*.　　　　　　　　fetlock

How many syllables?	Two
Where should you divide this word?	Between **t** and **l**
What sound comes between **f** and **t**?	/ ĕ /
What sound comes after the letter **o**?	/ k /
What sound is in front of the letter **c**?	/ ŏ /
What sound comes before the letter **t**?	/ ĕ /
What sound comes between **t** and **o**?	/ l /
Does this word have a strong syllable?	(Responses will vary.)

(Both syllables are strong in this word, but the first syllable is a little stronger. You can hear the short vowel in each syllable; there is no schwa sound.)

Say the word, then spell it.	(Names while forming letters)
(Discuss the meaning.)	

WORD FOCUS　　　　　　　　　　　　　　　　**Book Two: Lesson 14**

The first word is *cartridge*.　　　　　　　　cartridge

How many syllables?	Two
Where should you divide this word?	(Responses will vary.)

It's better to keep the **t** and **r** together because **tr**
is a consonant blend. So where should you divide?　　　Between **r** and **t**

Which syllable is the strong syllable?	The first syllable
Pronounce the first syllable.	/ kär /
Which syllable is the weak syllable?	The second syllable

Yes — even though the second syllable is weak, the
letter **i** does not have a schwa sound. It has a short **i**
sound. Remember, **i** sometimes is short in a weak
syllable. So, what sound does the letter **i** make?　　　/ ĭ /

Give the sound for the letters **d - g - e**.	/ j /
Pronounce the second syllable.	/ trĭj /
Say the word, then spell it.	(Names while forming letters)
(Discuss the meaning.)	

TEACHER SAYS:	STUDENT RESPONDS:

The next word is *abridge*.

	abridge
How many syllables?	Two
Where should you divide this word?	Between **a** and **b**
*(Right. The letter **a** by itself at the beginning of a word is a syllable.)*	
Give the sound for the letter **a**.	/ ə /
What is this sound called?	Schwa
Is it an open or closed syllable?	Open
*(Yes! The schwa **a** can be an open syllable.)*	
Which syllable is the strong syllable?	The second syllable
Give the sound for the letter **i**.	/ ĭ /
Give the sound for the letters **d - g - e**.	/ j /
What sound is in front of the letter **i**?	/ r /
What sound comes after the letter **b**?	/ r /
What sound comes between **b** and **i**?	/ r /
What sound comes before the letter **i**?	/ r /
Pronounce the first syllable.	/ ə /
Pronounce the second syllable.	/ brĭj /
Say the word, then spell it.	(Names while forming letters)
(Discuss the meaning.)	

The last word is *hodgepodge*.

	hodgepodge
How many syllables?	Two
Where should you divide this word?	Between **e** and **p**
*(That's right — you should not separate the combination **dge**.)*	
Pronounce the first syllable.	/ hŏj /
Pronounce the second syllable.	/ pŏj /
Do we hear a really weak syllable in this word?	No.
Give the sound for the letter **o**.	/ ŏ /
Give the sound for the letters **d - g - e**.	/ j /
Say the word, then spell it.	(Names while forming letters)
(Discuss the meaning.)	

TEACHER SAYS:	*STUDENT RESPONDS:*

The first word is *parcels*.

	parcels
How many syllables?	Two
Where should you divide this word?	Between **r** and **c**
Is the first syllable open or closed?	Closed
Pronounce the first syllable.	/ pär /
Is the second syllable open or closed?	Closed
Which syllable is the strong syllable?	The first syllable
Which syllable is the weak syllable?	The second syllable
Give the sound for the letter **e**.	/ ə /
What is this sound called?	Schwa
Give the sound for the letter **c**.	/ s /
How do you know that the **c** sounds like an **s**?	When **c** has **e**, **i**, or **y** after it, the sound of **c** is usually soft.
What sound is at the end of the word?	/ z /
What does the affix **s** mean?	"More than one"
Say the word, then spell it.	(Names while forming letters)
(Discuss the meaning.)	

The second word is *campuses*.

	campuses
How many syllables?	Three
Where should you divide this word? (Offer help.)	Between **m** and **p**, and between the first **s** and **e**
Is the first syllable open or closed?	Closed
Is the second syllable open or closed?	Closed
Is the third syllable open or closed?	Closed
Why is **e** - **s** added to this word, not just **s**?	If a word ends with the letter **s**, add **es**.
Pronounce the first syllable.	/ kăm /
Pronounce the second syllable.	/ pəs /
Pronounce the third syllable.	/ əz /
Which syllable is the strong syllable?	The first syllable
What vowel sound do you hear in the first syllable?	/ ă /
What vowel sound do you hear in the second syllable?	/ ə /
What vowel sound do you hear in the third syllable?	/ ə /
Say the word, then spell it.	(Names while forming letters)
(Discuss the meaning.)	

TEACHER SAYS:	STUDENT RESPONDS:
The third word is *hamlets*.	hamlets
How many syllables?	Two
Where should you divide this word?	Between the **m** and **l**
What sound comes between the letters **h** and **m**?	/ ă /
What sound comes before the letter **a**?	/ h /
What sound comes after the letter **a**?	/ m /
Pronounce the first syllable.	/ hăm /
Is this a strong or a weak syllable?	A strong syllable
What sound comes after the letter **t**?	/ s /
What does the affix **s** mean?	"More than one"
What sound comes between the letters **m** and **e**?	/ l /
What sound is in front of the letter **t**?	/ ə /
What sound comes after the letter **l**?	/ ə /
What is this sound called?	Schwa
What sound comes before the letter **s**?	/ t /
Pronounce the second syllable.	/ ləts /
Is this a strong syllable or a weak syllable?	A weak syllable
Say the word, then spell it.	(Names while forming letters)
(Discuss the meaning.)	

TEACHER SAYS:	STUDENT RESPONDS:
The last word is *athletes*.	athletes
How many syllables?	Two
Where should you divide this word?	Between **h** and **l**
Which syllable is the strong syllable?	The first syllable
Give the sound for the letter **a**.	/ ă /
Give the sound for the letters **t - h**.	/ th /
Pronounce the first syllable.	/ ăth /
What does the affix **s** mean?	"More than one"
Give the sound for the first letter **e**.	/ ē /
How do you know that it has a long e sound?	Because of the silent **e** at the end of the root word.
Give the sound for the letters **l - e - t - e**.	/ lēt /
Give the sound for the letters **l - e - t - e - s**.	/ lēts /
Say the word, then spell it.	(Names while forming letters)
(Discuss the meaning.)	

TEACHER SAYS: *STUDENT RESPONDS:*

The first word is *signs*.   **signs**

How many syllables?   One

The affix **s** at the end of this word can have two meanings.
It can mean "more than one sign," as in the sentence
Freeways have many traffic signs. It can also be the
s form of a verb, as we studied in this lesson. Can you
think of a sentence that uses this word as a verb?   (Responses will vary.)

What is the root word?   sign

Is this word spelled the way it sounds?   No

Give the sound for the letter **i**.   / ī /

Give the sound for the letter **g**.   No sound (silent)

What sound comes before the letter **i**?   / s /

What sound does the affix **s** make?   / z /

What sound comes after the letter **i**?   / n /

Say the word, then spell it.   (Names while forming letters)

(Discuss the meaning.)

The second word is *sings*.   **sings**

How many syllables?   One

Is this syllable open or closed?   Closed

Give the sound for the letter **i**.   / ĭ /

Give the sound for the letters **i - n - g**.   / ĭng /

Give the sound for the beginning letter **s**.   / s /

Give the sound for the ending letter **s**.   / z /

What sound is in front of the letter **n**?   / ĭ /

What sound comes after the first letter **s**?   / ĭ /

What sound follows the first letter **s**?   / ĭ /

What sound follows the letters **n - g**?   / z /

What sound follows the letter **i**?   / ng /

Say the word, then spell it.   (Names while forming letters)

(Discuss the meaning.)

TEACHER SAYS:	STUDENT RESPONDS:

The third word is *singes*.

<table>
<tr><td></td><td>singes</td></tr>
<tr><td>How many syllables?</td><td>Two</td></tr>
<tr><td>If you take away the affix s in this word, what is the root word?</td><td>singe</td></tr>
<tr><td>How do you know that the g is soft?</td><td>When g has e, i, or y after it, the sound of g is usually soft.</td></tr>
<tr><td>Listen to the word again: SIN ges (sĭn' jəz).</td><td></td></tr>
<tr><td>Which syllable is the strong syllable?</td><td>The first syllable</td></tr>
<tr><td>Pronounce the first syllable.</td><td>/ sĭn /</td></tr>
<tr><td>What sound comes after the first letter s?</td><td>/ ĭ /</td></tr>
<tr><td>What sound follows the first letter s?</td><td>/ ĭ /</td></tr>
<tr><td>What sound follows the letter i?</td><td>/ n /</td></tr>
<tr><td>Which syllable is the weak syllable?</td><td>The second syllable</td></tr>
<tr><td>Pronounce the second syllable.</td><td>/ jəz /</td></tr>
<tr><td>What sound follows the letter g?</td><td>/ ə /</td></tr>
<tr><td>What sound follows the letter e?</td><td>/ z /</td></tr>
<tr><td>Say the word, then spell it.</td><td>(Names while forming letters)</td></tr>
<tr><td>(Discuss the meaning.)</td><td></td></tr>
</table>

The last word is *snitches*.

<table>
<tr><td></td><td>snitches</td></tr>
<tr><td>How many syllables?</td><td>Two</td></tr>
<tr><td>What is the root word?</td><td>snitch</td></tr>
<tr><td>Can you divide the root word into syllables?</td><td>No</td></tr>
<tr><td>Which syllable is the strong syllable?</td><td>The first syllable</td></tr>
<tr><td>Which syllable is the weak syllable?</td><td>The second syllable</td></tr>
<tr><td>What sound comes after the first letter s?</td><td>/ n /</td></tr>
<tr><td>What sound follows the letter n?</td><td>/ ĭ /</td></tr>
<tr><td>Give the sound for the letters t - c - h.</td><td>/ ch /</td></tr>
<tr><td>Is the first syllable open or closed?</td><td>Closed</td></tr>
<tr><td>Pronounce the first syllable.</td><td>/ snĭch /</td></tr>
<tr><td>Pronounce the second syllable.</td><td>/ əz /</td></tr>
<tr><td>Give the sound for the letter e.</td><td>/ ə /</td></tr>
<tr><td>What is this sound called?</td><td>Schwa</td></tr>
<tr><td>What sound does the last letter s make?</td><td>/ z /</td></tr>
<tr><td>Say the word, then spell it.</td><td>(Names while forming letters)</td></tr>
<tr><td>(Discuss the meaning.)</td><td></td></tr>
</table>

TEACHER SAYS:	STUDENT RESPONDS:

The first word is *scrapped*.

scrapped

How many syllables?

One

What is the root word?

scrap

Why is the letter **p** doubled before adding the affix **ed**? (Offer help.)

If a one-syllable word ends with CVC, double the last consonant before adding an affix that starts with a vowel.

Can this word be divided into syllables?

No.

Tell me why.

(Wording will vary.)

What sound comes before the letter **c**?

/ s /

What sound is in front of the letter **c**?

/ s /

What sound comes after the letter **c**?

/ r /

What sound follows the letter **c**?

/ r /

Give the sound for the letters **s - c - r**.

/ scr /

What sound comes between the letters **r** and **p**?

/ ă /

Listen to the word again: SCRAPPED (scrăpt).

What sound do the letters **e - d** make?

/ t /

What does the affix **ed** mean?

"In the past"

Say the word, then spell it.

(Names while forming letters)

(Discuss the meaning.)

The second word is *gritting*.

gritting

How many syllables?

Two

Where should you divide this word?

Between the two **t**'s

Is the first syllable open or closed?

Closed

Pronounce the first syllable.

/ grĭt /

What sound follows the letter **g**?

/ r /

What sound follows the letter **r**?

/ ĭ /

What sound follows the letter **i**?

/ t /

What is the root word?

grit

Why is the **t** doubled in this word? *(Review Doubling Rule.)*

(Wording will vary.)

Pronounce the second syllable.

/ tĭng /

What sound comes before the letter **n**?

/ ĭ /

What sound is in front of the letter **r**?

/ g /

What is the affix in this word?

ing

Say the word, then spell it.

(Names while forming letters)

(Discuss the meaning.)

TEACHER SAYS:	STUDENT RESPONDS:
The next word is *crabby*.	**crabby**
What is the root word?	**crab**
What affix has been added to the end of this word?	**y**
Is **y** a vowel at the end of a word?	Yes.
Why is the **b** doubled?	(Wording will vary.)
(Review Doubling Rule.)	
How many syllables?	Two
Where should you divide this word?	Between the two **b**'s
Is the first syllable open or closed?	Closed
Give the sound for the letter **a**.	/ ă /
Give the sound for the letter **y**.	/ ē /
Pronounce the first syllable.	/ krăb /
Pronounce the second syllable.	/ bē /
Say the word, then spell it.	(Names while forming letters)
(Discuss the meaning.)	
The last word is *throbbed*.	**throbbed**
What is the root word?	**throb**
Give the sound for the letters **t - h**.	/ th /
What sound comes after the letter **r**?	/ ŏ /
What sound follows the letter **o**?	/ b /
Why is the **b** doubled?	(Wording will vary.)
(Review Doubling Rule.)	
Listen to the word again: THROBBED (thrŏbd)	
What sound does the affix **ed** make?	/ d /
Can this word be divided into syllables?	No
Tell me why.	(Wording will vary.)
Say the word, then spell it.	(Names while forming letters)
(Discuss the meaning.)	

TEACHER SAYS:	*STUDENT RESPONDS:*

The first word is *matted*.   **matted**

How many syllables?	Two
Where should you divide this word?	Between the two **t**'s
Which syllable is the strong syllable?	The first syllable
Which syllable is the weak syllable?	The second syllable
Is the first syllable open or closed?	Closed
Give the sound for the letter **a**.	/ ă /
Is the second syllable open or closed?	Closed
Give the sound for the affix **ed**.	/ əd /
What is the root word?	**mat**
Spell the root word.	**m - a - t**
Why is the **t** doubled in this word? *(Review Doubling Rule.)*	(Wording will vary.)
Say the word, then spell it.	(Names while forming letters)
(Discuss the meaning.)	

The second word is *mated*.   **mated**

What is the root word?	**mate**
What do you have to do before you add the affix **ed** to this word?	Drop the (silent) **e**
How many syllables are in this word?	Two
Give the sound for the letter **a**.	/ ā /
The letter **a** has a long sound, so where should you divide this word?	After the **a**
Is the first syllable open or closed?	Open
Pronounce the first syllable.	/ mā /
Pronounce the second syllable.	/ təd /
Is the second syllable open or closed?	Closed
Is the second syllable strong or weak?	Weak
Give the sound for the letter **e**.	/ ə /
Say the word, then spell it.	(Names while forming letters)
(Discuss the meaning.)	

TEACHER SAYS:	STUDENT RESPONDS:

The third word is *griping*. griping

What is the root word? **gripe**

What do you have to do before you add
the affix **ing** to this word? Drop the (silent) **e**

How many syllables are in this word? Two

Give the sound for the letter **i**. / ī /

Where should you divide this word? After the **i**

Is the first syllable open or closed? Open

Pronounce the first syllable. / grī /

Pronounce the second syllable. / pĭng /

What sound follows the letter **p**? / ĭ /

What sound follows the second letter **i**? / ng /

What sound comes before the letter **r**? / g /

What sound comes after the letter **r**? / ī /

What sound comes between the two **i**'s? / p /

Say the word, then spell it. (Names while forming letters)

(Discuss the meaning.)

The last word is *gripping*. gripping

How many syllables? Two

Where should you divide this word? Between the two **p**'s

Pronounce the first syllable. / grĭp /

What is the root word? **grip**

Spell the root word. **g - r - i - p**

Why is the **p** doubled in this word? (Wording will vary.)

Pronounce the second syllable. / pĭng /

In the second syllable, what letter is in front of **i**? / p /

What sound follows the letter **p**? / ĭ /

What sound comes after the second letter **i**? / ng /

Say the word, then spell it. (Names while forming letters)

(Discuss the meaning.)

Dictation

A main dictation exercise comes at the end of each regular lesson in all the Student Books. This carefully structured activity includes *WORDS, WORD GROUPS,* and *SENTENCE* which contain only words that have been presented in current or previous lessons.

Learning to take dictation acts as a springboard to further learning. It strengthens auditory memory, helps to increase attention span, and reinforces spelling. It establishes, in the students' minds, the close relationship between the oral and the written word.

Dictation practice—at a level that learners can handle—is a powerful way to build writing confidence. Ideally, a well-designed dictation exercise helps students test their newly learned skills, provides practice in proofreading, and leaves students with a feeling of success.

Many learners have trouble integrating their visual, auditory, and handwriting skills. Dictation helps them to do this, but much practice is needed. For this reason, extra practice material is provided in this Guide immediately after the regular dictation lessons. (Extra practice is optional and will have to be done on separate paper or in a separate dictation notebook.) The extra practice sentences can also be used for oral reading.

Learners seldom show as dramatic gains in spelling as in reading. Very poor spellers often benefit from being given the same dictation exercise, or block of extra practice sentences, repeatedly over a period of time. (Also see *Letter-Card Spelling,* pages 165-167, and the *Sight Word Study Method,* page 165 of this Guide.)

Instead of erasing, have students put a single horizontal line through any misspelled word. They should rewrite the word correctly next to the word with the line through it. This procedure strengthens visual-kinesthetic memory—seeing the correct spelling of the word and, at the same time, sensing how it feels to write the whole word accurately.

After dictating a sentence, allow time for students to write, read out loud, and edit their sentences. Then ask, "Does your sentence look like a sentence?" This question reminds them to begin with a capital letter and end with a period, a question mark, or (later on) an exclamation point.

PROCEDURE FOR DICTATION

The main dictation for each lesson is presented in a box. Each dictation exercise has three parts:

    (1) *Words* (sight words first; then phonetically-regular words),

    (2) *Word Groups* (phrases and clauses), and

    (3) *Sentences*.

Preparing for Dictation

Have students number the lines to be used. For example, say "Under WORDS, number each line from 1 to 14." Then, "Under WORD GROUPS, number each line from 1 to 5." Finally, "Under SENTENCES, number every other line from 1 to 3."

Dictating Words and Word Groups

Under *WORDS*, dictate both sight words and phonetically-regular words. The sight words are listed first. Next, dictate the *WORD GROUPS*.

Write each word or word group on the chalkboard where it can be seen as soon as the students have written their own. (If you are working with an individual learner and no chalkboard is available, write the words or word groups on a sheet of paper.) The spelling can thus be verified immediately and corrected, if necessary. This procedure sets up learners for success at the sentence level.*

Dictating Sentences

Before you begin dictating sentences, erase the chalkboard and have students cover the words and word groups they have just written.

Ask the students to lay down their pencils and listen while you read the entire sentence. Read it twice. Have students repeat it together, out loud, before picking up their pencils and writing. (Repeating the sentence orally helps individuals to develop auditory memory.) If necessary, read the sentence a third time, phrase by phrase, as the students write.

If working with a large group, write each sentence on the chalkboard so that students can proofread their own work. If working with only one person or a small group, go over the sentences individually with each learner.

---

* Some individuals have difficulty copying and "proofreading" from a chalkboard. If being moved closer to the board doesn't help, they will need individual attention from the teacher or another learner, who may take on the role of a tutor.

WORDS (Sight Words* are listed first) (13):

the, a**
at, lab, ran, lap, Jess, wet, met, vet, Jill, on, sod

WORD GROUPS:

1. *a* vet at *the* lab
2. ran *a* lap
3. met Jess
4. on wet sod

SENTENCES:

1. Jill met *the* vet at *the* lab.
2. Jess ran *a* lap on wet sod.

ADDITIONAL EXERCISE 1 (for students who need intensive practice at this level) — short **a**

WORDS (8):

the, a
had, hat, fat, ran, man, tan

WORD GROUPS:

1. *the* fat man
2. *a* tan rat
3. had *the* hat

SENTENCES:

1. *The* man had *a* tan hat.
2. *The* fat rat ran.

---

* Throughout the dictation for Student Book 1, sight words are in italics. Students, especially those with a weak visual memory of words, should review sight words at the beginning of each dictation lesson. (See *Sight Word Study Method* on page 165 of this Guide.) For the purposes of this program, the list of sight words includes not only phonetically-irregular words, but any word whose components have yet to be introduced. For example, until the **or** combination is introduced, the word **for** will be listed as a sight word.

The sight words **the and **a** should be pronounced naturally, with an unstressed / ŭ / sound, NOT as "thē lab," or "ā vet."

ADDITIONAL EXERCISE 2 — short **i**

WORDS (11):

the, a
hid, kid, kit, hit, in, pin, Tim, rib, Liz

WORD GROUPS:
1. *a* pin in *the* kit
2. Liz hid
3. hit *the* kid
4. in *the* rib

SENTENCES:
1. Liz hid *the* pin in *a* kit.
2. *The* kid hit Tim in *the* rib.

ADDITIONAL EXERCISE 3 — short **e, i**

WORDS (11):

the, a
Ted, fed, red, pen, hen, bell, will, in, Jim

WORD GROUPS:
1. sell *the* bell
2. fed *the* red hen
3. will Jim
4. in *a* pen

SENTENCES:
1. Ted fed *a* hen in *the* pen.
2. Will Jim sell *the* red bell?

ADDITIONAL EXERCISE 4 — short **i, u**

WORDS (11):

the
did, hill, in, hid, Kim, up, Russ, run, pup, hut

WORD GROUPS:
1. hid in *the* hut
2. run *the* pup
3. did Russ
4. up *the* hill

SENTENCES:
1. Did Russ run up *the* hill?
2. Kim hid *the* pup in *the* hut.

ADDITIONAL EXERCISE 5 — short **a**, **i**, **o**, **u**

WORDS (11):

the
had, sat, it, in, hot, mop, Tom, on, mud, sun

WORD GROUPS:
1. had Tom
2. on *the* mop
3. hot mud on it
4. sat in *the* sun

SENTENCES:
1. *The* mop had mud on it.
2. Tom sat in *the* hot sun.

ADDITIONAL EXERCISE 6 — short **a**, **e**, **i**, **u**

WORDS (15):

the, a
had, map, Pam, van, fed, tell, Bill, will, in, if, Bud, us, pup

WORD GROUPS:
1. had *the* map
2. if Bud
3. *a* pup in *the* van
4. had fed us
5. will tell Pam

SENTENCES:
1. Bud had *a* map in *the* van.
2. Pam will tell us if Bill fed *the* pup.

EXTRA PRACTICE

For students who are reading at this level, these sentences may be used for oral reading practice as well as dictation.

1. *The* pup bit *the* man on *the* lip.
2. *The* kid had fun in *the* tub.
3. Did *the* kid fill *the* tub?
4. Did *a* vet win *the* bet?
5. *A* vet did not win it.
6. Bill had *a* job at *the* mill.
7. Will *the* bed fit in *the* den?
8. *The* bed will not fit.
9. Ten men sat in *the* red bus.

10. Did *the* ten men fill *the* bus?
11. *The* pup had fun in *the* mud.
12. *The* pup sat in it.
13. Pam fed *the* pet rat.
14. *The* pet rat ran.
15. Sam had *a* bat in *the* van.
16. *The* bat fell on *the* mat.
17. Did Kim tell *a* fib?
18. Kim did not.
19. Bob fed *the* wet hen.
20. *The* wet hen ran up *the* hill.
21. Will *the* tan hat fit *the* man?
22. *The* hat will not fit.
23. *A* mad man sat on *the* tan hat.
24. *The* ill man had *a* pill.
25. Bob met *the* ill man on *the* bus.
26. Did *a* tan van hit *the* red bus?
27. *A* tan van did not hit it.
28. *The* pan had *a* hot lid.
29. *The* hot lid fell.
30. Did *the* man sell *the* lot?

WORDS 1 DICTATION

WORDS:

1.	kit	10.	not
2.	mad	11.	at
3.	hop	12.	fin
4.	pin	13.	mat
5.	tub	14.	rod
6.	rob	15.	win
7.	tap	16.	bit
8.	rip	17.	mop
9.	dim	18.	nap

ADDITIONAL WORDS (Optional):

1.	pan	6.	jut
2.	tot	7.	pet
3.	lop	8.	man
4.	rat	9.	pal
5.	van	10.	fat

WORDS (13):

the, a

had, men, did, in, dip, name, take, Pete, same, nine, lake

WORD GROUPS:

1. did Pete take
2. same nine men
3. had *the* name
4. dip in *a* lake

SENTENCES:

1. Nine men had *the* same name.
2. Did Pete take *a* dip in *the* lake?

ADDITIONAL EXERCISE (Optional)

WORDS (13):

the, a, for

us, hum, at, bell, will, Wade, wake, five, tune, Sue

WORD GROUPS:

1. *a* tune *for* Wade
2. will wake Sue
3. hum *for* us
4. *the* bell at five

SENTENCES:

1. Sue will hum *for* us.
2. Will *the* bell wake Wade at five?

EXTRA PRACTICE (Review **to** and **into**.*)

1. Rod rode *a* mile on *the* bike.
2. Kate ran *a* mile, but Mike ran five.
3. Did Pete take *a* nap?
4. Tell Pete *to* take *a* hike.
5. Tell him *to* hike up *the* hill.
6. Did Jake take *the* job at *the* mill?

---

* Sight words under Review will appear four or more times in the Extra Practice sentences.

7. Will Jake ride *a* bike *to the* mill?
8. Tell him *to* take *the* bus.
9. *The* bell will wake us up.
10. Will it wake Jake at *the* same time?
11. Kate ate in *the* hot hut.
12. *A* pup ran *into the* same hut.
13. *The* fat pup had *a* bone.
14. Did *the* pup hide *the* bone?
15. *The* pup made *a* fine mess.
16. Did *the* rude man sit on *the* hat?
17. *The* rude man sat on *the* fine hat.
18. *A* bike ran *into the* red van.
19. Dale will hike *to the* lone hut.
20. *The* lone man sat on *a* mule.
21. *The* mule rode *into the* sunset.
22. *A* mole made *a* hole in *the* hill.
23. *A* rat ran *into the* mole hole.
24. *The* fat mole sat in *the* hole.

(Review **from**.)

25. Did *the* rat run *from the* mole?
26. Rod rode *a* bike *from the* lake.
27. *The* bike fell *into a* hole.
28. Ron ran, but Dale rode in *the* van.
29. Will *the* men take *a* bus *from the* mill?
30. *A* fat man ran up *to the* mule.
31. Did *the* mule run *from the* man?

(Focus on words ending in Vowel + **e**.)

32. Will *the* man tell *a* lie *to* Lee?
33. *The* man will not lie *to* Lee.
34. Will *the* doe run *from* us?
35. *The* doe will run *to the* lake.
36. Will Moe take *a* jet?
37. Will Moe take *a* jet *from* Rome?
38. Tie *the* bike *to the* van.
39. Tie *the* mule *to a* pole.
40. Luke wore *a* red tie.
41. *The* tie had *a* hole in it.
42. Did Joe hide *the* hoe?
43. Joe hid *the* hoe in *the* hut.
44. Sue will take *the* late bus.
45. Mom made *a* homemade pie.
46. *The* pup ate *the* hot pie.

WORDS:

1.	fade	6.	net	11.	mule	16.	hike
2.	doze	7.	mile	12.	tube	17.	fin
3.	rude	8.	home	13.	dim	18.	vote
4.	sod	9.	lot	14.	puff	19.	wave
5.	safe	10.	mess	15.	mill	20.	vine

ADDITIONAL WORDS (Optional):

1.	toe	7.	jut	13.	bedtime
2.	due	8.	pet	14.	hilltop
3.	lie	9.	man	15.	homemade
4.	doe	10.	fat	16.	makeup
5.	fee	11.	foe	17.	inside
6.	tie	12.	pie	18.	sunset

SIGHT WORD PRACTICE (Optional):

1.	a	7.	from	13.	love
2.	the	8.	into	14.	are
3.	her	9.	for	15.	come
4.	to	10.	one	16.	move
5.	of	11.	have	17.	were
6.	do	12.	done	18.	some

WORDS (12):

the

is, bus, on, at, sun, Jan, up, rise, sunrise, woke, time

WORD GROUPS:

1. woke Jan up
2. is on *the* bus
3. at sunrise
4. rise on time

SENTENCES:

1. Jan woke up at sunrise.
2. Is *the* bus on time?

WORDS (13):

to, the, a

is, has, in, it, van, bike, hose, hole, safe, ride

WORD GROUPS:

1. *a* safe bike
2. has *a* hose
3. is in *the* van
4. *to* ride *the* bike
5. *a* hole in it

SENTENCES:

1. Is *the* bike safe *to* ride?
2. *The* hose in *the* van has *a* hole in it.

EXTRA PRACTICE

1. *A* hose is in *the* mud.
2. *The* hose has mud on it.
3. Did Don use *the* hose on his van?
4. Joe has *the* same size hat as mine.
5. *The* size is five.
6. His hat has *a* hole in it.
7. *The* home on *the* hill is not safe.
8. *The* hillside is on fire.
9. *The* home is not safe *from the* fire.
10. *The* kid is safe.
11. *The* pup has *a* fine nose.
12. Did *the* pup use his nose *to* save *the* kid?
13. Sue sat in *the* bus.
14. Sid sat on *the* same side as Sue.
15. Sid has *the* same name as his dad.
16. Russ will not take his van.
17. His van has *a* bad tire.

(Review **was**.)

18. *Was the* kid safe *from the* fire?
19. *The* kid *was* safe.
20. *Was the* home on *the* hill safe?
21. *The* home *was* not safe *from the* fire.
22. *Was the* tire on sale?
23. *The* tire *was* on sale.

(Focus on **vase** and **base**. Tell students that these two words ending in Vowel-**s-e** contain the sound of / s / instead of the usual / z /. The words **dose** and **case** also have the / s / sound.)

24.   A rose *was* in *the* vase.
25.   *The* rose in *the* vase *was* red.
26.   *The* vase *was* on *the* sill.
27.   *Was the* vase safe on *the* sill?
28.   Did *the* man run to *the* base?
29.   *Was the* man on base safe?
30.   *The* man on base *was* safe.

WORDS 1 DICTATION   Lesson 6, page 45

WORDS (14):

the, you, to
yes, my, did, men, job, yell, like, note, home, type, sis

WORD GROUPS:

1.   yes, *the* men
2.   yell at *you*
3.   like *to* type at home
4.   at my job
5.   did my note *to* my sis

SENTENCES:

1.   Yes, *the* men on *the* job like *to* yell.
2.   Did you type *the* note *to* my sis?

EXTRA PRACTICE (Review **you** and **your**. Focus on **I**, **my**, and **no**.)

1.   *Was your* bus on time?
2.   No, my bus *was* late.
3.   *Was your* wife late?
4.   Yes, but I did not yell.
5.   *The* rude man will yell if *the* bus is late.
6.   Is *your* sis at home?
7.   No, my sis is not home yet.
8.   Did *you* bake a ham?
9.   Yes, I did.

10. Will *you* type *the* note *to* Nate?
11. Yes, I will type it.
12. Did *the* yam rot in *the* hot sun?
13. No, *a* yam will not rot in *the* sun.
14. *The* yam did not rot.

(Focus on **he** and **by**.)

15. Will Sam bake *the* yam in a pan?
16. Will he yell if *the* pan is hot?
17. Yes, he will yell.
18. Did *the* rude man sit on *your* tie?
19. Yes, he sat on my tie.
20. Did *the* rude man sit by Ron in *your* van?
21. Yes, he sat by Ron.
22. Did he see *the* fire by *the* home on *the* hill?
23. Did you see a bike by *the* van?
24. *The* bike by *the* van *was* mine.

WORDS 1 DICTATION

Lesson 7, page 52

WORDS (10):

the, was
did, men, six, Max, pass, quiz, quite, late

WORD GROUPS:

1. did Max
2. pass *the* six men
3. was *the* quiz
4. quite late

SENTENCES:

1. Did *the* six men pass *the* quiz?
2. Max *was* quite late.

ADDITIONAL WORDS (Optional):

1. box	5. tax	9. fix	13. six
2. ax	6. quake	10. quiz	14. tux
3. ox	7. mix	11. wax	15. quote
4. quit	8. quip	12. quite	16. fox

EXTRA PRACTICE

1. Did *you* take *your* quiz?
2. I will take my quiz at six.
3. Tex will fix *the* hose in my van.
4. Will Tex wax *the* van?
5. A hen ran *from the* fox.

(Review **one**.)

6. A fox ate *one* hen.
7. *One* fox hid *from the* six men.
8. Max quit his job at *the* lab.
9. *The* quake at *the* lab *was* bad.
10. *One* quake *was* quite bad.
11. *The* tux has *one* hole in it.
12. Did *the* man fix *the* hole in *the* tux?
13. *The* box has *one* pill in it.
14. Did *the* pillbox fit in *the* kit?
15. *One* ox fell *into the* pit.
16. *One* fat ox *was* fed by Max.

WORDS 1 DICTATION   Lesson 8, page 59

WORDS (14):

come, you
pass, hill, will, cab, can, cop, on, in, if, Ken, cite, home

WORD GROUPS:

1. if Ken can pass
2. cite *the* cab
3. if *you* pass *the* cop
4. will *come* home
5. on *a* hill

SENTENCES:

1. Can Ken *come* home in a cab?
2. A cop will cite *you* if *you* pass on *the* hill.

EXTRA PRACTICE (Review **have**.)

1. A cub hid *from* us.
2. *The* cub had *a* cute face.
3. *The* cute cub hid in *a* cave.
4. *The* cave *was* by *a* cove.
5. Did *the* cave *have* ice in it?
6. My cup has *one* ice cube.
7. I *have one* ice cube in my cup.
8. *The* cute cat sat on *your* cap.
9. *Your* cap *was* on *the* cot.
10. Did *the* cat *have a* nap on *the* cot?
11. Did Cal *have a* cut on his face?
12. *Have you* cut *the* cake yet?
13. *Have you* had *one* cupcake?
14. His cat ran *into the* cave.
15. Did his cat hiss at *the* cub?
16. Ken had *a* race in his cab.
17. Did *the* cab set *the* pace?
18. Yes, his cab set *the* pace.
19. Did Ken win *the* race?
20. No, he did not win *the* race.
21. Did *a* cop see *the* race?
22. Did *the* cop cite Ken?
23. Did Ken *have a* red face?
24. A can *of* cod *was* on *the* sill.
25. *The* can had no lid.
26. *One* cat ate *the* cod in *the* can.
27. Can Bob fix *the* hole in *the* hose?
28. No, he cannot.
29. Can *you* pass *the* bus?
30. No, we cannot pass it.

(Review **come**. Focus on **we**.)

31. Has Cal *come* home yet?
32. No, he has not *come* home.
33. He will *come* home at nine if he can.
34. Will *you come to the* cove in June?
35. We will *come* if we can.
36. We like *to* sit in *the* sun at *the* cove.
37. We *came* home on *the* bus.
38. Yes, we *came* home on *the* late bus.

(Review **her**.)

39. Kit had *a* cut on *her* toe.
40. Kit cut *her* toe on *a* can.
41. Kate had lace on *her* cuff.
42. *Her* cuff had red lace.
43. Kim let *her* cat *have a* nap in *her* lap.
44. *Her* cat had *a* nice nap.

WORDS (10):

did, pen, ride, hole, pig, dig, big, got, Gene, gym

WORD GROUPS:

1. in *a* pig pen
2. dig *a* hole
3. *to the* big gym
4. got Gene *a* ride
5. did *the* pig

SENTENCES:

1. Gene got *a* ride *to the* gym.
2. Did *the* pig dig *a* hole in *the* big pen?

ADDITIONAL EXERCISE (Optional)

WORDS (12):

from
on, his, cat, fed, cut, Gus, gull, gate, bag, leg, huge

WORD GROUPS:

1. fed *the* huge cat
2. *from* Gus
3. *from* his bag
4. *a* gull on *the* gate
5. cut *a* leg

SENTENCES:

1. Gus fed *the* gull *from* a huge bag.
2. *The* cat cut his leg on *the* gate.

EXTRA PRACTICE (Review **gift**, **girl**, and **give**.)

1. Did *the* pup nip *the girl*?
2. Yes, *the girl* got *a* nip on *her* leg.
3. *The* bite *was* not bad but *her* leg was red.
4. Gus met *a girl* at *the* gym.
5. Did Gus *give the girl a* ride?
6. Yes, he gave *her a* ride *to the* game.
7. Did *the girl give her* age?
8. Yes, *the girl* is *the* same age as Gus.
9. *One* gull sat on *a* gate.

10. *The* gull *was* quite big.
11. *The* gull on *the* gate had *a* huge bill.
12. Did *you give the* gull *a* bit *of* cod?
13. Did Gene *give* his wife *a gift*?
14. Yes, he gave *a* gem *to* his wife.
15. His *gift was a* red gem.
16. His wife gave him *a* huge hug.

(Focus on **me**.)

17. *One girl* gave me *a gift*.
18. *The gift* is *a* tote bag.
19. My tote bag is huge.
20. I will *give her* a hug.
21. *The* jug is huge.
22. Did Jill fill *the* huge jug?
23. Give *the* jug *to* me.
24. *The* cub *was* in *a* big cage.
25. *The* cage had *a* hole in it.
26. Can Gabe fix *the* cage?
27. Did *the* cat take *a* nap on *the* rug?
28. *Give* me *a* rag *from the* bag.
29. *The* wet bug hid in *the* rag bag.
30. *The* rice *was* in *a* huge bag.

(Review **get**.)

31. Did mice *get into the* rice?
32. Yes, mice got *into* it.
33. *Get the* bag and *give* it *to* me.
34. Gabe set *a* mug on *the* sill.
35. *Was the* mug hot?
36. Get *the* mug *from* Gabe.
37. *Give the* hot mug *to* me.
38. *The girl* in *the* cab had *a* red wig.
39. Did *the* wig *get* wet?
40. Yes, *the* wig got quite wet.
41. Did Ned nod at *the girl*?
42. Ned did not nod at *her*.
43. *The* rug is on sale.
44. *The* tag on *the* rug is red.
45. Let me see *the* tag sale.
46. Will *you get the* rug?
47. *The* rug will make *a* fine *gift*.

Write the *key word* for each short vowel sound that you hear:

/ă/, /ĭ/, /ŏ/, /ĕ/, /ŭ/

The teacher will dictate 14 Sight Words (including Exceptions):

1. was	5. you	9. her	13. your
2. gone	6. give	10. one	14. into
3. from	7. get	11. have	
4. gift	8. come	12. girl	

ADDITIONAL WORDS (Optional)

1. safe	6. quit	11. yet	16. hug
2. got	7. quite	12. quiz	17. huge
3. miss	8. cub	13. page	18. cope
4. fox	9. face	14. has	19. cop
5. yell	10. gym	15. my	20. mix

WORDS:

1. snip	3. spin	5. slop	7. spit	9. glob
2. glad	4. twin	6. plum	8. trip	10. slim

WORDS (10):

from, girl
Glen, slip, class, glass, step, flat, stone, broke

WORD GROUPS:

1. on *the* flat stone
2. *from* Glen
3. a *girl* in his class
4. did slip on *the* step
5. broke *a* skate

SENTENCES:

1. Glen broke *the* glass on a flat stone.
2. Did *a* girl *from the* class slip on *the* step?

EXTRA PRACTICE (Review **do**.)

1. *Do you have a* plum tree?
2. Yes, we *do*.
3. It is time to prune *the* plum tree.
4. Stan can prune it.
5. Stan will trim it well.
6. *Do you* like *to* drive?
7. Yes, I *do*.
8. *Do* not step on *the* snake.
9. If *you* step on *the* snake, it will bite.
10. *The* twig *was* dry.
11. *The* dry twig fell *from the* tree.
12. If *you* step on *the* twig, it will snap.

(Review **of** and **two**.)

13. *Two of* us drove *to the* game.
14. *Two of* us sat on *the* grass by *the* lake.
15. *Two of* us rode on *the* sled.
16. Did *the* sled slide off *the* ice?
17. Yes, *the* sled slid.
18. *The* ride on *the* sled *was a* lot *of* fun.
19. Fred has *a* big slice *of* ham.
20. Can he fry *the* ham?
21. Tell Fred *to* cut *the* slice in *two*.
22. He can fry it in *a* pan on *the* stove.
23. He cannot use *the* grill.
24. *The* grill has grime on it.
25. *The* grave *was* in *a* grove.
26. *Two* men sat by *the* grave in *the* grove.
27. Do not step on *the* grass.
28. *The* grass by *the* grave *was* dry.
29. Will *one of the* men cut *the* grass?
30. *The* hat had *a* wide brim.
31. *The* brim *of the* hat *was* blue.
32. *A* glum man drove *two of* us *to the* bus stop.
33. Did *the* glum man smile at *the girl*?
34. Steve made *the* pot *of* rice on *the* stove.
35. *Two of* us ate *the* rice.
36. *One of* us will scrub *the* pot.
37. *Two* men will scrub *the* grill.

ADDITIONAL WORDS (Optional. Focus on compounds.)

1. flagpole
2. sunset
3. skyline
4. classmate
5. drugstore
6. fireplace
7. sideswipe

EXTRA PRACTICE (Focus on compounds.)

1. *The* flag at *the* top *of the* pole is blue.
2. *The* flagpole fell on *the* grass.
3. Did Gwen see *the* sunset?
4. *The* skyline at sunset *was* red.
5. Fran is *a* classmate *of* mine.
6. Gwen met Fran at *the* drugstore.
7. *Two* men set *the* place on fire.
8. Do *you have a* fireplace?
9. Did *the* bus sideswipe the van?

WORDS 1 DICTATION   Lesson 12, page 89

The teacher will pronounce 12 words. Write the *letter* of the vowel in each word.

1. fact	4. bulb	7. tram	10. task
2. must	5. limp	8. blend	11. slept
3. tilt	6. pond	9. gulp	12. crisp

WORDS 1 DICTATION   Lesson 12, page 95

WORDS (10):

has, his, men, and, went, hand, plant, Brent, splint, strike

WORD GROUPS:

1. Brent and *the* men
2. has *a* splint
3. went on strike
4. on *the* hand
5. at his plant

SENTENCES:

1. Brent has *a* splint on his hand.
2. *The* men at *the* plant went on strike.

EXTRA PRACTICE (Review **buy** and **for**.)

1. Kent went *for* a drive.
2. His fan belt broke.
3. He had *to buy a* fan belt *for* his van.
4. *Have* Gwen and Glen left yet?
5. Yes, Glen and Gwen went *to* see *a* film.

6. *Do you have a* stamp?
7. No, I *have to buy a* stamp.
8. Fran *was* late *for* class.
9. Did Fran *buy a* pass *for the* bus?
10. Stan went *to buy a* tire *for* his bike.
11. He ran *into a* huge spike.
12. *The* spike split *the* tire.
13. *The* spike made *a* huge slit in his best tire.
14. Will *you buy the* tire *for* scrap?
15. Take it *to the* dump.
16. Will *the* man at *the* dump *buy* it?
17. *The* dump has dust and *a* bad smell.
18. *The* dust at *the* dump made us ill.
19. We left and went home.
20. We still felt ill.
21. Greg and his twin went *for a* hike.
22. *The two* men set up camp by *a* lake.
23. Greg slept by *a* tree.
24. His twin slept on *a* flat stone.
25. Did Greg and his twin rest well?
26. Greg slept well but his twin did not.
27. Greg felt fine.
28. His twin felt stiff.

(Review **gone**.)

29. *The* lamp *was* not on.
30. Did *the* lamp *have a* bulb?
31. No, *the* bulb *was gone.*
32. I had *to buy a* bulb *for your* lamp.
33. Did Brent *buy a* bag *of* sand?
34. Yes, he left it by *the* gate.
35. Can *you* lift *the* bag *of* sand?
36. No, we *have to* drag *the* bag.
37. Ask Brent *to* help us lift it.
38. Brent is *gone.*
39. Ask Grace *for a* glass *of* milk.
40. Grace left *the* glass on *the* desk.
41. Did *the* milk spill on *the* desk?
42. Is *the* glass *gone*?
43. *Do you have to* gulp *the* milk?
44. Will Steve weld *the* pipe?
45. No, but Bruce will weld it.
46. Did *you* see *the* rust on *the* pipe?
47. No, *the* rust is *gone.*
48. Did *you* ask Grace *to* save us *a* place in line?
49. Next time, I will ask *her.*
50. *Do you* plan *to* take *a* bus *to the* plant?
51. *The* bus is gone.
52. Next time, I plan *to* take it.

1.	ant	7.	brute	13.	*herself*
2.	stripe	8.	trade	14.	*your*self
3.	bond	9.	quest	15.	grandstand
4.	slope	10.	clamp	16.	blueprint
5.	drum	11.	himself	17.	myself
6.	risk	12.	campfire	18.	sandpile

ADDITIONAL SENTENCES, including compound words (Optional.)

1. *Do you* plan *to* hike by *yourself?*
2. *Was the* grass cut by Greg himself?
3. We lit *a* campfire at dusk.
4. I lit *the* fire myself.
5. Did *you* sit on *the* grass *or* did *you* stand?
6. I sat by myself in *the* grandstand.
7. *The* sand by *the* pond *was* wet.
8. *The* girl made *a* sandpile next *to the* pond.
9. Did *the* girl make *the* sandpile by *herself?*
10. *The* flag had *one* blue stripe.
11. Print *your* name on *the* top line.
12. Did *you* see *the* blueprint on *your* desk?

WORDS 1 DICTATION Lesson 13, page 102

WORDS (10):

was
us, my, man, old, sold, colt, host, blind, kind

WORD GROUPS:

1. sold my colt
2. *was the* host
3. *to the* blind old man
4. *was* kind *to* us

SENTENCES:

1. *The* old man sold *the* colt *to* us.
2. My host *was a* kind old blind man.

ADDITIONAL WORDS (Optional.)

1.	gold	5.	wild	9.	most
2.	hold	6.	mild	10.	post
3.	told	7.	find	11.	jolt
4.	sold	8.	blind	12.	volt

EXTRA PRACTICE (Review **money**.)

1. Did *you* find *your* money?
2. *Was* it in *your* billfold?
3. My *money was* not in my billfold.
4. *The money was* in my old vest.
5. Most *of the* time, I save *money*.

(Focus on **a** and **an**. Remind students that "a" is used before words beginning with a consonant, while "an" is used before words beginning with a vowel; e.g. "a billfold," "an ice cube.")

6. I fold *a* bill and hide it.
7. I fold it and hide it in an old vest.
8. I spend most *of* my *money*.
9. I spend it as fast as I get it.
10. An old man fell on *a* ramp.
11. We told him *to* hold on.
12. We told him not *to* run.
13. *The* ramp is cold.
14. Can *you* help an old man?
15. Will *you* help me *to* hold him?
16. Hold on, and lift him up.
17. Do not jolt him.
18. He is old and cold.
19. Is *the* old man blind?
20. No, he is not blind.
21. He is just quite old.
22. He has had quite *a* jolt.
23. Find *a* place *for* him *to* sit.
24. Find *a* place for an old man *to* rest.
25. Let *the* old man sit in *the* sun and rest.
26. Stan sold *the* old gate.
27. He sold *the* gate *to* buy an ax.
28. Did Stan *buy* an ax *to* fell *a* tree?
29. *A* wild cub hid in *a* cave.
30. *The* cave *was* as cold as an ice cube.
31. *The* cub hid *from the* wild man.
32. *Do you* mind if I find *a* place *to* sit?
33. *Do you* mind if we sit next *to you*?

WORDS (15):

pup, lot, and, made, like, hall, wall, walk, talk,
Marge, Art, yard, car, bark, mark

WORD GROUPS:

1. and talk *to* Marge
2. like *to* walk in *the* yard
3. on *a* hall wall
4. made *a* mark on *the* car
5. bark *a* lot

SENTENCES:

1. Did *the* pup in *the* yard bark at *the* car?
2. Art made *a* mark on *the* wall in *the* hall.
3. Marge and I like *to* walk and talk a lot.

EXTRA PRACTICE

1. Bart rode his mule *into the* barn.
2. *The* tall mule went *into a* small stall.
3. A spark set *the* stall on fire.
4. Did *the* pup in *the* barnyard bark?
5. Did *the* fire start in *the* barnyard?
6. A spark can start *a* fire.
7. *The* fire made *a* wall *of* smoke.
8. Bart ran *from the* tall wall *of* smoke.
9. Bart had *to* call Walt.
10. Walt and Bart set *the* mule free.
11. *The* tall mule ran *from the* smoke in *the* barn.
12. Will my car stall on *the* hill?
13. If you step on *the* brake, *the* car will stall.
14. A cop told *the two* men *to* halt.
15. Did *the two* men halt?
16. Did *the* tall man trip and fall?
17. Did Marge spill *the* salt?
18. Did *the* salt spill on *her* plate?
19. *The* fireman had a scar on his arm.
20. *The* scar *was* on his left arm.
21. It *was a* large scar.
22. Part *of the* scar *was* on his hand.

(Focus on **talk** and **walk**.)

23. Five old men met in *the* park.
24. *The* men went *for a* walk.
25. It is *a* large park.
26. All *of the* men like *to* walk.
27. *The* five old men walk and talk.
28. *The* old men talk *a* lot.
29. Can we walk *to the* baseball park?
30. Yes, *the* baseball park is not far *from* home.
31. All *of* us like *to* walk.
32. We walk and talk *a* lot.
33. We all walk *to the* ball park.

WORDS 1 DICTATION

Lesson 15, page 120

The teacher will dictate 18 sight words.

1. do	7. from	13. her
2. buy	8. of	14. two
3. gone	9. sign	15. give
4. money	10. your	16. come
5. you	11. here	17. was
6. one	12. for	18. have

Write the *key word* for each short vowel sound that you hear:

/ĭ/, /ĕ/, /ă/, /ŭ/, /ŏ/

ADDITIONAL WORDS (Optional.)

1. drip	7. yard	13. brute
2. grope	8. bled	14. lisp
3. start	9. milk	15. dusk
4. walk	10. pond	16. hold
5. just	11. volt	17. find
6. small	12. tramp	18. clam

WORDS 1 DICTATION

Lesson 16, page 131

If a word that is dictated under the *WORDS* or *WORD GROUPS* column contains the **ed** affix, have students underline the affix.

WORDS (16):

was, of
and, six, nine, film, grill, car, end, ended,
start, started, dent, dented, rust, rusted

WORD GROUPS:

1. and start *the* car
2. end at six
3. *was* rusted
4. *of the* dent in *the* grill
5. started *the* film
6. *was* ended

SENTENCES:

1. *The* film started at six and ended at nine.
2. *Was the* grill of *the* car dented and rusted?

EXTRA PRACTICE (Review **some**.)

1. Did *the* ice on *the* lake melt?
2. *Some* of *the* ice melted.
3. Did *the* cat spill all *of the* milk?
4. *Some of the* milk *was* spilled.
5. Did *you* miss *the* bus?
6. *Some of* us missed it.
7. Did *the* old men talk *to you*?
8. *Some of the* old men talked *to* me.
9. Did *the* pup gulp *the* milk?
10. *The* pup gulped *some of* it.
11. Will *the* gas man fix *the* stove?
12. He has fixed it.
13. Did Walt walk *to the* gym?
14. Yes, Walt and his wife walked *to the* gym.
15. Did *the* large car stall on *the* hill?
16. Yes, *the* large car stalled.
17. Did *you* see *a* dent in *the* side *of the* bus?
18. Yes, *the* side *of the* bus *was* dented.
19. Did *the* last race start on time?
20. Yes, *the* last race started at five.

(Focus on **want** and **water**.)

21. Walt had a jug *of* water.
22. Did *you* want water?
23. Yes, we wanted water.
24. We all wanted *some* water.
25. *The* water in *the* jug *was* not cold.
26. Walt wanted *some* ice in his water.
27. Grace wanted *a* large glass *of* cold water.
28. I wanted just *a* sip *of* water.

If a word dictated under the _WORDS_ or _WORD GROUPS_ column contains an **ed**, **ing**, or **y** affix, have students underline the affix.

WORDS (16):

was, were
cot, Kim, hole, pothole, Max, tire, flat,
rest, rested, fill, filling, filled, fix, fixed

WORD GROUPS:

1. _were_ resting on the cot
2. fixed _the_ flat tire
3. _were_ Kim and Max
4. filled _the_ pothole
5. fixing _a_ hole in _the_ tire

SENTENCES:

1. Kim was resting on _the_ cot.
2. _Were the_ men filling in _the_ potholes?
3. Max is fixing his flat tire.

EXTRA PRACTICE

1. _The_ ice on _the_ lake is melting.
2. Did _you_ see _the_ jumping bug?
3. _The_ bug jumped _into the_ pie filling.
4. Steve has _a_ job at _the_ smelting plant.
5. _Some_ old men _were_ talking.
6. Smoke _from the_ stove _was_ filling _the_ hall.
7. _The_ hall _was_ filled with smoke.
8. _The_ sun is melting _the_ ice on _the_ sidewalk.
9. My cat and I went walking in _the_ park.
10. _The_ next race is starting at ten.
11. _Two_ men started _to_ yell _for_ help.
12. _The_ last film _was_ ending.
13. Clark went _to_ park his car.
14. Clark is parking his car in _the_ lot.
15. His car _was_ parked in _a_ red zone.

(Review **are**.)

16. _What are you_ fixing?
17. We _are_ fixing _the_ fan belt on _the_ van.
18. _What are the_ firemen holding?
19. _The_ firemen _are_ holding _a_ huge hose.
20. _What are you_ sending _to_ Kent?
21. We _are_ sending him _money for_ his rent.
22. His rent is due, but he has no job yet.
23. We _are_ lending him _some money for_ his rent.

(Review **were**.)

24. *What were you* and Rose *doing?*
25. We *were* waxing *her* car.
26. *What* did Rose ask *for?*
27. Rose asked *for a* rag and *some* wax.
28. *What were the* men lifting?
29. *The* men *were* lifting *a* crate.
30. *The* huge crate *was* lifted by *a* crane.
31. *What were you* welding?
32. I *was* welding *a* pipe.
33. I welded it by myself.
34. *What were you* asking *for?*
35. I *was* asking *for a* glass *of* water.
36. Walt *was* asking *for some* ice.

WORDS 1 DICTATION Lesson 18, page 148

In this lesson, a paragraph is dictated for the first time. Tell students that a paragraph is a group of sentences built around an idea or topic. Lines in the workbook should not be numbered when a paragraph is dictated, but most students need to be taught to indent the first word. Demonstrate on the chalkboard or a sheet of paper.

In dictating a paragraph, read aloud the entire paragraph; then dictate one sentence at a time, or one phrase at a time, if necessary. At the end, re-read the paragraph aloud, giving students a chance to edit.

When dictating words under the *WORDS* and *WORD GROUPS* columns, remind students that if a word contains the affix **ed**, **ing**, or **y**, the affix should be underlined.

WORDS (15):

money, for
by, old, wall, his, Steve, stove, save, saved, saving,
smoke, smoked, smoking, smoky

WORD GROUPS:

1. his smoking stove
2. saved it *for* Steve
3. by an old wall
4. is smoky
5. by saving *money*

PARAGRAPH:

    Steve is saving money *for* a stove. His old stove is smoking. *The* wall by *the* stove is smoky.

---

1. *Do you live* by yourself?
2. Yes, I *live* by myself.
3. I am *living* next *to a* park.
4. *Do you* plan *to move*?
5. Yes, I am *moving* in June.
6. Did *the* man *live* in an old tent?
7. Yes, he *lived* in *a* tent on *a* small plot *of* land.
8. Did he *move* the tent by himself?
9. We *moved* it *for* him.
10. *The* man *moved* to *a* small farm.
11. *The* farm is *a* big plot *of* land.
12. He is *living* on *the* farm by himself.
13. Did *you* like *the* film?
14. No, but Glen liked it.
15. Can Lee drive *the* big van?
16. Yes, he is driving us *to the* mall.
17. Did *you* wave at *the* bus *to* make it stop?
18. Most *of* us *were* waving.
19. We waved and called.
20. Most *of the* time I try *to* save *money*.
21. We saved *some* money at *the* sale.
22. I am saving *money for* a bus trip.
23. Did *the* mice hide *from the* cat?
24. *Two* mice *were* hiding.
25. Grace is saving us *a* place in line.
26. Jake told us *a* joke.
27. *Was* Jake joking?
28. Fred had *to* take *a* test.
29. He *was* taking *a* test *for* his welding class.
30. *The* sidewalk has ice on it.
31. It is icy.
32. *Do* not step on *the* icy sidewalk.
33. Did *the girl* smile and wave?
34. *The* smiling *girl* broke *her* skate.
35. *The girl was* skating on *the* pond.
36. *Her* nose is like *a* rose.
37. *The girl* has a rosy nose.
38. Did *the* tall man hire Fred *for the* job?
39. Yes, Fred *was* hired by *the* tall man.
40. Did Lynn shine *the* top of *the* desk?
41. Lynn *was* shining it, and I *was* helping.
42. *The* top *of the* desk is shiny.

If a word dictated under the *WORDS* or *WORD GROUPS* column contains an affix, have students underline the affix.

WORDS (16):

got, sat, wet, ran, log, dog, fog, frog, soft, lost, off,
fell, jump, jumped, jumps, jumping

WORD GROUPS:

1. jumping off
2. fell on *the* wet log
3. ran up *to the* soft frog
4. and *the* lost dog
5. sat on *a* log in *the* fog

PARAGRAPH (Remind students to indent.):

A frog sat in *the* fog on *a* soft log. A lost dog ran up and got on *the* wet log. *The* frog jumped, and *the* dog fell off.

EXTRA PRACTICE

1. *Some* sand got *into the* pipe.
2. Will *the* sand clog *the* pipe?
3. Yes, *the* sand will clog it.
4. Did *the* fog come in?
5. *The* fog is *coming* in.
6. *Do you* like *to* drive?
7. I like driving but not in *the* fog.
8. A hog ran *into the* barn.
9. Can Ross grab *the* hog?
10. Ross will grab it if he can.
11. Did *your* boss *move*?
12. Yes, he *moved* in June.
13. We helped my boss *to move*.
14. Did it cost him *a* lot *of money*?
15. He rented *a* small moving van.
16. My boss drove *the* van himself.
17. It did not cost *a* lot *of money*.
18. My dog got lost in *the* fog.
19. *Two* old men sat on *a* log.
20. *Were the* old men lost?
21. No, *the* men *were* not lost.

(Focus on **full**, **pull**, and **put**.)

22. *The* pipe is full *of* sand.
23. *The* plate is full *of* rice.
24. Put *some* salt in *the* rice.
25. *The* glass is full *of* water.
26. Put *the* glass on *the* sill.
27. Put *some* ice in *the* water.
28. Mark put his *money* in his vest.
29. Mark lost his billfold.
30. He lost *the* billfold but not *the money*.
31. *Your* glass fell off *the* sill.
32. *Your* pen fell off *the* desk.
33. *The* top *of the* desk is glossy.
34. *The* old desk has *a* glossy top.
35. Ross put *the* hog in *the* pen.
36. Ross made *a* fire in *the* fireplace.
37. He put *a* huge log on *the* fire.
38. Can *you* put *the* desk in *the* moving van?
39. No, *the* moving van is full.

WORDS 1 DICTATION   **Lesson 21, page 172**

The teacher will dictate 20 sight words.

1. the	6. what	11. to	16. done
2. love	7. live	12. two	17. are
3. were	8. have	13. said	18. money
4. said	9. often	14. gone	19. into
5. come	10. her	15. move	20. buy

WORDS 2 DICTATION   **Review of Student Book 1, page 6**

1. hide	8. dump
2. spend	9. grape
3. plot	10. left
4. task	11. brute
5. quiz	12. wax
6. cove	13. Pete
7. bulb	14. belt

SIGHT WORDS:

1.	do	7.	money	13.	some
2.	move	8.	one	14.	have
3.	are	9.	were	15.	was
4.	you	10.	gone	16.	into
5.	give	11.	her	17.	live
6.	to	12.	from	18.	buy

PARAGRAPH:

Glen has to take a test. He is taking a class in welding. Will he pass the test?

ADDITIONAL REVIEW WORDS (Optional.)

Other Sight Words and Exceptions introduced in Student Book 1, and frequently-used words containing the / ȯ / sound of **a** and / o͝o / sound of **u**:

1.	all	9.	love	17.	what	25.	wall	33.	water
2.	the	10.	have	18.	father	26.	mall	34.	want
3.	to	11.	eye	19.	guard	27.	small	35.	put
4.	into	12.	get	20.	said	28.	tall	36.	full
5.	of	13.	girl	21.	often	29.	hall	37.	pull
6.	for	14.	begin	22.	all	30.	salt	38.	bull
7.	come	15.	gift	23.	call	31.	talk	39.	push
8.	done	16.	sign	24.	fall	32.	walk	40.	bush

Word Families (closed-syllable words containing the long vowel sound) introduced in Student Book 1:

1.	old	6.	sold	11.	blind	16.	post	21.	jolt
2.	cold	7.	told	12.	find	17.	host	22.	volt
3.	fold	8.	wild	13.	kind	18.	ghost		
4.	gold	9.	mild	14.	mind	19.	bolt		
5.	hold	10.	child	15.	most	20.	colt		

1. traffic
2. wombat
3. invent
4. mascot
5. zigzag
6. disgust
7. admit
8. comment

Two-syllable words are introduced in this lesson. Many students have difficulty making the transition from spelling one-syllable words to two-syllable words. For students who need intensive spelling practice at the two-syllable level, refer to the procedure titled *Spelling Practice—Phonetically-Regular Two-Syllable Words* in the multisensory section of this Guide, page 173.

Remind students to underline the affix of words dictated under the *WORDS* or *WORD GROUPS* columns.

WORDS (Sight Words are listed first) (17):

the
had, did, Brad, stop, map, game, Mike, like, liking, liked, film, filmed, filming, combat, campus, umpire

WORD GROUPS:

1. a film of the game
2. filming Brad and Mike
3. did not like the umpire
4. liked the map
5. on the campus
6. and stop the combat

SENTENCES:

1. Did Mike like the combat film?
2. Brad had a map of the campus.
3. Did the umpire stop the game?

ADDITIONAL WORDS

1. contest	6. invade	11. sitcom	16. napkin
2. nutmeg	7. mistake	12. trombone	17. escape
3. mascot	8. reptile (rĕp tīl)	13. comment	18. ignite
4. admit	9. umpire	14. misfit	19. dispute
5. hubcap	10. stampede	15. intend	20. baptize

ADDITIONAL WORD GROUPS

1. at the end of the contest
2. was asking the mascot
3. did not comment
4. nutmeg in the cake
5. if the hubcap has a dent
6. a small reptile
7. make a mistake
8. if the umpire
9. until the last film
10. asked him to admit

EXTRA PRACTICE

1. The umpire made a mistake.
2. Will he admit it?
3. What was the mistake?
4. A fan got up to yell at the umpire.
5. The mascot yelled at the fan.
6. What did the mascot yell?
7. The cake has nutmeg in it.
8. Is the nutmeg a mistake?
9. No, the cake will win the contest.
10. A snake is a reptile.
11. The reptile slept on a flat stone.
12. What time will the contest end?
13. The combat film lasted until nine.
14. The contest will last until ten.
15. Did you see a dent in the hubcap?
16. Yes, the hubcap is dented.
17. Brent made a comment to Vic.
18. What was the comment?
19. Did Ted get wet inside the tent?
20. No, the tent was dry.

ADDITIONAL WORDS (Nonsense; optional.)

1. tombat
2. hudmin
3. ventop
4. joblid
5. stumrep
6. amsist
7. agnate
8. witlime
9. yebnote
10. zanluke
11. metlope
12. bindome

WORDS 2 DICTATION   Lesson 2, page 23

1. pencil
2. carbon
3. sudden
4. atlas
5. tinsel
6. ballot
7. kennel
8. seldom
9. album
10. tonsil
11. gallon
12. lesson

WORDS 2 DICTATION   Lesson 2, page 28

Two-syllable words containing a schwa sound are introduced in this lesson. These words are especially challenging for the speller who relies heavily on auditory skills because one vowel sound is indistinct. For students who need intensive spelling practice at the two-syllable schwa level, refer to the procedure titled *Spelling Practice—Two-Syllable Words Containing the Schwa Sound* in the multisensory section of this Guide, page 174.

WORDS (20):

the, have, having, to, what
I, we, if, did, his, miss, missed, missing, will,
trip, class, Bret, happen, cancel, lesson

WORD GROUPS:

1. did Bret and I
2. what if the bus
3. missing his trip
4. will have to cancel
5. if we happen to have
6. having a lesson

SENTENCES:

1. What will happen if I miss the bus?
2. Did Bret have to cancel his trip?
3. We missed the lesson.

ADDITIONAL WORDS

1.	tonsil	6.	infant	11.	pencil
2.	helmet	7.	victim	12.	bottom
3.	basket	8.	husband	13.	absent
4.	seldom	9.	canvas	14.	carton
5.	cotton	10.	custom	15.	button

ADDITIONAL WORD GROUPS

1. a strap on the helmet
2. inside the basket
3. will you find
4. put the carton
5. happen to see
6. if the milk will spill
7. a button on the vest
8. in the bottom of
9. made of canvas
10. the flap on the tent
11. if a strap broke
12. and the pencil fell
13. was dry inside the desk

EXTRA PRACTICE

1. The tent was made of canvas.
2. The canvas tent was dry inside.
3. Did you happen to see the milk?
4. A cat spilled the carton of milk.
5. Did you happen to see the pencil?

6. I put the pencil on the desk.
7. Did you happen to see my helmet?
8. Your helmet fell in the mud.
9. The strap on the helmet broke.
10. Did you happen to see a red button?
11. Pat put a button in the basket.
12. You will find the button in the bottom of the basket.
13. Will I find some milk in the bottom of the carton?

WORDS 2 DICTATION

WORDS (20):

your, was, her, my, shy, hand, on, ate, fish, dish, Shannon, lunch, bench, shake, shaking, man, men, fresh, freshman, freshmen

WORD GROUPS:

1. her dish on the bench
2. ate my lunch
3. fresh fish
4. Shannon and the freshman
5. and shake your hand
6. was shy

SENTENCES:

1. The fish on my dish was fresh.
2. Did the shy freshman shake your hand?
3. Shannon ate her lunch on a bench.

EXTRA PRACTICE

1. Did the van crash?
2. Yes, it crashed into the shed.
3. Chan has a mark on his chin.
4. Chan hit his chin on a branch.
5. The fishbone is small and sharp.
6. Do not choke on the fishbone.
7. Shane got a job on a ranch.
8. One ranch hand had a shotgun.
9. He put his shotgun in a chest.
10. Shane put the chest in a shed.
11. Chad had a chess set.
12. He had a pet chimp.
13. Chad liked to win at chess.
14. The chimp was champ.

(Review **shoe**.)

15. Old man Josh had a lot of cash.
16. Josh hid his cash in a shoe box.
17. Shannon left her shoe by the lake.
18. The shoe fell into the lake.
19. Shannon had one dry shoe.
20. The wet shoe did not fit.

WORDS 2 DICTATION   **Lesson 4, page 44**

Write the vowel that you hear.

1. match	4. sketch	7. witch	10. Scotch
2. pitch	5. Dutch	8. stretch	11. ditch
3. botch	6. scratch	9. clutch	12. patch

WORD DICTATION:

1. latch	3. fetch	5. crutch
2. notch	4. switch	6. itch

WORDS 2 DICTATION   **Lesson 4, page 50**

WORDS (16):

into, can, did, drive, driving, fix, ball, dog, gate, ditch, latch, Mitch, fetch, fetched, fetching, Ellen

WORD GROUPS:

1. fetching the dog
2. a ball in the ditch
3. into the gate
4. did Ellen fix
5. driving Mitch
6. can latch it

SENTENCES:

1. Did Mitch drive into a ditch?
2. Can Ellen fix the latch on the gate?
3. A dog fetched the ball.

ADDITIONAL WORDS

| 1. pitch | 3. hutch | 5. itch | 7. crutch | 9. match |
| 2. pinch | 4. hunch | 6. inch | 8. crunch | 10. march |

ADDITIONAL WORD GROUPS

1. broke the latch
2. an old hatchet
3. lit the last match
4. matching my red handbag
5. and broke the hatchet
6. spoke Dutch to me
7. if the old dutchman
8. a patch of blue sky
9. patching the tire
10. if the scratch on his arm
11. scratched it on the gate
12. and sketch the face
13. a rabbit in the hutch
14. sketching the rabbit hutch
15. on the kitchen stove
16. smoke in the kitchen

WORDS 2 DICTATION   Lesson 6, page 60

1. motel	5. robot
2. bacon	6. human
3. virus	7. cabin
4. raven	8. clinic

WORDS 2 DICTATION   Lesson 6, page 62

1. dictate	6. ignite
2. visit	7. rodent
3. melon	8. vacate
4. female	9. planet
5. comet	10. focus

WORDS (20):

her, his, time, job, broke, Tom, last, wife, home, got, finish, finishing, finished, moment, habit, Jason, smoke, smoking, smoked, smoky

WORD GROUPS:

1. finishing the last job
2. broke her habit
3. smoking habit
4. got finished in time
5. a moment at home
6. can Jason and his wife

SENTENCES:

1. Can Jason finish the job on time?
2. His wife broke her smoking habit.
3. Tom got home at the last moment.

ADDITIONAL WORDS

1. limit	6. cabin	11. visit
2. motel	7. open	12. locate
3. humid	8. student	13. Jacob
4. human	9. invite	14. canyon
5. silent	10. rotate	15. humane

ADDITIONAL WORD GROUPS

1. a limit of one
2. at the old motel
3. quite a humid place
4. human skull
5. dark and silent
6. lit a fire in the cabin
7. if you open the gate
8. one student in the class
9. did she invite
10. will rotate the men on the job
11. if we wish to visit
12. and locate the place
13. as I spoke to Jacob
14. rode a mule in the canyon
15. a humane act

1.	city	5.	levy	9.	hazy
2.	duty	6.	study	10.	body
3.	pony	7.	navy	11.	ruby
4.	tidy	8.	silly	12.	lazy

WORDS (18):

Mrs., Ms., her, has, like, liked, liking, desk, dog, hot, job, ate, jumbo, tidy, Tony, city, Mrs. Clark, Ms. Finch

WORD GROUPS:

1. liked the hot dog
2. ate at her desk
3. has Mrs. Clark
4. tidy Ms. Finch
5. the jumbo city
6. did Tony

SENTENCES:

1. Ms. Finch has a tidy desk.
2. Tony ate a jumbo hot dog.
3. Did Mrs. Clark like her job in the city?

EXTRA PRACTICE (Focus on **Ms.** and **Mrs.**)

1. The lady gave the ivy to Mrs. Carson.
2. Did Mrs. Carson plant the ivy?
3. The pony ate grass by the barn.
4. A lady led the pony into the barn.
5. The pony was led by Mrs. Nelson.
6. Mrs. Nelson put the tiny pony into a stall.
7. Pluto is a planet.
8. Tiny Pluto is far from the sun.
9. Ms. Ivy had a dog named Pluto.
10. Ms. Ivy fed her dog gravy.
11. Did Ms. Ivy get Pluto from the kennel?
12. Did Ms. Marsh live in the city?
13. Yes, she lived in the city.
14. The city was ugly.
15. Ms. Marsh liked living in the ugly city.

WORDS (20):

girl, is, was, pass, test, take, taking, fine, tub, man, Ted, that, this, thin, Beth, bath, bathtub, math, athlete, fifth

WORD GROUPS:

1. that thin athlete
2. this fine bath
3. Ted and Beth
4. to pass the fifth girl
5. was in this tub
6. will take that math test

SENTENCES:

1. That thin girl is a fine athlete.
2. Ted was the fifth man to take a bath in this tub.
3. Will Beth pass the math test?

ADDITIONAL WORD GROUPS (Focus on **both**.)

1. this child
2. these children
3. both of the children
4. both of the men
5. these three men
6. that gravy
7. this thin gravy
8. that fireman
9. both of the firemen
10. those three firemen
11. this witness
12. both of those men
13. this bath water
14. the water in that bathtub

EXTRA PRACTICE (Focus on **truth**.)

1. This gravy is thin.
2. I like thin gravy.
3. Did Tod win the tenth race?
4. No, Tod came in fifth.
5. This is the fifth time that I called.
6. Do you like milk with your lunch?
7. Yes, I like cold milk with lunch.

8. Do you see that witness?
9. Did that witness tell the truth?
10. Yes, the witness told the truth.
11. Did those firemen tell the truth?
12. Yes, they told the truth.
13. Both of them told the truth.
14. The three children were taking a bath.
15. This bath water is hot.
16. Those children like to splash water.
17. The children were splashing water in the bathtub.

(Review **they**.)

18. Did they call that witness?
19. Yes, they called the witness.
20. This is the fifth time that they called him.
21. Did they like the thin gravy?
22. Yes, they liked it.
23. Were they calling the firemen?
24. They were calling three of them.
25. Were the three children taking a bath?
26. Yes, they were.

WORDS 2 DICTATION

WORDS (20):

you, his, will, sell, selling, take, taking, his, van, Phil, photo, phone, phoned, phoning, Ralph, Joseph, when, why, white, which

WORD GROUPS:

1. when Phil
2. a photo of the white van
3. and why did Joseph
4. which Ralph will sell
5. if you phone
6. taking a photo

SENTENCES:

1. When will Joseph phone you?
2. Why did Ralph sell his white van?
3. Which photo did Phil take?

EXTRA PRACTICE

1. That dolphin was big.
2. The baby whale was small.
3. Was the dolphin as big as the baby whale?
4. The top of the wave was white.
5. That whitecap is a tiny wave.
6. Why do they call it a whitecap?
7. Why did Ralph park in my path?
8. When will the race start?
9. When will Ralph move his car?
10. When did Philip get a phone?
11. Why did they cancel the race?
12. Why did the whale dive?
13. When did the whale splash you?
14. When will Philip call?

(Review **who**, **whose**, **what**, and **where**.)

15. Who put the cup on the sill?
16. Who spilled milk on the rug?
17. Whose cup has a chip in it?
18. Who made the ham and rice?
19. Whose hat is this?
20. Whose phone is that?
21. Who ate the pot of rice?
22. What time did you wake up?
23. Where did Joseph invest his cash?
24. Who got to class on time?
25. Where did you hide that phone bill?
26. Where did Ralph hide his cash?
27. Whose phone bill is it?
28. Where are the children?
29. Whose children are they?
30. Where is the carton of milk?
31. What time did Joseph get home?
32. What did you do with the cup that has the chip in it?
33. What are the children doing with the phone bill?
34. What did you do with the rest of the carton of milk?

(Focus on **which**.)

35. Which child is calling?
36. Which bus did Joseph take?
37. Which phone is it?
38. Which class are you taking?
39. Which cup has a chip?

The teacher will dictate 16 sight words.

1.	have	5.	what	9.	shoe	13.	move
2.	were	6.	both	10.	truth	14.	gone
3.	buy	7.	two	11.	her	15.	live
4.	they	8.	from	12.	where	16.	your

1.	table	6.	puzzle
2.	bottle	7.	bugle
3.	rifle	8.	handle
4.	simple	9. .	sparkle
5.	tremble	10.	gobble

WORDS (20):

who, her, of, Mr., Mr. Hubble, Dr., Dr. Biddle, lit, gate, broke, car, lot, park, parked, parking, this, handle, candle, table, middle

WORD GROUPS:

1. broke this handle
2. middle of the table
3. Dr. Biddle and Mr. Hubble
4. in the parking lot
5. as Mr. Hubble parked the car
6. the man who lit the candle

SENTENCES:

1. Mr. Hubble broke the handle on this gate.
2. Who lit the candle on the table?
3. Dr. Biddle parked her car in the middle of the lot.

EXTRA PRACTICE

1. Where is the bottle of glue?
2. The glue in the bottle is old.
3. Put some water in the kettle.
4. Put on the kettle and make the water bubble.
5. Is the handle hot?

6. The handle is not hot.
7. Where did the ranch hand put the rifle?
8. The ranch hand put the rifle in the shed.
9. Where did Mr. Grable put the saddle?
10. Mr. Grable put the saddle in the stable.
11. My club is holding a raffle.
12. What is the raffle prize?
13. The big raffle prize is a bike.
14. What prize will Mr. and Mrs. Hubble donate?
15. They will donate an apple pie.
16. What is your middle name?
17. Did they bundle up the baby?
18. What is the title of the film?
19. Did they fumble the ball?
20. Did the wine in the bottle sparkle?
21. Yes, the red wine sparkled in the bottle.
22. The little girl pressed her hand in the wet sand.
23. The girl left an imprint of her little hand in the sand.

WORDS 2 DICTATION   **Lesson 12, page 125**

WORDS (20):

your, will, line, name, party, print, printed, printing, rope, swing, swinging, Hank, hang, hanging, bring, bringing, blank, sang, song, Frank

WORD GROUPS:

1. a rope to swing on
2. printed your name
3. sang the song
4. on a blank line
5. to the party
6. bringing Hank and Frank

SENTENCES:

1. Hank will bring a rope and hang the swing.
2. Frank sang a song at the party.
3. Print your name on the blank line.

EXTRA PRACTICE

1. Did you bring some string?
2. Was the string strong?
3. The string was long but not strong.
4. Did the phone ring?
5. The phone rang for a long time.

6. The cable is strong.
7. Hank will hang the cable.
8. Mr. King broke his arm.
9. His arm is in a sling.
10. Did Ms. Fink sing your song?
11. Did you thank Ms. Fink for singing it?
12. I think I thanked her.
13. Did they fill the tank with gas?
14. Yes, they filled the tank.
15. Which phone was ringing?
16. Which sink has pink tile?
17. Which bank was not open?

(Review **there** – *"in that place."*)

18. Was your soft drink on the sink?
19. Yes, my soft drink was there.
20. Was the cable in the trunk of the car?
21. Yes, the cable was there.
22. Is the bunk bed in the shed?
23. No, the bunk bed is not there.
24. Where was Mrs. King?
25. Mrs. King was there in the bank.
26. Where is the gas tank?
27. The tank is there on the left side.
28. Where are your children?
29. My children are there by the swing.

WORDS 2 DICTATION

Lesson 13, page 132

1. ticket
2. socket
3. chuckle
4. jacket
5. duckling
6. rocket
7. freckle
8. bucket
9. chicken
10. tickle

WORDS (20):

her, of, when, we, can, bike, cash, cashes, cashed, cashing, rode, rack, back, Chuck, check, pickup, Mrs. Spock, lock, locked, locking

WORD GROUPS:

1. locking up the cash
2. rode in the pickup
3. a bike in the rack
4. Mrs. Spock and Chuck
5. when we rode in the back
6. cashed her check

SENTENCES:

1. Mrs. Spock locked her bike in the rack.
2. When can we cash the check?
3. Chuck rode in the back of the pickup.

ADDITIONAL WORDS

1. shack	8. mock
2. quack	9. pluck
3. check	10. struck
4. trick	11. flock
5. smock	12. homesick
6. cluck	13. quicksand
7. brick	14. backpack

ADDITIONAL WORD GROUPS

1. in the back lot	11. that big black cab
2. opened this bank	12. if the page is blank
3. thick gravy	13. one duck on the lake
4. will think of you	14. will dunk it in the gravy
5. if I crack the code	15. sticking it with glue
6. fixing the crank	16. stinking up the basement
7. in the back of the truck	17. sat on a tack
8. at the bottom of the trunk	18. the size of a tank
9. was sick in bed	19. lit the candlewick
10. to scrub the sink	20. as fast as you can wink

EXTRA PRACTICE

1. Mack hid his cash in a sock.
2. He hid the sock in a bucket.
3. The tin bucket was black.
4. Mack put the bucket in a trunk.
5. He locked the trunk.
6. Mack hid the trunk in a shack.
7. He locked the shack with a padlock.
8. A rat got into the sock.
9. The rat had a quick lunch.
10. Do you see that duck?
11. Did that duck quack?
12. This hen has one chick.
13. Where is the chick?
14. The chick is there with the hen.
15. Did the hen cluck at the chick?
16. Yes, the hen clucked.
17. Where was the truck?
18. The truck was there in the backyard.

ADDITIONAL TWO-SYLLABLE WORDS

1.	sickle	5.	fickle	9.	pocket	13.	thicket
2.	crackle	6.	tackle	10.	picket	14.	racket
3.	pickle	7.	trickle	11.	packet	15.	rocket
4.	heckle	8.	buckle	12.	locket	16.	bucket

WORDS 2 DICTATION   Lesson 14, page 139

Write the vowel that you hear.

1.	fudge	6.	hedge
2.	ridge	7.	judge
3.	dodge	8.	pledge
4.	smudge	9.	bridge
5.	edge	10.	lodge

WORDS (20):

who, for, ball, base, baseball, on, this, fix, fixing, fixed, ate, gate, lunch, umpire, hinge, dodge, dodging, dodged, fudge, judge

WORD GROUPS:

1. ate this fudge
2. and who is fixing
3. dodging the baseball
4. lunch for the umpire
5. for this judge
6. a hinge on the gate

SENTENCES:

1. The umpire dodged the baseball.
2. Who fixed the hinge on this gate?
3. The judge ate fudge for lunch.

EXTRA PRACTICE

1. Who was standing on the ledge?
2. Bridget was standing there.
3. Who will trim the hedge?
4. Marge will trim it.
5. Who ate all of the fudge?
6. The judge ate it.
7. Who got stuck on the bridge?
8. A strange man got stuck there.
9. Where did Bridget sit?
10. She sat on the edge of the ledge.
11. Where did the judge get the fudge?
12. Mrs. Dodge gave the fudge to the judge.
13. Where is the large trash can?
14. The large trash can is at the edge of the sidewalk.
15. What is that strange man doing?
16. The strange man is dodging traffic on the bridge.
17. Why did Marge trim the hedge?
18. Why was Bridget standing on the ledge?
19. Why did Mrs. Dodge give the fudge to the judge?
20. Why is the strange man on the bridge?
21. Why is the trash can there at the edge of the sidewalk?

The teacher will dictate 10 sight words.

1. shoe
2. strange
3. they
4. live
5. where

6. there ("in that place")
7. what
8. have
9. some
10. buy

WORDS (20):

two, four, eight, car, cars, bridge, bridges, skunk, skunks, path, paths, dog, time, same, met, bark, barked, collide, colliding, collided

WORD GROUPS:

1. two barking dogs
2. four times
3. met eight skunks
4. at the same bridge
5. collide on the path
6. two colliding cars

SENTENCES:

1. Four cars collided on the bridge.
2. Two skunks met on the path.
3. Eight dogs barked at the same time.

EXTRA PRACTICE (Review **four** and **eight**.)

1. Four girls got off the bus.
2. Eight girls sat at the bus stop.
3. Did the girls miss the bus?
4. They missed four buses.
5. The eight girls got on the fifth bus.
6. The bus made eight stops.
7. Four students got off.
8. The students got off at the campus.
9. Eight carts were missing.
10. Beth put four cartons of milk in the cart.
11. Mr. Dodge had eight bags of cement.
12. He left four bags in his truck.
13. He put one bag of cement in the trunk of his car.

14. Mr. Dodge put the rest of the bags in his backyard.
15. A cactus has sharp spines.
16. Some plants are spiny.
17. Cactuses are spiny plants.
18. Were the rocks large?
19. Most of the rocks were large.
20. Were the shops open?
21. Most of the shops were closed.
22. Were the waves huge?
23. Some of the waves were huge.
24. Were the banks still open?
25. Not all of the banks were open.
26. Was the bench dry?
27. Both of the benches were dry.
28. Was your lunch small?
29. All of the lunches were small.
30. Was that dress long?

MORE PRACTICE

31. All of those dresses were long.
32. Were the students in class?
33. Not all of the students were in class.
34. Some students were absent.
35. Did the classes begin on time?
36. Both classes began on time.
37. Tadpoles have no legs.
38. Frogs begin life as tadpoles.
39. The apples on the trees were ripe.
40. Some apples were falling.
41. We picked eight boxes of apples.
42. Was your boss on time?
43. Both of the bosses were late.
44. Were the frogs in the pond?
45. Four frogs were in the pond.
46. Eight frogs sat on the bank of the pond.
47. Was the box full?
48. No, all of the boxes were empty.
49. Was the fox in the den?
50. No, the den was empty.
51. Both of the foxes were gone.
52. Some happy fans ate hot dogs.
53. All of the fans yelled at the umpire.

WORDS (20):

four, money, my, which, when, dog, phone, program, thrift, thrifty, save, saves, bark, barked, barks, ring, ringing, rings, start, starts

WORD GROUPS:

1. when the program
2. four ringing phones
3. when his dog barked
4. thrifty man
5. which started to ring
6. saving money

SENTENCES:

1. The thrifty man saves his money.
2. My dog barks when the phone rings.
3. Which program starts at four?

EXTRA PRACTICE

1. Ed yells when he cuts his chin.
2. That dentist tells jokes.
3. This program ends at eight.
4. The bus stops eight times.
5. A stitch in time saves nine.

(Review **does** and **goes**.)

6. Does a cat have nine lives?
7. Does that dog bark at the frogs in the pond?
8. Does your child like puzzles?
9. Does the dentist tell funny jokes?
10. Does the table have a mark on it?
11. Where does Mr. Marvin go on the bus?
12. Mr. Marvin goes to see his dentist.
13. Where does Chuck go in his truck?
14. He goes to the junk yard in his truck.
15. Where does this bus go?
16. It goes to the ballpark.
17. Does the bus stop there?
18. Where does Mrs. Spock shop?
19. She goes to that market to shop.
20. Does her child go with her?
21. Yes, the child goes with Mrs. Spock.

WORDS (20):

girl, four, went, Trish, trash, tunnel, post, postcard, ape, trip, tripped, tripping, trips, skin, skinny, shop, shopped, grin, grinned, grinning

WORD GROUPS:

1.   an ape and a girl (*Note:* Remind students that "an" is used before words
                                         that begin with a vowel sound; e.g., *an ox, an uncle.*)
2.   four tunnels
3.   tripping on the trash
4.   skinny girls on a postcard
5.   and grinned at Trish
6.   went shopping

SENTENCES:

1.   Trish tripped on the trash in the tunnel.
2.   Four skinny girls went shopping.
3.   An ape on a postcard is grinning.

EXTRA PRACTICE

1.   Did the cloth rip?
2.   Yes, the cloth ripped seven times.
3.   Did you scrub the table?
4.   Yes, I scrubbed it.
5.   Did Trish mop the kitchen?
6.   Yes, she mopped it.
7.   Will Kevin trim the seven hedges?
8.   He is trimming all seven of them.
9.   Will the children run?
10.   They are running.
11.   Did the men drop the trunk?
12.   Yes, they dropped it.
13.   Did you slip on the step?
14.   Yes, I slipped.
15.   Did Judge Gomez slam the gate?
16.   Yes, he slammed it.
17.   When did the music stop?
18.   The music stopped when we got up to dance.
19.   Does the girl like to shop?
20.   The girl goes shopping a lot.
21.   Does Shannon like to swim?
22.   Shannon goes swimming a lot.
23.   Does the baby like to pet the pup?
24.   The baby is petting the pup.
25.   The puppy likes the baby.

WORDS (20):

was, to, into, told, she, I, kitchen, kitchens, went, Sally, quit, quitting, mope, moped, moping, mop, mopped, mopping, slop, sloppy

WORD GROUPS:

1. Sally and I
2. into the kitchen
3. started moping
4. mops the sloppy kitchen
5. told her to quit
6. mopped up

PARAGRAPH (Remind students to indent the first word.):

    I told Sally not to mope. She quit moping. She went into the kitchen and mopped up the slop.

EXTRA PRACTICE

1. Did the lady slip on the slope?
2. Yes, she slipped.
3. The slop on the slope was wet.
4. The wet slope was sloppy.
5. The slope had mud on it.
6. The lady slipped on the muddy slope.
7. Did the sun shine on the hill?
8. No, the sun was not shining.
9. The sun was hiding.
10. Did Ken grope in the dark?
11. Yes, Kenny did.
12. He groped for the switch.
13. Did you see those sleds slide on the ice?
14. Yes, the sleds were sliding.
15. They were sliding on the icy slope.
16. Do you hope to win the race?
17. Yes, I am hoping to win it.
18. Did the seven men rob the bank?
19. Yes, the seven men robbed it.
20. Mr. Spock collects scrap.
21. Did he scrape his arm?
22. No, he scraped his hand.
23. He scraped it on some scrap metal.

The teacher will dictate 20 sight words.

1. were	6. eighth	11. live	16. move
2. buy	7. money	12. some	17. goes
3. does	8. give	13. there	18. what
4. shoe	9. where	14. four	19. two
5. eight	10. they	15. fourth	20. one

WORDS 3 DICTATION   **Review of Student Book 2**

PART 2

The teacher will dictate 5 words.

1. public
2. rotate
3. circus
4. wiggle
5. athlete

14 COMMON SIGHT WORDS:

1. her	6. they	11. four
2. move	7. were	12. are
3. where	8. buy	13. from
4. two	9. does	14. eight
5. some	10. who	

PARAGRAPH:

Mr. Nelson ran up the slope. The sloping hill was wet. He slipped on a rock and fell.

WORDS 3 DICTATION   **Lesson 1**

The teacher will dictate 10 words.

1. say	6. tray
2. clay	7. slay
3. sway	8. gray
4. way	9. stray
5. sway	10. lay

The teacher will dictate 12 words.

1. wait	5. faint	9. trail
2. raid	6. plain	10. faith
3. stain	7. nail	11. raise
4. jail	8. main	12. gain

WORD DICTATION:

1. contest
2. expand
3. impress
4. punish
5. transit
6. commit
7. funnel
8. picnic
9. include
10. female

WORDS:

who, all, truck, trucks, Ray, gray, day, days, Sunday
paint, painted, painting, paints, aid, aided, aiding, ail, ails, ailed, ailing

WORD GROUPS:

1. painted all day
2. who is aiding
3. on his gray truck
4. the man who ails
5. rained on Ray
6. ailed on Sunday

SENTENCES:

1. It rained all day on Sunday.
2. Ray is painting his gray truck.
3. Who will aid the ailing man?

EXTRA PRACTICE

1. Did Mrs. Clay wait for the mail?
2. Yes, she waited all day.
3. Mrs. Clay waited all day for the mailman.
4. She was waiting for her paycheck.
5. She got the paycheck when the mail came.
6. The mail came at the end of the day.

(Review **always**.)

7. When does Mr. Grayson get paid?
8. He always gets paid on the same day.
9. Does Mr. Grayson get paid on Friday?
10. Yes, he always gets his check on Friday.
11. His boss always pays him.
12. The boss always hands Mr. Grayson his check.
13. Payday is always on Friday.
14. Who says that it is raining?
15. The mailman says so.
16. Who says that the train will not be late?
17. This ticket man says so.
18. The ticket man says that the train will be on time.

(Review **said**.)

19. Who said that the jail was full?
20. The judge said so.
21. Judge Gray said so last Friday.
22. The paint on the rail is wet.
23. Who said that the paint is wet?
24. Ray said so.
25. Did Ray paint the rail with a can of spray paint?
26. No, he said that he painted it with a brush.
27. Did your landlady say when the rent is due?
28. My landlady said that the rent is due on May tenth.

WORDS 3 DICTATION   Lesson 2

WORD DICTATION:

1. legal
2. minus
3. open
4. siren
5. rival
6. habit
7. lemon
8. panel
9. denim
10. model

WORDS:

from, was, off, mile, home, far, barn, lid, that, this, broke, rip, ripping, ripped, rips, Morris, cord, born, forty, horse

WORD GROUPS:

1. ripping off the cord
2. far from this barn
3. broke the lid
4. was Morris
5. forty horses
6. miles from home

SENTENCES:

1. Forty miles is far from home.
2. This horse was born in that barn.
3. Morris broke the cord and ripped off the lid.

EXTRA PRACTICE

1. My landlord likes to sit on the porch.
2. He likes to tell a story.
3. My landlord told me this story.
4. He said that the dogs were on the porch.

5. A stork landed in the parking lot.
6. The dogs started barking.
7. They were barking at the stork.
8. He said that the dogs barked for forty days.
9. Did a storm hit your state?
10. Yes, a storm is hitting part of my state.
11. The storm is from the north.
12. Four ships sailed into port.
13. The four ships sailed into port this morning.

(Review **work**.)

14. When do you go to work?
15. I go to work at four in the morning.
16. Does Mrs. Jordan go to work?
17. When does Mrs. Jordan work hard?
18. She goes to work at six in the morning.
19. On Friday, she goes at ten in the morning.
20. Mrs. Jordan works from ten to six on Friday.

WORDS 3 DICTATION   Lesson 3

WORD DICTATION:

1. locust
2. gallon
3. limit
4. moment
5. timid

6. robin
7. slogan
8. duplex
9. agent
10. even

WORDS:

wash, washed, washes, they are, they're, we are, we're, I will, I'll, this, story, dish, dishes, tell, take, taking, go, going, way, subway

WORD GROUPS:

1. and they're telling
2. washing dishes
3. this time I'll
4. going to tell a sad story
5. on this subway
6. if we're taking

SENTENCES:

1. I'll wash the dishes this time.
2. They're telling a sad story.
3. We're going to take the subway.

EXTRA PRACTICE

1. Where's Mrs. York?
2. She is working.
3. She's painting the porch.
4. Will you call?
5. Yes, we'll call you.
6. We'll call you at eight.
7. Let's go to the game.
8. Let's help Mrs. York.
9. Where's Gordon?
10. Let's call Gordon.
11. What time is it?
12. Is it seven o'clock?
13. No, it's eight o'clock?
14. It's time to go.

WORDS 3 DICTATION   Lesson 4

WORD DICTATION:

1. infant
2. drastic
3. helmet
4. canvas
5. muffin
6. bottom
7. dental
8. magnet
9. seldom
10. tonsil

WORDS:

why, work, working, worked, does, does not, doesn't, is not, isn't,
did not, didn't, stop, stopped, stopping, bark, barked, train, Mr. Kent,
Jackson, Trenton

WORD GROUPS:

1. barking dogs
2. isn't Mr. Kent
3. doesn't work on the train
4. stopping in Trenton
5. worked in Jackson
6. and why didn't

SENTENCES:

1. Why didn't the dogs stop barking?
2. Mr. Kent doesn't work in Jackson.
3. Isn't this the train to Trenton?

---

1. Are we late for the train?
2. No, we aren't late.
3. Can you get tickets for the game?
4. No, I can't get tickets.
5. Were you home this morning?
6. No, we weren't.
7. Was the mail late?
8. No, it wasn't.
9. Have you fed the dogs?
10. I haven't fed them yet.
11. Did it rain on Sunday?
12. No, it didn't rain.

WORDS 3 DICTATION   Lesson 6

The teacher will dictate 8 words.

1. alive   5. amaze
2. adult   6. arise
3. alone   7. amuse
4. abuse   8. apart

WORD DICTATION:

1. plenty   6. gravy
2. study   7. sentry
3. candy   8. fancy
4. puny   9. holy
5. tiny   10. lazy

WORDS:

again, live, living, lived, lives, husband, husbands, uncle, uncles, baby, old, rich, wife, ring, ringing, alone, adopt, adopts, adopted, adopting

WORD GROUPS:

1. living alone
2. did ring again
3. my uncle and his wife
4. adopting a baby
5. the rich husbands
6. old phones ringing

SENTENCES:

1. My rich old uncle lives alone.
2. The wife and husband adopted the baby.
3. Did the phone ring again?

EXTRA PRACTICE

1. dressing alike
2. long ago and far away
3. setting it aside
4. at the adult class
5. waiting awhile
6. did not amuse Linda
7. at home alone
8. two pandas from China
9. afraid of the dark
10. on the soft sofa
11. tuna for lunch
12. walking away from the sofa
13. had a talk with Lorna
14. Did the twins dress alike?
15. Most of the time, they dressed alike.
16. What time does the adult class start?
17. The adult class started long ago.
18. What did Mona have for lunch?
19. Mona had a tuna sandwich.
20. Was Donna awake when the alarm went off?
21. No, the alarm woke Donna.
22. What is Lorna doing?
23. Lorna is painting again.

WORDS 3 DICTATION   Lesson 7

The teacher will dictate 14 words.

1.	germ	5.	nerves	9.	merging	13.	percent
2.	term	6.	nervy	10.	alert	14.	shelter
3.	midterm	7.	clerk	11.	person		
4.	nerve	8.	merge	12.	perhaps		

The teacher will dictate 20 words.

1.	girl	6.	birth	11.	third	16.	circus
2.	stir	7.	birthday	12.	thirst	17.	dirt
3.	stirred	8.	shirt	13.	thirsty	18.	dirty
4.	stirring	9.	skirt	14.	thirty	19.	squirt
5.	bird	10.	first	15.	circle	20.	squirm

The teacher will dictate 12 words.

1.	hurt	4.	churches	7.	disturb	10.	surprise
2.	hurting	5.	surf	8.	Thursday	11.	burger
3.	church	6.	curb	9.	Saturday	12.	hamburger

WORD DICTATION:

1.	hello	3.	ego	5.	lotto	7.	memo	9.	tempo
2.	jumbo	4.	pinto	6.	veto	8.	polo	10.	solo

WORDS:

was, all, is not, isn't, last, my, gold, that, her, nurse, nurses, purse, purses, forgot, sister, glitter, glitters, thirty, birth, birthday

WORD GROUPS:

1. forgot the nurse
2. did not glitter
3. that gold purse
4. was her last birthday
5. thirty nurses
6. all of my sisters

SENTENCES:

1. The nurse forgot her purse.
2. My sister was thirty on her last birthday.
3. All that glitters is not gold.

EXTRA PRACTICE

1. Turn at the first corner.
2. Turn left at the church.
3. The church is on the corner.
4. My turn signal is stuck.
5. Use your arm for a turn signal.
6. Summer is hot.
7. Winter is cold.
8. What did that person order for dinner?
9. That person ordered a burger.
10. Where is my partner?
11. My partner went to get lumber.
12. He is getting lumber at the lumber yard.
13. This is his third trip.
14. Ms. Sherman makes pancakes.
15. She puts butter in the pancake batter.
16. The batter is better with butter.
17. Who left the ladder in the rain?
18. Who left the paint can on the ladder?
19. Who spilled paint on the church steps?
20. A man on a ladder is painting the rafters.
21. My sister runs a dog kennel.
22. The kennel holds thirty dogs.
23. The dogs got thirsty and started to bark.
24. Thirty thirsty dogs started barking at the same time.
25. Fred got a free dinner for fixing the flat tire.
26. The nurse left her purse on a bench in the church.

WORD DICTATION:

1. city
2. mascot
3. photo
4. hazy
5. motto

6. copy
7. bonus
8. hobo
9. lady
10. invest

WORDS:

girl, girls, all, truck, trucks, three, got, Linda, Carla, Mona, splash, splashed, splashing, splashes, large, larger, largest, wet, wetter, wettest

WORD GROUPS:

1. splashing Mona
2. got Linda wetter
3. splashed all three
4. the largest truck
5. Carla and the girls
6. wettest of all

PARAGRAPH (Remind students to indent the first word.):

A large truck splashed the three girls. Carla got wet. Linda got wetter. Mona got the wettest of all.

EXTRA PRACTICE

1. Mr. Becker paints.
2. He is a painter.
3. Mrs. Jordan shops.
4. She is a shopper.
5. Mr. Jordan welds.
6. He is a welder.
7. Mr. Duffy trims trees.
8. He is a tree trimmer.
9. Rose and Brenda swim.
10. They are swimmers.
11. That man and his wife have a farm.
12. They are farmers.
13. Those men cut logs.
14. They are loggers.
15. Judge Crosby likes to jog.
16. She is a jogger.

(Review **woman, women**.)

17. That woman talks a lot.
18. She is a talker.
19. Those women dance.
20. They are dancers.
21. This woman trains dogs.
22. She is a dog trainer.
23. These women sing.
24. They are singers.
25. That woman drives a bus.
26. She is a bus driver.
27. Those women play tennis.
28. They are tennis players.
29. Those women play softball.
30. They are softball players.
31. Judge Crosby jogs fast.
32. Her sister jogs faster.
33. Your wife jogs the fastest.
34. That girl is a strong swimmer.
35. Her sister is stronger.
36. Brenda is the strongest.
37. My slice of cake is thin.
38. Your slice is thinner.
39. The slice on the plate is the thinnest.
40. April has long days.
41. May has longer days.
42. The days in June are the longest.
43. The planet Mars is small.
44. Venus is a smaller planet than Mars.
45. Pluto is the smallest planet of all.

WORDS 3 DICTATION   Lesson 9

The teacher will dictate 12 words.

1.	Monday	5.	money	9.	none
2.	come	6.	mother	10.	nothing
3.	front	7.	love	11.	son
4.	done	8.	some	12.	month

WORD DICTATION:

1.	ignite	6.	textile
2.	octane	7.	enclose
3.	reptile	8.	costume
4.	suppose	9.	unite
5.	athlete	10.	immune

WORDS:

two, had, baseball, girl, sport, sports, like, liking, liked, better, son, sons, one, mother, brother, brothers, love, loving, loved, loves

WORD GROUPS:

1. likes his brother
2. a better sport
3. loved the mother
4. had a baseball
5. than girls
6. two loving sons

PARAGRAPH (Remind students to indent the first word.):

   The mother had two sons. One son loved baseball. His brother liked girls better than sports.

EXTRA PRACTICE

1. Did you turn on the oven?
2. Yes, I turned the oven on.
3. Did you cover the pot of rice?
4. Yes, I covered it.
5. Is the rice done?
6. No, it is not done.
7. The rice isn't done.
8. Did it rain on Monday?
9. Yes, it rained on Monday.
10. Did they lock the front gate?
11. The front gate was not locked.
12. The front one was open.
13. Were the other gates open?
14. Yes, the other ones were open.
15. Not one of the gates was shut.
16. None of them was locked.
17. Did your brother win a trophy?
18. Yes, he won a swimming trophy.
19. My brother has three sons.
20. Two of his sons were born in April.
21. The other son was not born in that month.
22. He was born in the month of May.
23. What color is the rug?
24. The rug is a dark blue color.
25. Do you have another color?
26. No, the rug comes in just one color.
27. Where is the pepper?
28. The pepper is above the stove.
29. It is not on the shelf above the stove.
30. The shelf has nothing on it.
31. I see nothing on the shelf.

The teacher will dictate 8 words and 8 word groups.

1.	bright	9.	with a brighter light
2.	might	10.	might start a fight
3.	slight	11.	a slight problem
4.	right	12.	making a right turn
5.	bought	13.	bought and sold old cars
6.	fought	14.	and fought for her brother
7.	brought	15.	brought her three sons
8.	thought	16.	had not thought of it

WORD DICTATION:

1.	ballot	6.	problem
2.	gossip	7.	bullet
3.	method	8.	canyon
4.	pennant	9.	dental
5.	rapid	10.	gallon

WORDS:

was not, wasn't, would not, wouldn't, old, older, oldest, cash, check, checks, take, taking, with, price, prices, Mr. Hill, right, bought, sell, seller

WORD GROUPS:

1. bought the old car
2. taking a check
3. would not take
4. right price for Mr. Hill
5. but the seller
6. with cash

PARAGRAPH:

   The car was old, but the price was right. Mr. Hill bought it with cash. The seller would not take a check.

EXTRA PRACTICE

1. Could they see the bats in the dark?
2. No, they could not.
3. Would you open the gate?
4. I would, but the gate is locked.
5. I would if I could.
6. Which way should the driver turn?
7. The driver should turn right.
8. He should use his turn signal.
9. Where should he park?
10. He should park by that parking meter.

11. Did Mr. Ludlum buy a paper?
12. Yes, he bought a paper.
13. Did the nurse buy a purse?
14. Yes, she bought a white purse.
15. Did Mrs. Ludlum buy a jacket?
16. Yes, she bought a black jacket.
17. Is the size right?
18. Yes, the size is right.
19. The jacket ought to fit.
20. Did the nurse bring her white purse?
21. Yes, she brought it.
22. She brought her purse to the clinic.
23. Would you like to work at the clinic?
24. Yes, I would.
25. I would like to work with sick children.
26. When did the Ludlums bring gifts for the children?
27. They brought the gifts on Sunday night.
28. Did the three dogs fight?
29. Two of them fought.
30. One dog did not fight.
31. When did the two dogs fight?
32. They fought in the middle of the night.
33. Did you think of a name for the baby?
34. Yes, I thought of a name in the middle of the night.

WORDS 3 DICTATION   **Lesson 12**

WORD DICTATION:

1.	duty	3.	public	5.	unit	7.	vital	9.	demon
2.	mammal	4.	ruby	6.	slogan	8.	tablet	10.	sinus

WORDS:

was, her, milk, hole, cup, baby, grab, grabbing, shine, shining, play, playful, playfully, bright, brightly, use, useful, useless, pocket, pocketful

WORD GROUPS:

1. has a useful pocket
2. grabbed the baby
3. bright and shining sun
4. a hole in the cup of milk
5. was playing
6. playfully grabbing her pocket

SENTENCES:

1. Her playful baby grabbed the cup of milk.
2. The sun was shining brightly.
3. This useless pocket has a hole in it.

EXTRA PRACTICE WORDS

1.	hope	11.	restful
2.	hoping	12.	restfully
3.	hopeful	13.	safe
4.	hopeless	14.	safer
5.	hopelessly	15.	safest
6.	hopefully	16.	safely
7.	rest	17.	quick
8.	resting	18.	quicker
9.	rested	19.	quickest
10.	rests	20.	quickly

EXTRA PRACTICE

1. Kirk is a safe driver.
2. He drives safely.
3. Mona is a quick worker.
4. She works quickly.

(Review **people**.)

5. Those people had no home.
6. They were homeless.
7. Most of the homeless people had no jobs.
8. They were jobless.
9. The jobless people felt restless.
10. Those people felt useless.
11. Some of the people got jobs.
12. Those people felt useful and hopeful.

WORDS 3 DICTATION
Lesson 13

The teacher will dictate 20 words.

1.	study	11..	cry
2.	studied	12.	cries
3.	studying	13.	cried
4.	studies	14.	crying
5.	lazy	15.	happy
6.	lazier	16.	happier
7.	laziest	17.	happiest
8.	fry	18.	happily
9.	fried	19.	lady
10.	frying	20.	ladies

WORD DICTATION:

1.	babble	6.	handle
2.	muzzle	7.	little
3.	kettle	8.	saddle
4.	bundle	9.	dimple
5.	rattle	10.	puzzle

EXTRA PRACTICE WORDS

1.	play	11.	story	21.	baby
2.	plays	12.	stories	22.	babies
3.	played	13.	try	23.	luck
4.	playing	14.	tries	24.	lucky
5.	player	15.	tried	25.	luckier
6.	playful	16.	trying	26.	luckiest
7.	playfully	17.	monkey	27.	copy
8.	stay	18.	monkeys	28.	copies
9.	stays	19.	turkey	29.	copying
10.	stayed	20.	turkeys	30.	copier

EXTRA PRACTICE SENTENCES

1. When does Mr. Lopez study?
2. Mr. Lopez studies at night.
3. When does the baby cry?
4. She cries at night.
5. Did the landlord tell a story?
6. He told two stories.
7. Did Mr. Lopez copy his notes?
8. Yes, he copied them.
9. Did the baby try to stand up?
10. Yes, she tried.
11. Did the wet shirt dry in the sun?
12. Yes, the wet shirt dried.
13. When does a bat fly?
14. It flies at night.

The teacher will dictate 8 words and 8 word groups.

1. sleep
2. deep
3. need
4. needless
5. teeth
6. three
7. street
8. freeze

9. in a deep sleep on the cot
10. sleeping deeply
11. not in need of help
12. a needless stop
13. three baby teeth
14. two or three green trees
15. sweeping the street
16. if you open the freezer

WORD DICTATION:

1. expose
2. collect
3. admire
4. lily
5. umpire

6. fancy
7. invade
8. commute
9. hundred
10. immune

WORDS:

who, do not, don't, will not, won't, off, Lee, hand, bite, biting, slice, slicing, sliced, road, roast, roasted, jeep, feed, feeding, beef

WORD GROUPS:

1. the man who won't
2. not feeding Lee
3. parked off the road
4. biting the roast beef
5. a hand on the jeep
6. if we don't slice it

SENTENCES:

1. Who sliced the roast beef?
2. Don't bite the hand that feeds you.
3. Lee won't park the jeep off the road.

EXTRA PRACTICE

1. Did Mr. Green try to sleep?
2. Yes, he tried to sleep on the cot.
3. Mr. Green spent a sleepless night.
4. Don't slip on the street.
5. The street is full of slush.
6. I slipped on the slush in the street last week.
7. Will you meet Lee?
8. I won't meet Lee this week.
9. The truck hit a rut in the road.

10. This road is full of deep ruts.
11. Will Mr. Green get a load of coal?
12. Yes, but he won't load the coal into his truck.
13. Is your throat sore?
14. No, I don't have a sore throat.
15. Did the soap float in the bathtub?
16. Yes, the soap floated.
17. Keep off the green grass.
18. Who keeps the grass so green?
19. Did the van exceed the speed limit?
20. Yes, the speeding van exceeded the limit.
21. Do you drive home on the freeway?
22. No, I don't use the freeway.
23. I use the city streets to get home.
24. Why is the baby still sleeping?
25. Babies need a lot of sleep.
26. Who gave the speech at the meeting?
27. The coach gave the speech.
28. Coaches like to give speeches.
29. Have you ever seen a queen bee?
30. Have you ever seen grass that is three feet tall?
31. Have you ever got a ticket for speeding on the freeway?

(Review **been.**)

32. Who has been feeding the deer?
33. Who has been sleeping on this cot?
34. Who has been keeping this grass so green?
35. Who has been sweeping these streets?
36. Have you ever been on that road?

WORDS 3 DICTATION   **Lesson 16**

WORD DICTATION:

1. graphite
2. pamphlet
3. dolphin
4. photo
5. siphon
6. Ralph
7. orphan
8. aphid
9. Joseph
10. phonics

WORDS:

was, sign, signed, unsigned, resign, forgot, Mr. Carter, form, reform, reformed, unformed, tax, taxes, fund, funded, refunding, turn, return, returning, returned

WORD GROUPS:

1. was signing the form
2. and forgot Mr. Carter
3. returning late
4. a refund on his taxes
5. his unsigned form
6. forgot to return it to him

PARAGRAPH:

Mr. Carter forgot to sign his tax form. The unsigned form was returned to him. His tax refund will be late.

EXTRA PRACTICE

1. Did your brother resign?
2. Yes, he resigned his job.
3. Did your brother pack and move?
4. Yes, he packed his bags and moved.
5. We helped him to load his car.
6. We loaded up the trunk.
7. Did his mother get a report from him?
8. Yes, he reported to his mother.
9. My brother did not like to live alone.
10. He repacked his bags.
11. He reloaded the trunk of his car.
12. Then, he returned home.
13. He unloaded the trunk of his car.
14. He unpacked his bags alone.
15. Did his old boss hire him back?
16. Yes, my brother got rehired.
17. He returned to his old job.
18. Was the old switch safe?
19. No, the old switch was unsafe.
20. Did you test it?
21. Yes, I tested it.
22. The switch needed to be replaced.
23. Did you replace it?
24. I replaced the old switch.

WORD DICTATION:

1. cyclone
2. hydrant
3. gypsy
4. tyrant
5. symbol
6. mystic
7. system
8. python
9. cypress
10. nylon

WORDS:

her, under, hid, spot, spotting, spotted, shout, shouting, shouted, trout, Mrs. Trout, mouse, house, couch, couches, out, loud, louder, loudest, loudly

WORD GROUPS:

1. spotting a trout
2. under the couches
3. a loud shout
4. shouted at Mrs. Trout
5. hid the mouse
6. out of her house

PARAGRAPH:

Mrs. Trout spotted a mouse in her house. The mouse hid under the couch. Mrs. Trout shouted loudly and ran out.

EXTRA PRACTICE WORDS

1. spouse
2. spouses
3. cloud
4. cloudy
5. proud
6. proudly
7. prouder
8. sound
9. soundless
10. soundlessly
11. round
12. around
13. ground
14. grounder
15. groundless
16. mouth
17. mouthful
18. grouch
19. grouchy
20. thousand
21. bound
22. rebounded
23. about
24. amount
25. count
26. recount
27. uncounted
28. counter
29. hour
30. hourly

EXTRA PRACTICE WORD GROUPS

1. if the wife and her spouse
2. rain clouds in the sky
3. on a cloudy day
4. around the clock
5. a grouchy spouse
6. with his proud mother
7. smiling proudly
8. when we counted the money
9. stepped around the corner
10. a thousand times faster
11. a mouthful of mush
12. mush on the counter
13. two hours later
14. thousands of hours
15. bounding back
16. getting the rebound
17. just about to open
18. if they sound alike
19. opened his mouth
20. counting the money

The teacher will dictate 8 words and 8 word groups.

1.	youth	9.	her youthful smile
2.	youthful	10.	four players on the court
3.	group	11.	a group of youths
4.	tour	12.	taking four courses
5.	toured	13.	of course
6.	court	14.	when the court convenes
7.	course	15.	were taking a tour
8.	courses	16.	keeping on the course

WORD DICTATION:

1.	lesson	6.	magnet
2.	expire	7.	collide
3.	until	8.	solid
4.	complete	9.	second
5.	habit	10.	enclose

WORDS:

buy, buying, young, younger, youngest, cousin, cousins, country, countries, big, bigger, biggest, save, saving, plan, planning, planned, unplanned, house, houses

WORD GROUPS:

1. has a bigger house
2. my youngest cousin
3. saving up to buy
4. buying my house
5. a big country
6. is younger

PARAGRAPH:

My young cousin has big plans. He is saving up to buy a house. He is planning to buy a house in the country.

EXTRA PRACTICE WORDS

1.	soup	11.	double
2.	soups	12.	doubling
3.	group	13.	doubled
4.	grouping	14.	trouble
5.	regrouped	15.	couple
6.	tour	16.	couples
7.	detour	17.	pour
8.	detouring	18.	poured
9.	youth	19.	court
10.	unyouthful	20.	course

1. Did Jason pour the coffee?
2. Of course, he poured it.
3. Jason poured four cups of hot coffee.
4. The coffee is hot, but the soup is not.
5. You do not have to sip that soup.
6. The soup is not hot.
7. A group of fans shouted and stamped.
8. They were shouting at the umpire, of course.
9. Our son went on tour with group of students.
10. The large group filled the tour bus.
11. The students toured the White House.
12. The tour bus had to make a detour on the way home.

WORDS 3 DICTATION   Lesson 19

WORD DICTATION:

1.	victim	6.	fatal
2.	explode	7.	compel
3.	humid	8.	tribute
4.	baptize	9.	inquest
5.	cabin	10.	cremate

WORDS:

most, mostly, ever, hole, pants, denim, work, workable, unworkable, worker, wash, washable, unwashable, rugged, ruggedness, hard, harder, hardest, hardly, hardness

WORD GROUPS:

1. hardly ever gets
2. rugged workers
3. my washable denims
4. a hole in his pants
5. most denim pants
6. ruggedness of most workers

PARAGRAPH:

Most workers like denim pants. Denim is washable and rugged. I hardly ever get a hole in my denims.

EXTRA PRACTICE WORDS

1. fresh	11. rest	21. unused
2. freshly	12. restful	22. usable
3. freshness	13. restfulness	23. unusable
4. happy	14. like	24. move
5. happiness	15. likable	25. movable
6. unhappiness	16. unlikable	26. removable
7. thought	17. port	27. love
8. thoughtless	18. portable	28. lovable
9. thoughtful	19. use	29. lovely
10. thoughtfulness	20. reuse	30. loveliness

WORDS 4 DICTATION   Review of Student Book 3

PART 2

The teacher will dictate 8 words containing the schwa **a**.

1. awake	5. apart
2. adult	6. soda
3. alone	7. comma
4. abuse	8. tuna

SIGHT WORDS:

1. love	5. woman	9. people
2. says	6. they	10. where
3. brother	7. been	11. four
4. goes	8. work	12. sign

PARAGRAPH:

Mrs. Ludlum unpacked her bags and sat on the couch. The baby woke up and cried. Mr. and Mrs. Ludlum spent a sleepless night.

WORDS 4 DICTATION   Lesson 1

The teacher will dictate 12 words.

1. tooth	5. noon	9. noodle
2. shampoos	6. afternoon	10. shoot
3. food	7. cartoon	11. cool
4. aloof	8. soon	12. gloomy

The teacher will dictate 4 sentences.

1. My cat sat aloofly on the roof.
2. That horse has a sore hoof.
3. The tramp was a man without roots.
4. Was the stove pipe filled with soot?

WORD DICTATION:

stable, raffle, saddle, cuddle, stifle, dribble, marble, idle, noble, muffle, cradle, bundle, rifle, tremble, shuffle

---

WORDS:

money, dip, dipped, drop, dropped, three, play, player, part, parted, foot, football, took, cook, cookbook, pool, cool, fool, soon, sooner

WORD GROUPS:

1. dropped her money
2. a cool dip in the pool
3. fooled the cook
4. are football players
5. took three cookbooks
6. soon will be parting

SENTENCES:

1. Three football players took a dip in the cool pool.
2. The cook dropped the cookbook on her foot.
3. A fool and his money are soon parted.

EXTRA PRACTICE WORDS

1. child	6. sisterhood	11. state	16. likely
2. childhood	7. false	12. statehood	17. likelihood
3. man	8. falsehood	13. woman	18. live
4. manhood	9. brother	14. womanhood	19. lively
5. sister	10. brotherhood	15. like	20. livelihood

WORDS 4 DICTATION   Lesson 2

The teacher will dictate 12 words.

1. use	5. bright	9. count
2. misuse	6. brighten	10. discount
3. cover	7. judge	11. gold
4. discover	8. misjudge	12. golden

WORD DICTATION:

thunder, later, member, sober, center, after, order, shutter, timber, gander, elder, fiber, number, tender, better

WORDS:

under, lady, ladies, bench, benches, glass, glasses, just, them, think, thinker, place, misplace, misplaced, displaced, wood, wooden, step, stepped, misstep

WORD GROUPS:

1. stepped on the glass
2. did the lady
3. has misplaced them
4. under her glasses
5. sat on the wooden bench
6. just thinking

SENTENCES:

1. The lady has misplaced her glasses.
2. Did you see them under the wooden bench?
3. No, but I think I just stepped on them!

WORDS 4 DICTATION   Lesson 3

WORD DICTATION:

kettle, wiggle, puzzle, nozzle, bugle, dazzle, little, bottle, smuggle, muzzle, gargle, title, shuttle, haggle, drizzle

WORDS:

they, two, have, both, unite, united, United States, U.S., U.S. Navy, uncle, Uncle Sam, boy, boys, join, joined, joining, employ, employed, employing, employment

WORD GROUPS:

1. having two employers
2. both of my boys
3. by Uncle Sam
4. United States Navy
5. the same employment
6. joining the U.S. Navy

PARAGRAPH:

My two boys have the same employer. They both joined the U.S. Navy. They are employed by Uncle Sam.

WORD DICTATION:

planet, attic, expel, plastic, frantic, repel, propel, hornet,
garnet, linnet, drastic, compel

WORDS:

you, your, must, this, zone, zoning, rezone, lane, speed, speeding,
block, blocked, unblock, reduce, reducing, reduced, hospital, hospitals,
ambulance, ambulances

WORD GROUPS:

1. blocking your lane
2. not a hospital
3. a speeding ambulance
4. this hospital zone
5. ambulance lane
6. must reduce speed

PARAGRAPH:

This is a hospital zone. You must reduce your speed. Do not block the
ambulance lane.

The teacher will dictate 3 sentences.

1. The runner has a blister on his heel.
2. The blister may heal in time for the next race.
3. If not, he'll have to wait until next time.

The teacher will dictate 8 words and 8 word groups.

1.	meat	9.	eating meat for dinner
2.	each	10.	if you look at each one
3.	treat	11.	at the treatment center
4.	clean	12.	cleaning up that mess
5.	scream	13.	screamed and ran away
6.	please	14.	displeasing the public
7.	meal	15.	ate a meatless meal
8.	lead	16.	his misleading statement

WORD DICTATION:

local, dental, final, penal, total, vital, fiscal, spinal,
vocal, rascal, signal, rental

WORDS:

you, your, have, too, water, look, horse, drink, before, can, cannot, can't, eat, eating, eater, lead, leader, leap, leaped, leaping

WORD GROUPS:

1. leading the horse
2. can't make the leap
3. looking at the water
4. eating your cake
5. before you drink it, too
6. have to leap

SENTENCES:

1. You can't have your cake and eat it, too.
2. You can lead a horse to water, but you can't make it drink.
3. Look before you leap.

EXTRA PRACTICE WORDS

1.	dear	11.	fearless	21.	unclear
2.	deepest	12.	near	22.	unclearly
3.	hear	13.	nearly	23.	clearer
4.	hearing	14.	nearness	24.	clearest
5.	unhearing	15.	nearer	25.	smear
6.	year	16.	nearest	26.	smeared
7.	yearly	17.	rear	27.	smearing
8.	fear	18.	clear	28.	beard
9.	fearful	19.	clearly	29.	bearded
10.	fearfully	20.	clearness	30.	beardless

WORDS 4 DICTATION Lesson 7

The teacher will dictate 8 words and 8 word groups.

1.	school	9.	stoppping at the school crossing
2.	ache	10.	my last toothache
3.	stomach	11.	like the stomach of a rooster
4.	Christmas	12.	two Christmas gifts
5.	mechanic	13.	has a mechanical problem
6.	technical	14.	technical books
7.	chef	15.	eating with the chef
8.	machine	16.	when I oil the machines

WORD DICTATION:

content, pretend, indent, intend, prudent, extend, intent, potent, extent, rodent, extend, attend, student

EXTRA PRACTICE WORDS

1.	write	24.	kneecap	47.	dumb
2.	writer	25.	kneel	48.	dumbly
3.	writing	26.	kneeling	49.	comb
4.	rewrite	27.	know	50.	combing
5.	rewrote	28.	knowing	51.	uncombed
6.	written	29.	unknowable	52.	limb
7.	unwritten	30.	knife	53.	climb
8.	wrong	31.	knot	54.	climber
9.	wrongly	32.	knotted	55.	lamb
10.	wrongful	33.	knob	56.	oft
11.	wrap	34.	knobless	57.	often
12.	wrapping	35.	knobby	58.	soft
13.	unwrapped	36.	knock	59.	soften
14.	wrist	37.	knocked	60.	softener
15.	wrists	38.	knockout	61.	listen
16.	wiring	39.	knit	62.	listener
17.	wringer	40.	knitted	63.	listening
18.	wreck	41.	knuckle	64.	listened
19.	wrecked	42.	thumb	65.	fast
20.	wrench	43.	crumb	66.	fasten
21.	wrenches	44.	numb	67.	unfastened
22.	knee	45.	numbly	68.	machine
23.	knees	46.	numbness	69.	machines

EXTRA PRACTICE SENTENCES

1. Does that coffee machine work?
2. No, it does not.
3. The coffee machine doesn't work.
4. I just lost my money in that coffee machine.
5. Did you press the button?
6. Yes, I pressed the button.
7. I pressed it with my thumb.
8. Maybe it was the wrong button.
9. It was not.
10. It wasn't the wrong one.
11. Didn't a light go on?
12. Yes, a green light went on.
13. Didn't some coffee come out?
14. Not a drop of coffee came out.
15. Did you pull the coin return knob?
16. Yes, I pulled the knob, but I didn't get my money back.
17. Did you knock on the machine?
18. Yes, I knocked on it.
19. Did you knock with your knuckles?
20. I knocked with my knuckles, and I knocked with my knee.
21. No money came out.
22. Did you kick the machine?
23. Yes, I kicked it hard with my sandal.
24. Didn't you stub your toe?
25. Yes, I stubbed my toe.
26. Is your toe numb?
27. Yes, my toe is numb.
28. The machine has my money, and I have a numb toe.

WORDS 4 DICTATION   Lesson 8

The teacher will dictate 8 words and 8 word groups.

1. bread
2. heavy
3. dead
4. threat
5. instead
6. health
7. ready
8. head

9. spreading jelly on the bread
10. not too heavy to lift
11. dead or alive
12. a deadly threat
13. instead of giving up
14. two healthy babies
15. never ready on time
16. heading the list

WORD DICTATION:

silver, differ, farther, quiver, further, over, wafer, pilfer, bather, panther, suffer, fever

```
WORDS:

push, pushed, pushing, won, Linda, race, raced, racing, pace,
head, headed, ahead, steady, unsteady, breath, breathless, breathlessly,
sweat, sweater, sweating

WORD GROUPS:

1.  pushing ahead
2.  won the race
3.  was Linda
4.  out of breath
5.  at a steady pace
6.  sweating and breathless

PARAGRAPH:

    The race was run at a steady pace. At the end, Linda pushed ahead
and won. She was out of breath and sweating.
```

EXTRA PRACTICE WORDS

1.	earth	9.	learning	17.	unheard	25.	greatest
2.	earthly	10.	relearn	18.	search	26.	greatly
3.	unearthly	11.	early	19.	searcher	27.	greatness
4.	earthen	12.	earlier	20.	searches	28.	break
5.	unearthed	13.	earliest	21.	research	29.	breaks
6.	learn	14.	pearl	22.	researching	30.	breaking
7.	learner	15.	pearly	23.	great	31.	steak
8.	learned	16.	heard	24.	greater	32.	steaks

WORDS 4 DICTATION   Lesson 9

The teacher will dictate 6 words and 6 word groups.

1.	cause	7.	causing no problems
2.	applaud	8.	applauded the band
3.	launch	9.	at the launching of the ship
4.	fault	10.	a faultless game
5.	faucet	11.	fixing the leaky faucet
6.	August	12.	on a hot August night

WORD DICTATION:

decent, event, recent, moment, pigment, ointment, prevent, invent, accent

WORDS:

caught, taught, daughter, Paul, fish, fished, fishing, size, sizes, bass, help, helped, helpful, helpless, basket, haul, hauled, hauling, laundry, laundries

WORD GROUPS:

1. caught a bass
2. taught her to fish
3. hauling in the bass
4. the size of Paul
5. laundry baskets
6. helping his daughter

PARAGRAPH:

Paul taught his daughter to fish for bass. She caught a bass the size of a laundry basket. He helped her to haul it in.

EXTRA PRACTICE WORDS

1.	fruit	12.	juiceless
2.	fruitful	13.	bruise
3.	fruitfully	14.	bruised
4.	fruitless	15.	recruit
5.	unfruitful	16.	recruiter
6.	suit	17.	build
7.	suitable	18.	builder
8.	unsuitable	19.	rebuild
9.	juice	20.	building
10.	juices	21.	built
11.	juicy	22.	rebuilt

(Focus on affix **be**.)

23.	became	29.	behave
24.	become	30.	behind
25.	before	31.	beyond
26.	belong	32.	beside
27.	because	33.	betray
28.	between	34.	beneath

EXTRA PRACTICE WORD GROUPS

1.	soon became lazy	7.	between you and me
2.	before the end of the year	8.	beyond the trees
3.	does not belong to them	9.	walking beside her
4.	because of the rain	10.	never betrayed us
5.	were behaving well	11.	beneath the bench
6.	the screen behind the umpire	12.	will become restless

The teacher will dictate 8 words and 8 word groups.

1. chief
2. brief
3. diesel
4. priest
5. piece
6. niece
7. field
8. cashier

9. asking the chief
10. spoke briefly
11. ran out of diesel
12. two priests in an old church
13. four pieces of pie
14. my oldest niece
15. to the left fielder
16. paid the cashier

WORD DICTATION:

gritty, sandy, chubby, shifty, tidy, duty, lobby, windy, party, flabby, tardy, shabby

---

WORDS:

full, fully, sermon, sermons, belong, belonged, belonging, black,
stole, stolen, Sunday, thief, brief, briefly, briefer, briefest, briefcase,
priest, priestly, priests

WORD GROUPS:

1. was a thief
2. brief sermons
3. stole it on Sunday
4. a black briefcase
5. full of priests
6. belongs to him

PARAGRAPH:

A thief stole a black briefcase. The briefcase was full of sermons.
It belonged to a priest.

EXTRA PRACTICE WORDS

1. grief
2. chief
3. chiefly
4. piece
5. pieces
6. field
7. fielder
8. outfield

9. infield
10. yield
11. yielded
12. unyielding
13. shield
14. shielded
15. fierce
16. fiercely

17. fiend
18. fiendish
19. believe
20. believing
21. believed
22. unbelievable
23. believer
24. belief

25. disbelief
26. achieve
27. achiever
28. achievement
29. achievable
30. relieve
31. relieving
32. relief

EXTRA PRACTICE WORD GROUPS

1. believes in his friends
2. friendly handshakes
3. relieved to be with her friend
4. lifelong friendship

EXTRA PRACTICE SENTENCES

1. A friend in need is a friend indeed.
2. Friendship is love without wings.
3. The only way to have a friend is to be one.
4. Home is where our friends are.

WORDS 4 DICTATION   **Lesson 12**

The teacher will dictate 3 sentences.

1. Their books are on the desk.
2. There are no marks in the books.
3. They're checking out two more books.

The teacher will dictate 8 words and 8 word groups.

1. receive
2. deceive
3. protein
4. ceiling
5. either
6. neither
7. weird
8. seize

9. receiving good advice
10. but deceived nobody
11. plenty of protein
12. looked up at the ceiling
13. either you or I
14. neither you nor I
15. a weird mistake
16. seized the shopping cart

WORD DICTATION:

level, channel, tunnel, even, raven, marvel, gravel, novel, haven, flannel, woven, kennel

---

WORDS:

their, lift, lifted, drink, drinking, morning, each, glass, glasses, weigh, weighing, weight, weights, eight, eighty, eighteen, eighth, neighbor, neighbors, neighborly

WORD GROUPS:

1. their glasses
2. drinking milk
3. eighteen miles a day
4. their neighbors
5. lifting weights
6. each morning

PARAGRAPH:

   Their neighbor lifts weights. He runs eighteen miles each morning. He drinks eight glasses of milk a day.

EXTRA PRACTICE WORDS

1.	caffein	8.	received
2.	protein	9.	receiving
3.	reindeer	10.	ceiling
4.	sleigh	11.	deceive
5.	weight	12.	deceived
6.	receive	13.	deceiving
7.	receiver	14.	undeceived

EXTRA PRACTICE SENTENCES (Focus on **there**, **their**, and **they're**. Note that "there"at the beginning of a sentence is often followed by "is," "are," "was," or "were.")

1. There is a cat on the fence.
2. There are two cats.
3. There was a dog in the yard.
4. There were three dogs.
5. Their apartment was on fire.
6. Their children ran out in time.
7. Their older son called for help.
8. Their home was saved, but it was full of smoke.
9. They're not spending the night at home.
10. They're staying with their uncle.
11. They're going home in the morning.
12. They're glad their home was saved.

(Focus on words containing **ei**.)

13. There is protein in milk.
14. There are eight mice in the basement.
15. There was caffein in the coffee.
16. There were eighteen spoons on the table.
17. Their sleigh broke.
18. Their neighbor helped them to fix it.
19. Their son received his diploma.
20. Their ceiling leaks.
21. They're not deceived by the lie.
22. They're gaining weight.
23. They're going to fix the ceiling.
24. They're lifting weights at the gym.

WORDS 4 DICTATION   Lesson 13

The teacher will dictate 4 words and 4 word groups.

1.	know	5.	knows when to stop
2.	window	6.	will open the window
3.	throw	7.	if you throw the ball
4.	follow	8.	followed the leader

WORD DICTATION:

baggy, frisky, bulky, ugly, oily, soggy, buggy, husky, foggy, holy, belly, pesky

---

WORDS:

nose, nosy, scratch, scratched, scratches, look, looked, tree, brown, growl, growler, growled, howl, howled, howling, down, power, powerless, powerful, powerfully

WORD GROUPS:

1. looking down
2. scratches on the nose
3. a powerful growl
4. howling at the dog
5. ran up the brown tree
6. growled at the cat

PARAGRAPH:

The big dog growled at the brown cat. The brown cat scratched him on the nose. The dog howled. The cat ran up a tree and looked down at the powerful dog.

EXTRA PRACTICE WORDS

1.	low	19.	grow	37.	yellow
2.	lower	20.	growing	38.	pillow
3.	lowest	21.	crow	39.	pillowless
4.	below	22.	blow	40.	window
5.	slow	23.	blower	41.	windowless
6.	slowly	24.	flow	42.	borrow
7.	row	25.	flowed	43.	borrower
8.	tow	26.	glow	44.	borrowing
9.	towed	27.	glowing	45.	sorrow
10.	towing	28.	throw	46.	sorrowful
11.	mow	29.	thrower	47.	arrow
12.	mower	30.	throwing	48.	narrow
13.	elbow	31.	sow	49.	narrowly
14.	elbows	32.	sowed	50.	shadow
15.	know	33.	follow	51.	shadowy
16.	knowing	34.	follower	52.	widow
17.	knowable	35.	followed	53.	widower
18.	unknowable	36.	fellow		

EXTRA PRACTICE SENTENCES

1. This spray kills household germs.
2. Spray around the shower.
3. Spray down the drains.
4. Spray in the toilet bowl.
5. Is the spray powerful?
6. Yes, it's powerful.
7. Keep it out of the hands of children.

The teacher will dictate:

1. law	lawful	unlawfully
2. awe	awful	awfully
3. flaw	flawless	flawlessly
4. yawn	yawned	yawning
5. crawl	crawler	crawled
6. awkward	awkwardly	awkwardness

WORD DICTATION:

credit, dentist, flutist, polish, blemish, vomit, audit, artist, punish, leftist, edit, banish

---

WORDS:

cover, covered, uncovering, chick, chicken, huge, hen, yard, barnyard, saw, hawk, hawkish, claw, claws, clawed, clawing, squawk, squawked, squawking, squawker

WORD GROUPS:

1. a hen in the barnyard
2. all of the claws
3. squawking hens
4. saw the huge hawk
5. squawked and ran
6. will cover the chickens

PARAGRAPH:

The hawk had huge claws. A hen in the barnyard saw the hawk. The hen squawked and all the chickens ran for cover.

EXTRA PRACTICE WORDS

1. few	13. chewed	25. nephew-in-law
2. fewer	14. chewing	26. curfew
3. fewest	15. crew	27. cashew
4. new	16. screw	28. mildew
5. newly	17. shrewd	29. mildewed
6. renew	18. shrewder	30. threw
7. renewal	19. shrewdest	31. drew
8. dew	20. shrewdness	32. withdrew
9. dewdrop	21. sewer	33. grew
10. pew	22. jewel	34. blew
11. stew	23. jewelry	
12. chew	24. nephew	

EXTRA PRACTICE WORD GROUPS

1. in a few years
2. fewer than ever
3. the fewest number
4. starting the new year
5. was the newest father
6. large crew of workers
7. sat on the chewing gum
8. ever met my nephew
9. as she threw the ball to her father
10. grew corn behind the house
11. drew a sketch of the little house
12. withdrew the last number

WORDS 4 DICTATION Lesson 16

The teacher will dictate:

1. commit	committee	committing
2. occur	occurred	occurring
3. propel	propelled	propeller
4. cancel	canceled	canceling
5. suffer	suffering	sufferer

WORD DICTATION:

humor, collar, motor, actor, solar, dollar, tremor, doctor, tutor,
cellar, rumor, armor

WORDS:

were, they, father, children, new, New York, three, window,
sleep, sleeping, open, opened, begin, beginner, beginning,
permit, permitted, travel, traveler, traveled

WORD GROUPS:

1. not beginning
2. traveling to New York
3. three fathers
4. they opened
5. permitted the children
6. were sleeping by an open window

PARAGRAPH:

A father and his three children traveled to New York by bus. In the
beginning, they had a hard time sleeping. They were not permitted to open
the window.

The teacher will dictate 7 words and 7 word groups.

1.	fair	8.	unfair to ask
2.	pair	9.	one pair of socks
3.	chair	10.	were on the chair
4.	repair	11.	was repairing the roof
5.	staircase	12.	met Cindy on the stairs
6.	aircraft	13.	where the aircraft landed
7.	dairy	14.	the dairy on the corner

The teacher will dictate:

1.	care	careful	careless
2.	prepare	preparing	unprepared
3.	share	shared	sharing
4.	aware	unaware	awareness
5.	compare	compared	comparing

WORD DICTATION:

freedom, custom, bottom, wisdom, lemon, phantom, dragon, felon, seldom, symptom, prison, stardom

---

WORDS:

head, survive, survival, surviving, yet, our, close, closer, drink, eat, can, cannot, can't, with, without, air, airy, airless, hair, hairless

WORD GROUPS:

1. eating and drinking
2. without air
3. close to our heads
4. but cannot survive
5. can see our hair
6. can't see the air

PARAGRAPH:

   Air is as close as the hair on our heads. We can't eat or drink it. We can't see it. Yet, we cannot survive without air.

EXTRA PRACTICE WORDS

1.	carry	7.	married	13.	parents	19.	Gary
2.	carries	8.	marrying	14.	parenthood	20.	Mary
3.	carried	9.	parrot	15.	Larry	21.	Carol
4.	carrying	10.	carrot	16.	Barry	22.	Sharon
5.	marry	11.	barrel	17.	Harry	23.	Karen
6.	marries	12.	parent	18.	Darren		

EXTRA PRACTICE SENTENCES

1. Gary is selling his car.
2. Do you want to buy it?
3. Is it in good shape?
4. It's in fair shape.
5. The brakes are not good.
6. Will Gary repair the brakes?
7. Yes, he'll repair them himself.
8. He'll put on new brake pads.
9. Two hubcaps are missing.
10. He'll buy a new pair of hubcaps.
11. Do the tires need air?
12. No, the tires have plenty of air.
13. There is a spare tire.
14. There is a good spare in the trunk.
15. Are you aware that the brake light is out?
16. I was not aware of that.
17. Gary will replace the brake light.

WORDS 4 DICTATION   Lesson 18

The teacher will dictate 7 words and 7 word groups.

1.	famous	8.	when you are famous
2.	hazardous	9.	not so hazardous
3.	joyous	10.	joyous event
4.	nervous	11.	were nervously jumping
5.	dangerous	12.	if the job is dangerous
6.	package	13.	asking for the package
7.	bandage	14.	were replacing bandages

The teacher will dictate:

1.	prevent	prevented	preventive
2.	expense	expenses	expensive
3.	impress	impressed	impressive
4.	protect	protecting	protective
5.	construct	constructed	constructive
6.	addict	addicted	addictive

WORD DICTATION:

admit, clinic, timid, valid, commit, permit, solid, panic, toxic,
rapid, omit, comic

WORDS:

story, stories, fair, fairs, grew, outgrew, like, liked, unlikely, enter, entered, age, cabbage, cabbages, act, active, actively, humor, humorous, humorously

WORD GROUPS:

1. liked his humor
2. was entered in the fair
3. a humorous story
4. an active old age
5. grew cabbages
6. telling stories

PARAGRAPH:

He was active in his old age. He liked to tell a humorous story. He grew cabbages and entered them in the fair.

WORDS 4 DICTATION   Lesson 19

The teacher will dictate:

1.	act	acted	action
2.	object	objected	objection
3.	inject	injected	injection
4.	infect	infected	infection
5.	affect	affected	affection
6.	note	noted	notion
7.	relate	related	relation
8.	translate	translated	translation
9.	complete	completed	completion
10.	digest	digested	digestion

WORD DICTATION:

carton, cartoon, nation, pontoon, cotton, mutton, station, portion, lotion, glutton, festoon, spittoon

WORDS:

nurse, nursing, gave, sing, singing, throat, TV, sore, clinic, clinical, prevent, prevented, preventive, prevention, infect, infecting, infection, inject, injected, injection

WORD GROUPS:

1. will prevent the TV star
2. from a clinic
3. had a sore throat
4. gave an injection
5. singing on TV
6. prevented the infection

PARAGRAPH:

The TV star had a throat infection. The sore throat prevented her from singing. A nurse from the clinic gave her an injection.

EXTRA PRACTICE WORDS

1. instruct
2. instructed
3. instructing
4. instructive
5. instruction
6. reject
7. rejected
8. rejecting
9. rejection
10. construct
11. constructing
12. reconstruct
13. constructed
14. construction
15. promote
16. promoted
17. promoting
18. promotion
19. suggest
20. suggested
21. suggesting
22. suggestive
23. congest
24. congested
25. congestion
26. locate
27. located
28. relocated
29. location
30. operate
31. operating
32. operation
33. regulate
34. regulated
35. regulating
36. regulated
37. regulation

EXTRA PRACTICE EXERCISE FOR ADVANCED STUDENTS

WORDS:

were, they, all, husband, work, worker, week, weekly, party, parties, invite, invitation, construct, construction, promote, promoted, promotion, celebrate, celebrating, celebration

WORD GROUPS:

1. the week that they celebrated
2. were all invited
3. promoted her husband
4. celebration party
5. last time he got a promotion
6. working in construction

PARAGRAPH:

Last week, her husband got a promotion. They gave a party to celebrate. All of the construction workers were invited.

EXTRA PRACTICE WORDS FOR ADVANCED STUDENTS

1. occupy
2. occupation
3. perfect
4. perfection
5. distract
6. distraction
7. convict
8. conviction
9. collect
10. collection
11. corrupt
12. corruption
13. state
14. station
15. correct
16. correction
17. correctional
18. motion
19. commotion
20. emotion
21. emotional
22. nation
23. national
24. subtract
25. subtraction
26. inspect
27. inspection
28. depress
29. depression
30. confess
31. confession
32. discuss
33. discussion
34. motive
35. motivate
36. motivation
37. educate
38. education
39. educational
40. separate
41. separation
42. dictate
43. dictation
44. operate
45. operation
46. invest
47. investigate
48. investigation
49. populate
50. population
51. vacate
52. vacation
53. civil
54. civilized
55. civilization

EXTRA PRACTICE SENTENCES FOR ADVANCED STUDENTS

1. Actions speak louder than words.
2. The people who need it the most never seem to get a vacation.
3. An ounce of prevention is better than a pound of cure.
4. Civilization begins with order.

SECTION III

Multisensory Teaching Techniques and Drills

INTRODUCTION

Some learners need even more intensive decoding and encoding practice than the Student Books provide. The multisensory teaching procedures presented in this section are designed specifically for extra, in-depth practice in reading, spelling, and writing.

In the *Getting Started* section of this Guide, page-by-page suggestions are offered on how to present the first three lessons in Student Book One, and specific multisensory exercises are recommended at certain stages of instruction.

Give yourself time to become familiar with the routines. Then, if the student shows a need, gradually introduce multisensory activities.

THE POWER OF MULTISENSORY LEARNING

The eyes do not learn to read, nor do the ears. The *brain* learns to read. How the brain gets its information from the outside world and how it organizes that information are all-important to the task of reading, spelling, and writing.

Most people have been taught to depend mainly on the visual channel to recognize words. Reading *is* a visual task, but it depends heavily on auditory input that allows a person to match the spoken sound and the written symbol.

In addition, speaking and writing are dependent upon messages sent to the brain through the sense of touch (*tactile* input) and through awareness of what the muscles are doing (*kinesthetic* input).

"Multisensory learning" means that several pathways to the brain are being stimulated at the same time. In multisensory learning, the learner:

- *sees* letters and words (visual input)
- *hears* the sounds of letters and words (auditory input)
- *"feels"* the sensations of touch and muscle movement when using the hand to write and/or using the mouth to speak (tactile-kinesthetic input).

Thus, through multisensory learning, the brain gets a multiple message. If one learning channel is weak, the others can reinforce it. The learner perceives, processes, stores, and communicates more successfully.

INTRODUCING STUDENTS TO THE CONCEPT OF MULTISENSORY LEARNING

The *WORDS* program contains important multisensory drills and learning routines. Learners participate enthusiastically once they are made aware of the effectiveness of the multisensory approach.

Begin a discussion about multisensory learning by asking learners how the brain gets its information from the outside world. Encourage responses such as "through the eyes" and "through the ears." Be sure that "doing"—the feeling of the muscles in motion—is included.

Use an analogy, such as learning to drive a car:

> *We may watch a driver turn the ignition key, set the gear lever, apply a foot to the accelerator, turn the steering wheel, etc. We may listen to the driver explain each of these steps. But few of us ever really learn to drive a car until we get "hands on" experience, along with looking and listening. Not until the proper sequence of movements is fixed firmly in our "muscle memory," which is the kinesthetic learning channel, do we become competent drivers.*

Similarly, in language learning, the action of "doing" (saying and forming letters, or "talking through" a language concept), along with seeing and hearing, speeds up the learning process for most students.

BRIEF DESCRIPTIONS OF THE MULTISENSORY TEACHING TECHNIQUES AND DRILLS

Following are brief descriptions of the multisensory exercises that begin on page 161.

1. The *Vowel Drill* can be used as a warm-up for the *Phonics Review* exercises found toward the end of most lessons in Student Book One (for example, see Lesson 2, page 14). Although emphasis should be on vowel sounds, consonant sounds can be practiced by learners in the same way, if needed.

2. *Blending Practice* helps learners who have difficulty pronouncing words or syllables correctly. It gives valuable oral practice in producing sounds in the right sequence. This activity can be introduced any time during or after Lesson 2 of Student Book One.

3. The *Sight Word Study Method* gives auditory and tactile-kinesthetic support to learners with poor visual recall for spelling nonphonetic words. This strategy for learning sight words can be introduced as early as Lesson 2 of Student Book One and used throughout the program.

4. *Letter-Card Spelling*, Level 1, greatly helps learners who have difficulty spelling (encoding) phonetically-regular words and syllables. This exercise can be introduced in Lesson 2 of Student Book One or any time thereafter. Level 2 is a more advanced version that can be used with individuals who have mastered Level 1.

5. *Visual-Motor Patterning* trains learners to distinguish between letter shapes for reading purposes and for writing printed materials. This individualized activity can be used any time during or after Lesson 1 of Student Book One.

6. *Auditory Spelling* gives learners practice in developing auditory memory for letter sequences in words. This technique can be introduced at any point in the program and continued as new spelling patterns are introduced in the Student Books.

7. *Pencil Tracking to Improve Reading Fluency* helps learners during the reading process to "keep their places" and overcome errors such as misread words, omissions, and insertions. This activity can be introduced any time after a learner has completed the first half of Student Book One.

8. *Pencil Tracking to Develop Phrase Reading* is designed for use with Student Books Three and Four. This technique helps very slow readers to acquire skill in reading word groups (units of thought). With continual practice, both reading and comprehension improve.

9. *Spelling Practice—Phonetically-Regular Two-Syllable Words* assists students in making the transition from spelling one-syllable words to spelling two-syllable words. This activity is designed to be used with Lesson 1 in Student Book Two.

10. *Spelling Practice—Two-Syllable Words Containing the Schwa Sound* helps learners deal with the issue of spelling two-syllable words that contain a weak vowel sound in the unstressed syllable. From Lesson 2 in Student Book Two onward, regular use of this exercise is recommended because the spelling of schwa words is a continual challenge.

VOWEL DRILL (3 to 5 minutes)

A brief multisensory exercise on vowel sounds (and consonant sounds, if necessary) can be given to the learners after they are introduced to the letter-sound relationships. This can be done after the Phonics Review exercise, which is given toward the end of each regular lesson in the Student Books, starting with Lesson 2 in Student Book One.

This activity is presented from two approaches: visual and auditory. First, students are shown the letter (visual input). They respond by:

- naming the letter
- naming the key word (see next page) and
- giving the appropriate sound.

Then the routine is reversed. This time, students are given the sound (auditory input). They respond the same way: by naming the letter, naming the key word, then giving the appropriate sound.

For tactile-kinesthetic reinforcement, encourage students to form each letter (the larger the better) on the desk or tabletop at the same time that they are naming the letter. This should be done with the fingertips (index and middle finger) without looking at the hand, keeping the wrist straight and the elbow bent, and moving the entire arm in a robot-like way.

Key Words for the Vowel Drill

SHORT VOWELS		
ă	—	at
ě	—	Ed
ĭ	—	if
ŏ	—	ox
ŭ	—	up

LONG VOWELS		
ā	—	safe
ē	—	eve
ī	—	dime
ō	—	hope
ū	—	mule
ōō	—	rule

INSTRUCTIONAL TECHNIQUE

Short Vowel Drill*

1. Write the five vowel letters in a column on the chalkboard. Make the letters large, with at least four inches between each letter. (If working individually, sit beside the student and write letters on a sheet of paper.)

   a

   e

   i

   o

   u

2. Point to the letter **a** (visual input).
3. Students respond: **a** – **at** – / ă /. Keeping wrists straight and moving the entire arm as they name the letter, they form a large **a** on their desks or tabletops with their fingertips.
4. Point to each vowel letter in the same way, and the students respond as in Step 3.
5. Next, give the sound of a letter without pointing (auditory input): / ă /.
6. Students respond the same way: **a** – **at** – / ă /, again forming the letter on their desktops with their fingertips.
7. As Step 6 is finishing up, point to the letter **a** for visual reinforcement.
8. Follow the procedure with all the vowel sounds, varying the sequence. Students respond in the same way for each vowel you present visually or auditorially.

---

* *Note:* **a** (in boldface) denotes the *name* of the letter; / ă / (enclosed with slashes) denotes the *sound* of the letter.

INSTRUCTIONAL TECHNIQUE
*Long Vowel Drill**

1. On the chalkboard or sheet of paper, write the five vowel letters with a line and **e** after each of the vowels. (The line signifies a consonant.) The arrangement should look like this:

$$\begin{array}{ccc}
\textbf{a} & \_\_ & \textbf{e} \\
\textbf{e} & \_\_ & \textbf{e} \\
\textbf{i} & \_\_ & \textbf{e} \\
\textbf{o} & \_\_ & \textbf{e} \\
\textbf{u} & \_\_ & \textbf{e}
\end{array}$$

2. Point to the vowel letter pattern (for example, **a __ e**) for visual input.

3. Students respond: "**a** with an **e** at the end – **safe** – / ā /." (Keeping wrists straight and moving the entire arm as they name the letter, they form large letters **a __ e** (with a line between the two letters) on the desktop with their fingertips.

4. Point to each vowel letter pattern in the same way, and the students respond as in Step 3.

5. Next, give the sound of a letter without pointing (auditory input): / ā /.

6. Students respond the same way: "**a** with an **e** at the end – **safe** – / ā /," again forming the letter pattern on the desk or tabletops with their fingertips.

7. As Step 6 is finishing up, point to the letter **a** for visual reinforcement.

8. Follow the procedure with all the vowel sounds, varying the sequence. Students respond in the same way for each vowel you present visually and auditorially.

BLENDING PRACTICE – Small Group or One-to-One Tutoring (3 to 5 minutes)

Once students are familiar with the short vowel sounds, they are ready for this blending exercise.

Blending is an auditory-oral task. It refers to the ability to blend a sequence of single sounds into a syllable. Blending helps learners to "sound out" and to spell phonetically-regular words.

The instructional technique for blending practice appears on the next page.

---

* *Note:* **a** (in boldface) denotes the *name* of the letter; / ā / (enclosed with slashes) denotes the *sound* of the letter.

INSTRUCTIONAL TECHNIQUE

1. Write the five vowel letters in a column on the chalkboard or sheet of paper as in the *Vowel Drill*, but the sequence will be different:*

i

e

a

u

o

2. Point to each vowel letter and have students say its short sound. Go through these short sounds several times, varying the sequence and gradually increasing speed as you point to the letters.

3. Next, have students write the letters in the same order on a sheet of paper. To the right of the vowels, they should place a consonant, such as **b**. The arrangement should look like this (demonstrate):

i

e

a   **b**

u

o

4. Demonstrate how the students should "track" with a sweeping motion with their pencils from each vowel to the letter **b** as they pronounce the syllable (the short vowel blending into / b /):

Lead students in pronouncing the syllables as they track with their pencils from each vowel to the consonant:

ib, eb, ab, ub, ob

5. Have them erase the letter **b** and replace it with another consonant — **k**, for example. As the students track from each vowel to the **k**, lead them in pronouncing the short vowel sounds blending into / k /:

ik, ek, ak, uk, ok

6. Continue this exercise for three to five minutes, having students use various consonant letters.

7. As students progress, have them add two consonant letters (ending blends). For example:

sk (isk, esk, ask, usk, osk)

sp, st, ft, mp, nd, nt, ct, pt, and **ps**

8. Finally, use real words from lists in the Student Book.

---

* This arrangement starts with the frontal vowels.

SIGHT WORD STUDY METHOD
for Memorizing Words with Nonphonetic Spellings

Sight words are the downfall of spellers with unstable visual recall of words. For these individuals especially, a multisensory study method and frequent review are very important. If visual memory is weak, this activity reinforces it with auditory and tactile-kinesthetic memory.

First demonstrate the method. Have students practice the method until everyone is able to follow the steps with ease and accuracy.

INSTRUCTIONAL TECHNIQUE

While demonstrating, say:

1. Copy the words you want to memorize on a strip of paper (lined notebook paper cut in half lengthwise).

2. Go over the word two or more times with a pencil. As you trace, *say the letters out loud*. Then say the word.

3. Put your pencil down. Write the word with your fingertips—index and middle finger—on the desk or tabletop. Make large letters. Keep your wrist and hand straight, with your elbow bent. Your entire arm should move. Say each letter as you form it. Say the word.

4. Turn the paper over and upside down. Write the word at the top of the paper. Say each letter as you write it. Now, fold the paper once, from bottom to top. Compare the word you just wrote with the first one. Is it spelled correctly? If not, repeat Steps 2, 3, and 4.

During Step 3, stress keeping the wrist straight, moving the whole arm (robot-like) and making large letter forms—the larger the better—to leave a permanent impression on the memory.

Repeat the demonstration often until the routine is automatic for all students.

LETTER-CARD SPELLING—Level I (5 to 7 minutes)

Letter-Card Spelling is a highly structured multisensory activity that is popular with learners who need intensive practice in encoding (spelling).

Materials

Each student will need a set of alphabet consonants, 2-1/2" x 3" or smaller, with one letter on each card—white for consonants, another color for vowels. (These cards may be made by the students by cutting in half 3" x 5" index cards.)*

---

* A sheet of letters is included in Appendix C of this Guide. The sheet may be reproduced—consonants on white paper, the vowels on colored paper. Cut the letters, keeping the heavy black line at the bottom of each letter so that the students know which is the bottom and which is the top, thus avoiding reversals or inversions. For indefinite use, laminate the reproduced sheets before cutting out the letters.

Setting Up

More advanced spellers may start with the entire alphabet. New learners should start with only one or two vowel cards (for example, **a** and **i**) and three or four consonant cards (perhaps **b**, **f**, **n** and **t**).

Have the students lay the cards out alphabetically at the top of their desks or table. A large open area should be left for tabletop writing and for placing letters when spelling a word or syllable.

Word or Syllable Lists

For new learners start with three-letter phonetic words containing short vowel sounds; for example, **fat, tin, fib, ban, fin, tan, bat, fan, tab, fit**.

If students are able to spell some of these words from memory, use "nonsense" syllables to give practice in phonetic spelling; for example, **bif, naf, tib, fab, taf, nib, baf**.

Select syllables from the Phonics Review exercises in the Student Book. As learners gain skill in phonetic encoding, gradually add the remaining vowels and consonants. Aim at mastery of syllables that contain four and five letters, such as **twen, lusk, drant,** and **scrib**.

INSTRUCTIONAL TECHNIQUE

Letter-Card Spelling—Level I

TEACHER: Pronounce the target syllable, **baf**.

STUDENT(S):
1. Repeats the syllable, **baf**.
2. Gives the first sound, / b /.
3. Names the letter and forms a large letter **b** on the desktop with two fingers.
4. Selects the alphabet card containing the letter **b** and places it on the desktop, below the rows of alphabet cards. This can be designated the "spelling area."
5. Repeats the syllable, **baf**.
6. Gives the next sound, / ă /.
7. Names the letter and forms a large **a** on the desktop.
8. Selects the letter card **a** and places it after the letter card **b** in the spelling area.
9. Repeats the syllable, **baf**.
10. Gives the next sound, / f /.
11. Names the letter and forms a large **f**.
12. Selects the letter card **f** and places it after the letter cards **b - a** in the spelling area.
13. Repeats the syllable, **baf**.
14. Spells the syllable out loud, forming each letter on the desktop.
15. Writes the syllable on a piece of paper, naming the letters as he or she writes; then says, **baf**.

LETTER-CARD SPELLING – Level II (5 to 7 minutes)

Not until mastery of *Letter-Card Spelling – Level I* is achieved is a student ready for Level II.

When the consonant and vowels are firmly established, begin this next step. Start with small words containing consonant digraphs. As learners progress through Student Books Three and Four, various spelling patterns may be included.

After the first word has been given, continue dictating words in which only one letter or digraph is changed, added, shifted, or omitted.

As in Level I, students line up letter cards alphabetically at the top of their desks or tables. At this level, they will be using all of the vowels and consonants, and the consonant digraphs as introduced.

INSTRUCTIONAL TECHNIQUE

Letter-Card Spelling—Level II

TEACHER:	Spell **chat**.
STUDENT:	(Chooses letter cards **ch** - **a** - **t** and places them in the spelling area. Repeats **chat**.)
TEACHER:	Now spell **chap**.
STUDENT:	(Removes letter card **t** and replaces it with **p**. Repeats **chap**.)
TEACHER:	Spell **chip**.
STUDENT:	(Removes **a** and replaces it with **i**. Repeats **chip**.)
TEACHER:	Spell **ship**.
STUDENT:	(Removes **ch** diagraph and replaces it with **sh**. Repeats **ship**.)
TEACHER:	Now spell **shin**.
STUDENT:	(Removes **p** and replaces it with **n**. Repeats **shin**.)
TEACHER:	Spell **thin**.
STUDENT:	(Removes **sh** and replaces it with **th**. Repeats **thin**.)
TEACHER:	Spell **chin**.
STUDENT:	(Removes **th** and replaces it with **ch**. Repeats **chin**.)
TEACHER:	Spell **inch**. (This is a "shift" or transposition.)
STUDENT:	(Removes **ch** from the beginning of the word and places it at the end. Repeats **inch**.)

Continue with **pinch, punch,** etc. The list of words that can be used for this exercise is seemingly endless. Remember to dictate words in which there will be only one change at a time.

Once students understand the procedure, the teacher's cue word "spell" can be omitted.

If students have difficulty encoding a word or words, revert to the Level I routine temporarily.

VISUAL-MOTOR PATTERNING
for Discriminating Between Letter Shapes

It is important that individuals learn to distinguish between letter shapes for accurate reading and to build up visual and muscle memory for forming letters when required to print (for example, application forms, order blanks, tax and registration forms, etc.).

When reading and writing printed material, some learners tend to reverse certain letters such as **b - d** and **p - q**. They often capitalize letters in inappropriate places: in the middle of a word, at the beginning of a word within a sentence or, as an example, mixing lower case and upper case letters in the exercise in Lesson 1 in Student Book One.

$$a \, B \, c \, D \, e \, F \, g \, h \, i \, J \, k \, l \, M$$
$$n \, o \, P \, q \, r \, s \, t \, u \, v \, W \, x \, y \, z$$

Visual-Motor Patterning also can be used with learners who sometimes leave out letter fragments (**n** for **m**, **v** for **w**) or, a less common problem, invert letters (**n** for **u**, **d** for **p**).

This activity can be started very early in the program on an individual basis. It must be done regularly, though, to be effective.

INSTRUCTIONAL TECHNIQUE

1. Make up a worksheet that concentrates on the target letter that a learner has difficulty with—the letter **b**, for example (see next page).

    On the upper half of the page, print five lines of large letters which randomly include the target letter. The learner must locate each target letter, then trace it while saying its name out loud.

2. The lower half of the page should contain five lines of words. The target letter should appear in most of the words. Again, the learner must locate the letter and trace it while saying its name out loud.

    Make sure that the learner traces the letter correctly. For example, if tracing **b**, the formation of the letter starts with a down stroke of the vertical line, stops, goes halfway up the line, around to the right for the "hump," then down and around to the bottom of the vertical line. It helps to verbalize each stroke if an individual has difficulty remembering the pattern.

3. Direct the learner to scan the line from left to right in reading style.

Note: Avoid using any letter that might directly cause confusion when learners start practicing the target letter. For example, if they are working with **b**, do not use **d** as a contrast until **b** is firmly established. They should concentrate on just one letter until it can be written automatically. At that point, prepare worksheets using a contrasting letter.

Some individuals may need several worksheets before starting practice on another letter. Use no more than one worksheet per session, because students can become fatigued if asked to do too much at one sitting.

(Don't forget to make copies of the worksheets you prepare—you will probably use them again with other students.)

VISUAL MOTOR PATTERNING SAMPLE WORKSHEET

Trace each letter **b**. Say the name of the letter as you trace.

h	p	o	b	j	b	k	b	q	f
m	b	r	t	u	q	s	i	j	b
b	f	l	k	b	y	a	q	b	h
t	b	c	g	p	q	b	f	b	u
r	q	b	l	k	g	x	z	q	a

Trace each letter **b**. Say the name of the letter as you trace.

web	bin	job	bite	rob	hub
but	buzz	bib	ebb	bop	tube
rip	jab	fib	bone	bum	bat
bell	bob	reb	pep	ban	robe
pub	bit	jibe	bus	sob	lip

AUDITORY SPELLING—Small Group or One-to-One Tutoring (3 to 5 minutes)

The purpose of this exercise is to give learners practice in developing auditory memory for letter sequences in words. The teacher spells a word orally. Students learn to hold in memory the sequence of letters they hear and form a mental picture of the complete word before saying the word out loud.

This activity can be used repeatedly for reinforcement and review as new words are introduced in the Student Books.

No matter at what point you wish to introduce *Auditory Spelling*, always begin with phonetic CVC (consonant-vowel-consonant) words until learners catch on to the procedure. Then add one-syllable words that contain silent **e** at the end, consonant blends, and some sight words that have been studied. When learners are succeeding at each step, start selecting a few words from a current lesson and include three or four words from previous lessons.

If working with a small group, decide on a prearranged signal for group response. In this way, you will control the responses so that some learners will not answer before others have a chance to process the word.

INSTRUCTIONAL TECHNIQUE

TEACHER:	(Spelling the word distinctly and at a moderate rate) Listen: **r - o - d**. Repeat that.
STUDENTS:	**r - o - d**
TEACHER:	Say the word.
STUDENTS:	**rod**
TEACHER:	Now write the word with your fingertips. Say the letters out loud as you write. (Lead a group until they learn the routine and respond together: **r - o - d**.) Listen: **f - i - n**. Repeat that.
STUDENTS:	(At your signal) **f - i - n, fin** (They form the word on a desk or tabletop while saying the letters out loud, then repeat the word.)
TEACHER:	Listen: **h - u - t**

Some learners will process words more quickly than others. In a group-teaching situation, make a note of those individuals who may be having difficulty, but do not remove them from the group. Have them pair up for a later short session to review the words together—they should take turns being the "tutor." Tell them to form the letters with their fingertips *immediately after the word is spelled to them*. Have them repeat each letter as they form it. Tell them to try to picture the word as they form it, *then* say the word. Gradually encourage them to say the word *before* forming it on the desk or tabletop.

PENCIL TRACKING TO IMPROVE READING FLUENCY—
One-to-One Tutoring (5 to 10 minutes)

Some learners have difficulty keeping their places while reading across a line of print. They may skip a line or drop down a line in the middle of a sentence.

An effective way to ease this problem is to have learners use a pencil (a red pencil is preferable) to underline as they read. The pencil acts as an extension of the hand and guides the eyes across the printed line. This exercise also helps learners overcome errors such as misread words, omissions (words left out), or insertions (words that are not in a sentence).

This activity can be started after a learner has completed the first half of Student Book One. Use sentences from the Student Books.

INSTRUCTIONAL TECHNIQUE

Explain to the learner why the use of a pencil is important. Then say, "As you read the sentence (paragraph, passage), I want you to underline with your pencil. You will start underlining at the beginning of each line. *Do not lift the pencil until you come to the end of the line, even if there is a period within the line.* When you come to the end of each line, lift the pencil and begin the next line. If you make a mistake, I will simply say, 'No.' Then I want you to try to find your own mistake."

Example

STUDENT: (underlining and reading aloud) Sue had a job at a hotdog stand in the park. A man come up to . . .

TEACHER: (gently) No.

STUDENT: (keeping pencil in place) A man . . . *came* up to the stand. He smelled . . .

TEACHER: No.

STUDENT: (keeping pencil in place) He sm . . . *smiled* at Sue and asked for a hotdog and a Sprite. As the man was holding the hotdog in his hand, a husky dog came running by and (and so forth)

If the learner cannot find his or her own error within five or six seconds, point it out, then continue.

After a short time, the learner will be making fewer errors. Encourage the use of a pencil for all reading activities as long as the individual needs it.

PENCIL TRACKING TO DEVELOP PHRASE READING—
Use with Student Books Three and Four (7 to 10 Minutes)

The pencil also may be used with those learners who are word-by-word readers. If they continue to plod along, one word at a time, without guidance, they remain slow readers and fail to grasp the meaning of sentences and passages.

During the process of reading, the eyes do not move smoothly across a printed page. They "fixate," or stop, several times in short, quick movements. The more fixations individuals make, the slower will be their rate of reading. Good readers will pace their reading rate according to the type of materials being read and the purpose for the reading. While "speed" reading certainly is not the goal in the *WORDS* program, learners should be taught how to read in *thought units* (word groups) for a better reading rate and better comprehension.

Learners who have completed Student Books One and Two are familiar with word groups (mostly phrases and clauses). They have had practice in reading word groups and writing them in Sentence Focus exercises and from Dictation.

INSTRUCTIONAL TECHNIQUE

Use sentences or paragraphs from a current lesson in Student Book Three or Four or from a dictation exercise. Insert large dots between units of thought.

Example

.The mailman . has worn . a hole . in the sole . of his shoe.

The student, using a pencil, reads the sentence out loud while underlining from dot to dot:

The mailman has worn a hole in the sole of his shoe.

Use the same procedure with a paragraph or passage.

My landlord was born on a farm. The farmhouse

was so small that he had to sleep in the barn

when he was young. He slept in a stall with a horse,

but he snored so loudly that the horse kicked him out.

After a while, lengthen the units of thought by using fewer dots.

Two-syllable words are introduced in Student Book Two, Lesson 1. Many learners have a hard time making the move from spelling one-syllable words to spelling two-syllable words. They need plenty of practice. For this purpose, a blank sheet for extra practice is provided in Appendix C (page 195), titled "Two-Syllable Word Dictation." (This sheet may be duplicated in quantity, cut in half, and used by students for frequent two-syllable word dictation practice.)

INSTRUCTIONAL TECHNIQUE

At the beginning, the student or group should follow these steps:

1. Pronounce the word.
2. Pronounce the first syllable.
3. Spell the first syllable out loud and write it.
4. Follow the same procedure with the second syllable.
5. Write the entire word, naming each letter as it is written.

Here is a sample script. (If working with a group, have students respond in unison.)

TEACHER:	The word is **contest**. Repeat that.
STUDENT:	**contest**
TEACHER:	Pronounce the first syllable.
STUDENT:	**con**
TEACHER:	Write the first syllable and name each letter as you write.
STUDENT:	(Writes **con** under the column labeled *First Syllable* while naming the letters, **c - o - n**.)
TEACHER:	Pronounce the second syllable.
STUDENT:	**test**
TEACHER:	Write the second syllable and name each letter as you write.
STUDENT:	(Writes **test** under the column labeled *Second Syllable* while naming the letters **t - e - s - t**.)
TEACHER:	Pronounce the word, then write it as you name each letter.
STUDENT:	(Writes **contest** under the column labeled *Word* while naming the letters, **c - o - n - t - e - s - t**.)

Follow the two-syllable spelling procedure as long as needed. Suggested lists for phonetically-regular two-syllable word dictation are on the next page.

Phonetically-Regular Two-Syllable Words

1. contest	1. until	1. invade	1. invite
2. invent	2. intend	2. costume	2. impose
3. admit	3. napkin	3. admire	3. stampede
4. combat	4. himself	4. immune	4. excite
5. album	5. submit	5. expose	5. ignore
6. upset	6. plastic	6. baptize	6. dictate
7. picnic	7. zigzag	7. escape	7. subside
8. mascot	8. unless	8. ignite	8. explode
9. cactus	9. traffic	9. mistake	9. include
10. public	10. nutmeg	10. entire	10. dispute

SPELLING PRACTICE—Two-Syllable Words Containing the Schwa Sound

In Lesson 2, Student Book Two, the *schwa* sound is introduced. The schwa sound is the source of countless spelling errors. Numerous two-syllable words in English contain a schwa sound in the unstressed syllable. When the word is pronounced, a learner cannot, by listening, tell which vowel letter to use in that unstressed syllable.

Explain the "schwa problem" to your students. For example:

- The word that sounds like / lĕs' ən / is spelled **lesson**.
- The word that sounds like / vĭc' təm / is spelled **victim**.
- The word that sounds like / kĕn' əl / is spelled **kennel**.
- The word that sounds like / hŭs' bənd / is spelled **husband**.

Write the word **canvas** on the chalkboard or on a sheet of paper. Tell the student or group that, for spelling purposes, each *schwa* word should be thought of as having two pronunciations. Say, "For example, look at this word, **canvas**. The *actual* pronunciation is / căn' vəs /." (Point to each syllable as you pronounce it.) "But the *spelling* pronunciation is / căn văs /." (Again, point to each syllable.)

Write the word **seldom** on the board. Say, "This word, **seldom**, should be thought of as having two pronunciations. The *actual* pronunciation is / sĕl' dəm /. But the *spelling* pronunciation is / sĕl dŏm /."

It is very important that learners understand this concept. The sample script on the next page will help to clarify the idea.

INSTRUCTIONAL TECHNIQUE

Hand out a blank practice sheet, "Two-Syllable Word Dictation," provided in Appendix C on page 195. If working with a group, have students respond in unison. Here is a sample script:

TEACHER: The word is / răn' səm /. Repeat that.

STUDENT: / răn' səm /

TEACHER: Pronounce the first syllable.

STUDENT: / răn /

TEACHER: Write the first syllable and name each letter as you write.

STUDENT: (Writes **ran** under the column labeled *First Syllable* while naming the letters **r - a - n**.)

TEACHER: The whole word is / răn' səm /. The second syllable is pronounced / səm /. Repeat the second syllable.

STUDENT: / səm /

TEACHER: Yes. The pronunciation is / səm /. But the *spelling* pronunciation is / sŏm /. Listen: / sŏm /. How is that *spelled*?

STUDENT: **s - o - m**

TEACHER: Write the second syllable and name each letter as you write.

STUDENT: (Writes **som** under the column labeled *Second Syllable* while naming the letters, **s - o - m**.)

TEACHER: Give the actual pronunciation of the whole word.

STUDENT: / răn' səm /

TEACHER: Give the *spelling* pronunciation of the word.

STUDENT: / răn sŏm /

TEACHER: Write the whole word as you name each letter.

STUDENT: (Writes **ransom** under the column labeled *Word* while naming the letters, **r - a - n - s - o - m**.)

After Lesson 2, Student Book Two, regularly review two-syllable words introduced in each current lesson, using the above procedure as needed.

WORD LISTS FOR DICTATION

Two-Syllable Words Containing the Schwa Sound

1. ransom	1. pencil
2. tonsil	2. ballot
3. basket	3. bottom
4. seldom	4. cancel
5. happen	5. atlas
6. cotton	6. common
7. canvas	7. husband
8. victim	8. sudden
9. tunnel	9. gallon
10. custom	10. infant

SECTION IV

Appendix A: Phonics Overview

INTRODUCTION

English is an alphabetic language. Each letter of the alphabet can represent one or more of the sounds that we *say* to form words that we can *read*.

The term *phonics* refers to the teaching of the relationships between speech sounds and letters of the alphabet. Phonics is the most practical method of teaching people word recognition and spelling. Yet many adults and adolescents were never given the opportunity to learn this basic skill. If our learners are ever to become independent readers and spellers, it is essential that they understand the written code of our language.

About 85% of English words are phonetic; they can be "sounded out." There are variations in spelling patterns, but these can be taught in a logical way so that students can learn how to rely on generalized patterns and basic rules. The Student Books are set up to make the job easy for you.

Pages 178 through 184 provide teachers and tutors with the sounds and descriptions of English vowels and consonants. If teaching phonics is a new experience for you, do not try to digest the entire range of sounds at one time. Instead, use the *Vowel Pronunciation Key* on page 178 and the *Consonant Pronunciation Key* on page 182. These two charts are for Student Book One only and will get you started in the right direction.*

TEACHING PHONICS THROUGH THE WORDS PROGRAM

The teaching of phonics requires direct instruction. First, be certain that the learners know the consonant sounds given in Lesson 1, Student Book One. Then go on to Lesson 2, which introduces the short vowels. The short vowels are presented first because the graphic patterns are clear and straightforward; for example, **rob**, **mat**, **win**.

Problems may arise because many learners cannot distinguish between short vowel sounds, such as / ĕ / and / ĭ / or / ŏ / and / ŭ /. For this reason, the short vowels are reviewed throughout the program, so keep moving. Otherwise, learners will feel they are "stuck" on the short vowels and not progressing.

Lesson 3 begins preliminary work with the long vowels, which are introduced in one-syllable words that end with silent **e**: **robe**, **mate**, **wine**. This gives learners the opportunity to compare the long and short sounds and pay attention to the differences in the spelling patterns.

---

* *Note:* **s** (in boldface) denotes the *name* of the letter; / s / (enclosed with slashes) denotes the *sound* of the letter (/ sss /).

Multisensory techniques are very valuable in teaching phonics. Students should see, hear, say, and write the letters and sounds at the same time whenever possible. They should receive visual and auditory input while getting feedback to the brain through the "feel" of simultaneously saying the sounds and writing the letters and words.

Make them aware of what their mouths, lips, and tongues are doing while pronouncing letters and words. Ask questions: *

> *Do you feel the tip of your tongue touching the gum ridge behind your upper teeth?* (The sound of the letter **d**)
>
> *Hold your lips together. Can you hear and feel the sound coming through your nose?* (The sound of the letter **m**)
>
> *Can you feel your jaw drop and your mouth open wider?* (Comparing / ŭ / with / ŏ /)
>
> *Do you feel the tip of your tongue press against the roof of your mouth?* (The sound of the letter **l**)
>
> *Put your thumb and finger on your throat under your chin. Can you feel the movement?* (The sound of the letter **g**)
>
> *Are your upper teeth touching your lower lip as you blow out air?* (The sound of the letter **f**)

During each session, use two or three multisensory exercises, such as *Short Vowel Drill* and *Blending Practice*, to review the vowel sounds, especially the short vowels. After students learn the routines of various drills, spend no more than three to five minutes on any one drill. These drills should be continued on a regular basis until students can respond automatically. After that, review the drills from time to time.

Keep in mind these sensory processes while teaching phonics:

- *Visual Discrimination* (interpreting what is seen),

- *Auditory Discrimination* (interpreting what is heard), and

- *Tactile-Kinesthetic Feedback* (the sense of touch and the "feel" of what the muscles are doing when pronouncing and writing words).

---

* See *"Sounding Out" the Consonants*, page 183 of this Guide.

VOWEL PRONUNCIATION KEY

(for Student Book One)

Vowel Letter	Sound	Dictionary Symbol	Key Words
a	Short a	ă	at, apple
a	Long a	ā	safe, name
a	ah	ä	father, car
a	aw	ȯ	ball, talk
e	Short e	ĕ	Ed, bed
e	Long e	ē	eve, me
i	Short i	ĭ	if, igloo
i	Long i	ī	dime, ice
o	Short o	ŏ	ox, olive
o	Long o	ō	hope, toe
o	aw	ȯ	dog, soft
u	Short u	ŭ	up, umbrella
u	Long u	ū, o͞o	mule, rule
u	oo as in "book"	o͝o	put, pull
y	Short i	ĭ	gym, cyst
y	Long i	ī	type, July
y	Long e	ē	happy, study

Note: Vowel combinations (diphthongs and vowel digraphs) and R-controlled vowels are thoroughly described in Student Books Two, Three, and Four when those spelling patterns are introduced. (Also see *Sounds of the English Vowels*, pages 179 through 182 of this Guide.)

SOUNDS OF THE ENGLISH VOWELS
(Teacher-Tutor Reference)

The pronunciation of a vowel can vary, depending on its position in a word. The rules that govern vowel sounds are clearly explained in the Student Books and are presented in orderly progression, one step at a time. Learners are given sufficient time to practice one concept before another is introduced.

The various sounds of the vowels given in this section are the ones used in the *WORDS* program.* The listings below and on the next few pages are for teacher and tutor reference only. A vowel that is introduced in Student Book One in one-syllable words will be introduced again in two-syllable words in Student Books Two and Three. Words of three and four syllables are presented in Student Book Four.

The Sounds of the Vowel a

/ ă /   at, cabin, shellac (short **a**, closed syllable)

/ ā /   safe, basement, locate (long **a**, silent **e** at the end of a syllable)

/ ā /   apron, bacon, relation (long **a**, open syllable)

/ ȯ /   all, false, sidewalk (**a** has the sound of "aw," usually followed by **l** or **ll**)

/ ä /   father, art, disarm (**a** has the sound of "ah," usually followed by **r**)

/ ə /   infant, atlas (schwa sound, closed syllable, unstressed)
        adult, tuna (schwa sound, open syllable, unstressed)

The Sounds of the Vowel e

/ ĕ /   bed, lesson, contest (short **e**, closed syllable)

/ ē /   eve, stampede, completely (long **e**, silent **e** at the end of a syllable)

/ ē /   equal, demon, torpedo (long **e**, open syllable)

/ ə /   travel, happen, moment (schwa, closed syllable, unstressed)

---

* *The Holt School Dictionary of American English*, Holt, Rinehart & Winston, New York, 1971, is used as a reference for the *WORDS* program. The diacritical marks (symbols above vowels to indicate their sounds) are taken from this source with one exception: the long **o** before the letter **r** as in the word **store**. This dictionary, along with a few others, shows a "hook" above the **o**. This sound actually is the long **o**, and this program treats it as a long vowel sound: / stōr /.

The Sounds of the Vowel i

/ ĭ /   if, river, omit (short i, closed syllable)

/ ī /   dime, iceberg, polite (long i, silent e at the end of a syllable)

/ ī /   idle, spider, horizon (long i, open syllable)

/ ə /   pencil, denim, April (schwa, closed syllable, unstressed)

The Sounds of the Vowel o

/ ŏ /   ox, comet, allot (short o, closed syllable)

/ ō /   hope, notebook, suppose (long o, silent e at the end of a syllable)

/ ō /   open, bonus, solo (long o, open syllable)

/ ȯ /   dog, song, across (closed syllable)

/ ŭ /   love, mother, money, govern ("Scribal O," closed syllable)

/ ə /   wagon, ballot, symbol (schwa, closed syllable, unstressed)

The Sounds of the Vowel u

/ ŭ /   up, mustard, instruct (short u, closed syllable)

/ ū / or / yo͞o /   mule, useless, barbecue (long u, silent e at the end of a syllable)

/ o͞o /   rule, rudeness, pursue (long u, silent e at the end of a syllable)

/ ū / or / yo͞o /   unit, computer, menu (long u, open syllable)

/ o͞o /   super, truly, Honolulu (long u, open syllable)

/ o͝o /   put, bulldog, bushel (closed syllable)

/ ə /   campus, sinus, hopeful (schwa, closed syllable, unstressed)

The Sounds of the Vowel y

/ ĭ /   gym, system, abyss (short i, closed syllable)

/ ī /   style, typewriter, analyze (long i, silent e at the end of a syllable)

/ ī /   fly, nylon, deny (long i, open syllable)

/ ē /   happy, bodyguard (long e at the end of a syllable)

The Sounds of the Vowel Combinations*

ai	/ ā /	aid, train (beginning and middle positions, Student Book Three)
ay	/ ā /	crayon, day (middle and ending positions, Student Book Three)
au	/ ȯ /	August, because (beginning and middle positions, Student Book Four)
ea	/ ē /	eat, clean, sea (all positions, Student Book Four)
ea	/ ĕ /	head, deaf, ready (middle position, Student Book Four)
ea	/ ā /	great, break, steak (middle position, Student Book Four)
ee	/ ē /	eel, green, tree (ending position, Student Book One; beginning and middle positions, Student Book Three)
ei	/ ē /	either, receive (beginning and middle positions, Student Book Four)
ei	/ ā /	eight, vein (beginning and middle positions, Student Book Four)
ie	/ ē /	chief, yield (middle position, Student Book Four)
oa	/ ō /	oat, coach (beginning and middle positions, Student Book Three)
oi	/ oi /	oil, voice (beginning and middle positions, Student Book Four)
oo	/ o͞o /	ooze, moon, shampoo (all positions, Student Book Four)
oo	/ o͝o /	book, good (middle position, Student Book Four)
oo	/ ō /	door, floor (middle position, Student Book Four)
oo	/ ŭ /	blood, flood (middle position, Student Book Four)
oy	/ oi /	boy, loyal (middle and ending positions, Student Book Four)
ou	/ ou /	out, south (beginning and middle positions, Student Book Three)
ou	/ o͞o /	you, soup (middle and ending positions, Student Book Three)
ou	/ ŭ /	touch, country (middle position, Student Book Three)
ou	/ ō /	four, court (middle position, Student Book Three)
ui	/ o͞o /	suit, juice (middle position, Student Book Four)

The Sounds of the R-Controlled Vowels

/ är /	car, landmark (Student Book One); heart (Student Book Four)
/ âr /	air, care, parent, carry (Student Book Four)
/ êr /	ear, beard, clear (Student Book Four)
/ ûr /	clerk, girl, nurse, word (Student Book Three); earth (Student Book Four)
/ ȯr /	born, northwest, landlord (Student Book Three)
/ ōr /	fort, story, four (Student Book Three); door (Student Book Four)
/ ər /	over, summertime, carpenter (Student Book Three)

---

* *Note:* Sometimes, when two vowels appear together, the first vowel has the long sound, and the second vowel is silent. However, research studies have shown this generalization is true only about 45% of the time. The old rhyme, "When two vowels go walking, the first one does the talking," can be misleading.

The Sounds of <u>aw</u>, <u>ew</u>, and <u>ow</u>

aw / ȯ /   law, crawl, jigsaw (Student Book Four)

ew / ū / or / yo͞o /   few, pewter, nephew (Student Book Four)

ew / o͞o /   crew, jewel, withdrew (Student Book Four)

ow / ō /   show, grown, follow (Student Book Four)

ow / ou /   owl, town, allow (Student Book Four)

CONSONANT PRONUNCIATION KEY

(for Student Book One)

Consonant Letter	Initial Position	Medial Position	Final Position
b	**b**ig	ca**b**in	tu**b**
d	**d**en	re**d**uce	sa**d**
f	**f**at	in**f**ant	pu**ff**
g	**g**um	wa**g**on	jo**g**
h	**h**ip	be**h**ave	—
j	**j**ob	ban**j**o	pa**ge**, fu**dge** (j)
k	**k**id	to**k**en	ya**k**
l	**l**ap	he**l**met	do**ll**
m	**m**ud	le**m**on	ha**m**
n	**n**et	ba**n**dit	pi**n**
p	**p**ad	na**p**kin	li**p**
r	**r**ob	pa**r**ent, hu**rr**y, ga**r**den	ca**r**
s	**s**it	pla**s**tic	bu**s**
t	**t**en	ho**t**el	ra**t**
v	**v**at	se**v**en	di**v**<u>e</u>
w	**w**ig	sand**w**ich	—
y	**y**es	can**y**on	—
z	**z**ip	la**z**y	bu**zz**

Note: Letters that have no sound of their own (**c**, **q**, and **x**) are not included in this list. (See *"Sounding Out" the Consonants*, next two pages.)

SOUNDS OF THE CONSONANTS
(Teacher-Tutor Reference)

When pronouncing consonants in isolation, do not say *buh* for / b /, *duh* for / d /, *luh* for / l /, etc. After all, we do not say *buh-ed-duh* for the word "bed." To avoid this problem, you might practice the voiced consonant sounds in the final position in words: **ta<u>b</u>**, **re<u>d</u>**, **leg**, **dol<u>l</u>**, or **e<u>dge</u>**. (The letter **j** is not used in the final position; the sound is represented by **ge** or **dge**). Also, it may take practice when pronouncing consonant blends not to say *guh-lad* for "glad" or *puh-lan* for "plan."

Following is an overview of the consonant letters and digraphs introduced in Student Books One and Two.

VOICED		VOICELESS	VOICED	VOICELESS
b	*and*	**p**	**l**	**h**
d	*and*	**t**	**m**	**sh**
v	*and*	**f**	**n**	**wh**
g	*and*	**k**	**r**	**ph** (f)
z	*and*	**s**	**w**	**ck** (k)
j	*and*	**ch**	**y**	
t̶h̶	*and*	**th**	**ng**	
These are paired sounds. Each pair is produced in essentially the same way.			**nk**	

Voiced consonants are produced by vibration of the vocal cords. *Voiceless* consonants are produced with a stream of breath; the vocal cords do not vibrate.

"SOUNDING OUT" THE CONSONANTS
(Teacher-Tutor Reference)

- **b** and **p** are paired sounds.* They are both produced by closing the lips, which momentarily stops the flow of breath, then quickly popping them open. / b / is voiced. / p / is voiceless. The / p / requires only a gentle puff of breath.

- **d** and **t** are paired sounds, produced essentially the same way. / d / is voiced. / t / is voiceless. The tongue is raised so that the tip firmly touches the upper gum ridge (not the upper teeth). The tongue is held in this position for a fraction of a second, then released quickly.

- **f** and **v** are paired sounds. / f / is voiceless. / v / is voiced. The lower lip lightly touches the upper teeth, and a stream of air is forced across the lower lip.

---

* Consonants that are called "paired sounds" are produced in almost the same way; that is, the tongue or lips are in the same position for both sounds. The difference lies in how much breath escapes and whether the sound is voiced or voiceless.

- **g** and **k** are paired sounds. / g / is voiced. (This is "hard" g—"soft" g sounds like / j /.) / k / is voiceless. The back of the tongue is raised firmly to the center of the roof of the mouth (the soft palate), then dropped quickly.

- **s** and **z** are paired sounds. / s / is a voiceless hissing sound. / z / is a voiced buzzing sound. For both, the tip of the tongue is placed behind the upper teeth *or* behind the lower teeth (it varies with individuals).

- **h** is voiceless and does not have a fixed position. The sound which immediately follows the / h / determines the position of the tongue and lips. But, generally, the mouth is open with a very gentle flow of air escaping from within the throat area.

- **j** and the digraph **ch** are paired sounds. / j / is voiced. / ch / is voiceless. The tongue is up against the roof of the mouth as though pronouncing / t /, but instead of following through with / t /, the tongue drops to say / sh /; immediately the stream of air is cut off.

- **l** is voiced. The tip of the tongue is flattened against the upper gum ridge. Sound escapes from the sides of the tongue.

- **m** is voiced. The lips are firmly closed, and the sound comes through the nose.

- **n** is voiced. The mouth is slightly open. The tongue is raised and the entire tongue tip touches the upper gum ridge. Sound comes through the nose.

- **r** is voiced. It is troublesome because there are slight variations in producing it. Generally, however, the tongue tip is raised slightly toward the roof of the mouth. The sides of the tongue slightly touch the upper back teeth. Sound comes out over the tip of the tongue.

- **w** is voiced. At the beginning of the word or syllable, it starts with the lips rounded in a pursed position with the sound of / $\overline{oo}$ /. (Say the words **will**, **well**, **wall** slowly. You will be able to hear and feel what is happening when you pronounce / w /.) The letter **w** at the end of a word takes on a vowel quality, as in the words **show**, **cow**, **saw**, and **new**.

- **y** is a consonant when it is the first letter of a word or syllable. It is voiced, beginning with the sound of / $\overline{e}$ /, the middle area of tongue touching the roof of the mouth. The tip of the tongue is down. Then the middle of the tongue quickly drops into position for whatever vowel sound is coming next.

- **c**, **q**, and **x** have no sounds of their own. **c** can sound like / k / or / s /. (See Student Book One for the rule governing this). **q** is always followed by the letter **u** in English words. (**qu** sounds like / kw /.) **x** usually sounds like / ks /, as in **box**, **extreme**, or **expose**. Before a vowel, **x** sometimes is pronounced / gz /, as in **example** and **exist**.

- **sh** is voiceless. The sides of the flattened tongue lightly touch the upper back teeth, the tip relaxed. A wide stream of air is released over the tongue.

- **th** and **th** are paired sounds. **th** is voiceless. **th** is voiced. The tongue is placed between the upper and lower front teeth, the tip barely showing. Air is forced between the tongue-tip and teeth.

- **wh** is produced as / hw / (the reverse of the spelling). / h / is quickly followed by / w /. A very gentle stream of air is released.

- **ng** and **nk** are both voiced with the mouth slightly open. The back of the tongue is raised to the center of the roof of the mouth while sound is being forced through the nose. **nk** ends with the sound / k /.

Appendix B: Word Lists for Decoding

DEVELOPING AUTOMATIC DECODING

Some learners need intensive training in "sounding out" words (phonetic decoding). Sample word lists for extra practice are given on the next few pages.

This type of activity gives students practice in visually detecting consonant and vowel changes within clusters of words (visual discrimination) and in "ear training" (auditory discrimination). Students learn to match what they see with what they hear themselves say.

Use these word lists, along with the multisensory exercises, to bring learners to the point where matching letters and sounds becomes automatic.

The goal is to speed up the word recognition process. As learners progress, decoding becomes more and more internalized and evolves into a natural flow of words in phrases and sentences.

PROCEDURE
(3 to 5 minutes)

Have the student underline while pronouncing the words on a page horizontally, vertically, or both, as the arrows indicate. Reading horizontal lists reinforces left-to-right patterning. Reading vertical lists helps the learner to quickly recognize letter groupings.

If decoding is difficult for a new learner, pronounce each word first and have him or her repeat after you. (If working with a group of students, encourage group response. Use a cue, such as saying, "Next . . ." so that they respond in unison.)

Spend no more than five minutes at a time on the word lists.

WORD LISTS FOR DECODING: Short Vowels

Directions: Read these words out loud to the teacher. Follow the arrows.

/ ĭ /	/ ĕ /	/ ă /	/ ŭ /	→
fin	fen	fan	fun	nap
pin	pen	pan	pun	map
bin	Ben	ban	bun	mat
bit	bet	bat	but	met
him	hem	ham	hum	net
miss	mess	mass	muss	nut
				not
				nob
				nab
				nub
				nun
				sun
				sum
				mum
				mud
				mad
				mod
				mid
				med
				men
				man
				Nan

/ ă /	/ ŏ /
map	mop
mat	mot
mad	mod
can	con
ran	Ron
Dan	Don
ax	ox

WORD LISTS FOR DECODING: Short Vowels

Directions: Read these words out loud to the teacher. Follow the arrows.

/ĕ/	/ĭ/	/ǎ/		/ǎ/	/ǒ/	/ŭ/	
bed	bid	bad		cat	cot	cut	bed
led	lid	lad		gat	got	gut	bid
red	rid			hat	hot	hut	bud
				rat	rot	rut	bad
bet	bit	bat		cap	cop	cup	dad
set	sit	sat		pap	pop	pup	did
let	lit			sap	sop	sup	hid
wet	wit			lap	lop		had
pet	pit	pat		map	mop		hod
				tap	top		hot
hep	hip						hat
pep	pip	pap		cab	cob	cub	hit
rep	rip	rap		nab	nob	nub	hut
yep	yip	yap			rob	rub	nut
					sob	sub	but
bell	bill			cad	cod	cud	bug
sell	sill			had	hod		beg
fell	fill			pad	pod		big
hell	hill			sad	sod		pig
tell	till				doll	dull	pit
well	will				loll	lull	
dell	dill				moll	mull	

WORD LISTS FOR DECODING: Short and Long Vowels

Directions: Read these words out loud to the teacher. Follow the arrows.

→ mad
made

bid
bide

nod
node

rob
robe

→ hope
hop

rid
ride

dot
dote

pin
pine

rat
rate

hat
hate

us
use

man
mane

nap
nape

fin
fine

pate
pat

not
note

pet
Pete

tot
tote

tap
tape

tap
tape

pal
pale

din
dine

dud
dude

van
vane

cape
cap

tub
tube

lop
lope

pip
pipe

jib
jibe

cop
cope

dim
dime

tam
tame

fat
fate

fad
fade

mope
mop

man
mane

same
Sam

WORD LISTS FOR DECODING: Consonant Blends/Short Vowels

Directions: Read these words out loud to the teacher. First read down the list, then across.

→		→		→	
rip	rap	**lit**	let	**tub**	tab
drip	drop	**slit**	slot	**stub**	stab
trip	trap	**flit**	flat	**tubs**	tabs
trips	traps	**kit**	cat	**sub**	sob
strip	strap	**kits**	cats	**snub**	snob
strap	strop	**skit**	scat	**nub**	nab
tap	top	**spit**	spat	**rub**	rib
zap	zip	**pit**	pet	**grub**	grab
lap	lop	**pot**	pat	**cub**	cab
laps	lops	**pots**	pats	**cob**	cub
slap	slop	**spot**	spat	**job**	jab
flap	flop	**slot**	slat	**lob**	lab
clap	clop	**lot**	let	**lobs**	labs
clip	clap	**jot**	jet	**slob**	slab
slip	slap	**got**	get	**blob**	blab
lips	laps	**sot**	sat	**glob**	glib
lip	lap	**set**	sit	**gob**	gab
lop	lip	**wet**	wit	**rob**	rub
top	tap	**jet**	jut	**rib**	reb
tops	taps	**vet**	vat	**crib**	crab
stop	step	**vets**	vats	**jib**	jab
sop	sap	**nets**	nuts	**fib**	fob

WORD LISTS FOR DECODING: Consonant Blends/Short Vowels

Directions: Read these words out loud to the teacher. Follow the arrows.

→ and	→ imp	→ dust	→ sent
hand	limp	gust	tent
land	blimp	just	went
gland	skimp	rust	dent
grand	crimp	crust	spent
brand	cramp	trust	bent
band	ramp	must	rent
stand	camp	mist	rant
strand	lamp	fist	grant
sand	clamp	twist	scant
send	stamp	list	slant
spend	tamp	last	plant
end	damp	blast	pant
lend	dump	fast	punt
mend	bump	mast	stunt
pend	jump	past	blunt
tend	lump	pest	grunt
trend	clump	rest	runt
vend	slump	crest	hunt
bend	pump	vest	hint
bond	pomp	west	mint
blond	romp	jest	tint
fond	stomp	zest	flint

WORD LISTS FOR DECODING: One-Syllable Words Ending with Double Consonants/Short Vowels

Directions: Read these words out loud to the teacher. Follow the arrows.

→	→	→	→
fuss	ill	biff	fizz
muss	sill	buff	fuzz
mass	will	bluff	buzz
pass	swill	fluff	jazz
brass	swell	puff	razz
crass	spell	huff	
grass	spill	guff	
glass	pill	gruff	
class	kill	scuff	
lass	skill	skiff	
less	mill	stiff	
bless	smell	staff	
cress	sell	stuff	add
dress	cell	snuff	odd
press	well	sniff	egg
stress	dwell	cliff	inn
mass	dell	tiff	butt
miss	dill	riff	mutt
hiss	grill	miff	mitt
kiss	trill	muff	
bliss	twill	duff	
Swiss	still	cuff	

WORD LISTS FOR DECODING: Consonant Blends/Short and Long Vowels

Directions: Read these words out loud to the teacher.

BL

blab	bluff
blob	blame
bless	blade
bliss	blaze
blend	blast
blond	blitz
blunt	blimp
blue	blip

CL

clam	clog
clan	clot
clone	clod
clip	clad
clap	club
clop	class
close	clasp
clove	cliff

FL

fly	flee
flit	fled
flat	fluff
flab	flame
flag	flake
flak	fluke
flex	flute
flask	flint

GL

glad	glob	glass
glib	globe	gland
glum	glue	glaze
glut	glint	glide

PL

plot	plum	plate
plan	plume	place
plane	plug	plump
plant	plus	plunge

SL

slit	sled	slop
slot	slid	slope
slug	slide	slant
slab	slice	slump

WORD LISTS FOR DECODING: Consonant Blends/Short and Long Vowels

Directions: Read these words out loud to the teacher.

SC

scan	scuff
scant	scoff
scab	scum
scope	scam
score	scale

SK

skip	skate
skid	skill
skit	skull
skin	skulk
skim	sky

SN

snug	sniff
snag	snuff
snob	snipe
snub	snip
snore	snake

SP

span	spin	spine	spend	spent
spy	space	spice	spade	spike

SW

swim	swam	swum	swell	swill
swig	swag	swift	Swiss	swipe

ST

step	stun	stint	stag	stamp	stomp	stove	state	stale	sty
stem	stunt	still	stage	stump	stone	store	stake	stand	style

WORD LISTS FOR DECODING: Consonant Blends/Short and Long Vowels

Directions: Read these words out loud to the teacher.

BR	
brag	brisk
brig	brave
brat	brand
bran	brass
brim	brace
bribe	brute
bride	broke

CR	
cram	crave
cramp	crane
crab	cry
crib	crust
crop	crisp
crud	craft
crude	craze

DR	
drab	drill
drop	drift
drip	drive
drag	draft
drug	drape
drum	dress
dry	drove

FR	
fry	frump
fret	frond
free	frog
frill	frost
frizz	froze
frisk	fringe
frame	France

GR	
grab	gruff
grub	grip
grin	gripe
grim	grape
grime	grope
grand	grove
grant	grave

PR	
press	prep
print	prop
prune	prom
prude	prod
prim	probe
prime	pride
pry	prize

TR	
trap	tram
trip	trim
tripe	tramp
trot	trump
trek	trust
tree	tribe
try	trade

TWO-SYLLABLE WORD DICTATION—PRACTICE SHEET

	First Syllable	*Second Syllable*	*Word*
1.	_____	_____	_____
2.	_____	_____	_____
3.	_____	_____	_____
4.	_____	_____	_____
5.	_____	_____	_____
6.	_____	_____	_____
7.	_____	_____	_____
8.	_____	_____	_____
9.	_____	_____	_____
10.	_____	_____	_____

- -

TWO-SYLLABLE WORD DICTATION—PRACTICE SHEET

	First Syllable	*Second Syllable*	*Word*
1.	_____	_____	_____
2.	_____	_____	_____
3.	_____	_____	_____
4.	_____	_____	_____
5.	_____	_____	_____
6.	_____	_____	_____
7.	_____	_____	_____
8.	_____	_____	_____
9.	_____	_____	_____
10.	_____	_____	_____

SENTENCE FOCUS Grid for Extra Practice

	SUBJECT	VERB	OBJECT				
Which? Whose? How Many?	Who? What?	Did? Does? Doing? Can Do? Will Do?	What? Whom?	Where?	When? How Often? How Long?	How?	Why?

Letters for Letter-Card Spelling

b	c	d	f	g	h	j	k
l	m	n	p	q	r	s	t
v	w	x	y	z	th	th	tch
wh	ph	sh	ch	ck	nk	ng	dge

a	e	i	o	u	y

Appendix D: The History of the English Language — A Summary

Where did the English language begin? Why is there such a diversity of English spelling patterns? What factors influenced the changes in pronunciation? How did our language acquire such an enormous vocabulary? Adult learners want to know why **night** is spelled the way it is and not *nite*; why **ed** is added to most verbs to show past tense but not added to "irregular" verbs; why the digraph **ch** is pronounced / ch / in **church** but not in the words **school** and **chef**.

Many of these questions are answered in the Student Books as word patterns are introduced. But additionally, if adult learners have some knowledge of the historical development of English, it helps to put in perspective our curious spellings, our extensive vocabulary, and our way of putting words together to form sentences.

THE DEVELOPMENT OF ENGLISH

The roots of English began in ancient Britain. From modest beginnings in that small island country some fifteen hundred years ago, English has emerged as the language of international communication in most parts of the world today.

English is classified as a Germanic language; that is, it belongs to the same group of languages as German, Dutch, Swedish, and Norwegian. Its basic sentence structure and function words are Germanic. However, more than half of the English vocabulary is derived from Latin, the language of the old Roman Empire. Some of our words come directly from Latin; some indirectly through other Romance languages such as French, Italian, and Spanish.

Over hundreds of years, English, like all languages, has shown gradual changes in pronunciation, spelling, meaning, and grammar. These changes are due to migrations, armed conquests, and various cultural contacts.

THE CELTS

People from Western Europe who spoke the Celtic language migrated regularly to the British Isles from the latter part of the Bronze Age until the first century, B.C. These Celts came to be called Britons. The words **Briton**, **Britain**, and **British** are of Celtic origin. Modern variants of the Celtic language can be heard today in Wales, northern Scotland, and western Ireland.

In A.D. 43, the Roman Emperor Claudius began his conquest of Britain. During their almost 400 years of occupation, Roman armies were never able to totally conquer the native Celts, especially in Wales and Scotland. When the Roman Empire crumbled and its troops had been withdrawn from Britain by A.D. 410, the Latin language had not greatly influenced the prevailing Celtic language except in a few place names and in some words such as *camp, disc* (**dish**), *win* (**wine**), and *mil* (**mile**). It was not until a few hundred years later that Latin started to play a vital role in the expansion of the English vocabulary.

THE ANGLO-SAXONS

During the middle of the fifth century, three Northern European tribes—the Angles, the Saxons, and the Jutes (called collectively the Anglo-Saxons)—began raiding Briton. Eventually these tribes settled and began farming. Words such as **earth**, **field**, **plow**, **ox**, and **swine** all come from the Anglo-Saxons.

The Anglo-Saxons spoke different Germanic dialects but were able to understand one another. Slowly, these dialects merged and became the foundation of the language we now refer to as Old English. Much of the basic vocabulary we use today consists of words from the Old English language. For example,

husbonda (**husband**)	*etan* (**eat**)	*milc* (**milk**)
wif (**wife**)	*drincan* (**drink**)	*bedd* (**bed**)
cild (**child**)	*bitan* (**bite**)	*toth* (**tooth**)

The word **English** itself was spelled *Englisc* but pronounced the same way because the **sc** spelling in Old English was given the same sound as the present day digraph **sh**. The word **England** was derived from *Anglecynn* ("Anglekin" or "race of the Angles") and later was written *Englaland* ("land of the Angles").

During the Old English period, Latin again was being slowly reintroduced into the British Isles through Christian missionaries. Christianity, with its center in Rome, used religious words derived from Latin, Greek, and Hebrew. As a result, words having to do with religious life became common in English: **altar**, **shrine**, **candle**, **minister**, **priest**, **deacon**, **bishop**, **verse**, **hymn**, and **Sabbath**.

THE SCANDINAVIANS (The Viking Age)

In the eighth century, fierce Viking* sea-warriors began attacking and plundering lands around the North and Baltic Seas. The Vikings, one-time neighbors of the Anglo-Saxons in Northern Europe and closely related to them by blood, came from the Scandinavian and Jutland Peninsulas.** Over a period of time, they began settling in various parts of the British Isles—the Danes in the north and east of England, the Norwegians in the northwest and Ireland.

There was a similarity between the Scandinavian and Anglo-Saxon languages. Some words intermingled; for example, the Anglo-Saxon word *scyrte* and the Old Norse (Scandinavian) word *skyrta* both meant "shirt." Today we use both

---

* The name *Viking* has been used interchangeably in language and history books with the terms *Scandinavian*, *Dane*, *Norwegian*, *Norse*, *Norseman*, and *Northman*.

**The Scandinavian Peninsula includes Norway and Sweden; the Jutland Peninsula comprises Denmark and a northern part of Germany.

words, but the old Norse developed into the meaning "skirt." Another example is our word **stick**. In Old English, it was *sticca*; in Old Norse, it was *stik*. Many of our one-syllable words containing the beginning blend **sk** come from Old Norse: **skate**, **sky**, **skid**, **skin**, **skill**, **skull**, **ski**.

THE NORMAN FRENCH

In 1066, William the Conqueror, Duke of Normandy, overwhelmed the English in the Battle of Hastings. The Norman Conquest had a tremendous influence on the English language. It marked the beginning of the Middle English period.

Normandy, a region on the northwestern coast of France, is situated directly across the English Channel from England. Normandy received its name from the Vikings (called "Normans," the French word for "Northmen"), who had settled there during the same period that other Viking bands were settling in England. The Normans quickly adopted the French language, although some elements of the Scandinavian language remained in certain pronunciations and spellings.

As a result of the Conquest, the English-speaking ruling class was replaced by the French-speaking Normans. This was the time when English had a great influx of Latin-derived words. French is a Romance language; that is, it is derived from Latin (*Romance* meaning "in the Roman manner"). Thus it was through French that the vocabulary of English has such a high percentage of Latin borrowings. If this had not happened, it is likely that English would be much more closely related to the Scandinavian and German languages than it is.

Of French origin are almost all words referring to government (such as **govern**, **public**, **council**, **court**); law (**judge**, **plea**, **plaintiff**, **punishment**, **innocent**); the military (**army**, **navy**, **guard**, **retreat**); fashion (**gown**, **coat**, **jewel**, **kerchief**, **apparel**); social life (**recreation**, **leisure**, **conversation**); the arts (**poet**, **sculptor**, **painter**, **performer**, **beauty**); and meals (**chef**, **feast**, **roast**, **poultry**, **appetite**).

Sometimes both English and French words were used, and both are used today.

English	French	English	French
cow, ox	beef	hide	conceal
sheep	mutton	work	labor
pig	pork	wish	desire
calf	veal	rot	decay
woods	forest	inn	hotel

Some borrowings were directly from Latin, as well as through French:

English	French	Latin
folk	people	population
ask	question	interrogate
help	aid	assist
reckon	count	compute
smart	sensible	intelligent

During the fifteenth and sixteenth centuries, major changes in vowel sounds occurred. One example is the shifting in sounds of the **oo** digraph. The pronunciation of the words **door** and **floor** are holdovers from Old English / dōr / and / flōr /, spelled with one **o**. Most words with **oo** developed into the sound heard in **moon** and **boot**. Others became "unrounded," as the sound in **blood** and **flood**, and some of these were shortened even more in the late sixteenth century to the sound heard in **book** and **good**.

The language now was making the transition to Modern English. The early Modern English period is noted for its increase in vocabulary, not only from Latin and French, but also Greek and Italian. This resulted in the English vocabulary being perhaps the largest of any language. Typically, English has not just one word to convey a meaning or shades of meaning, but several. The word **teach**, for example, has many synonyms: **instruct, educate, tutor, inform, direct, guide, drill, coach,** and so forth.

THE AMERICANS

American English evolved from the various English dialects brought to the colonies in the seventeenth and eighteenth centuries. Colonists from southern England settled in New England. Those from southeastern England colonized the Atlantic Coast area south from Chesapeake Bay. Those from northern England settled in Pennsylvania and later moved into the northern and central regions of the country. Add to that the French, Spanish, and other settlements in North America, and the result is a language that is a rich mixture of American dialects which never lost contact with the mother tongue of England.

New words came into English through our native American Indians (**pecan, hickory, squash, moose, skunk, raccoon**) including many of our states' names, such as Connecticut, Delaware, Idaho, Mississippi, Nebraska, Ohio, Oklahoma, Utah, etc.

Other "foreign" words that crept into American English include:

Arabic: **candy, magazine, sofa, zero, algebra**

Dutch: **cookie, coleslaw, boss, Santa Claus**

German: **pretzel, noodle, kindergarten**

African: **banjo, zebra, chimpanzee**

Italian: **pizza, umbrella, volcano, piano**

Mexican: **tomato, chocolate, chili, coyote**

West Indian / Cuban: **barbecue, hurricane, tobacco**

❧   ❧   ❧

For more in-depth reading on the history of English, consult a good dictionary (most contain a front section on the subject) or any of several publications that can be found in a library.

Appendix E: Glossary

Accent. The stress that is placed on one syllable in a word that contains two or more syllables; that is, one syllable is said with more force than another. See *Syllable*.

Affix. A prefix or a suffix attached to the beginning or the end of a word (e.g., **un** in **unkind** or **ing** in **farming**). (The term *affix* is used in the *WORDS* program to avoid the confusion that exists in remembering the difference between "prefix" and "suffix.")

Analysis. The separation of a whole into its parts. In "word analysis," an individual must be able to analyze a whole word into its parts by letters or letter combinations and their corresponding sounds, or by syllables, or by roots and their affixes. Compare *Synthesis*.

Antonym. A word having the opposite meaning of another word (**rich** is an antonym of **poor**).

Auditory. Refers to the sense of hearing or information going into the brain through the ear.

Auditory discrimination. The ability to distinguish one speech sound from another. Includes the ability to identify and choose between sounds of different pitch and intensity.

Auditory memory. The ability to remember a sequence of sounds within a word or a sequence of words (as in a sentence) in the order in which they are heard. Auditory memory affects the ability to respond to verbal directions. See *Memory*.

Auditory training (also referred to as *ear training*). Training to develop an individual's ability to hear the difference (discriminate) between speech sounds, including isolated vowel and consonant sounds, sound patterns, and sounds blended into syllables and words.

Closure. The process of completing a word, sentence, sequence, or picture when one or more parts of the whole are missing.

Compound word. A word composed of two or more smaller words (e.g., **windshield**, **gentleman**, **nevertheless**).

Consonant. Any letter of the alphabet except **a, e, i, o,** and **u**. The letter **y** is a consonant if it appears at the beginning of a word (**yes, yellow**) or at the beginning of a syllable within a word (**beyond, canyon**).

Consonant blend. Two or more consonant letters in a sequence (**brake, split, pond**), each of which is pronounced.

Consonant digraph. A combination of two consonant letters which are pronounced as a single sound (**ship**, **phone**, **bath**).

Contraction. A shortened word formed from two words by omitting a letter or letters and inserting an apostrophe (**they're** for **they are**; **can't** for **cannot**).

Decoding. The process of pronouncing a word through sound-symbol relationships ("breaking the code"). Decoding is complete when an individual understands the meaning of the printed symbols. Listening also is a decoding process, in which sounds (especially speech sounds) are heard and understood.

Diphthong. A combination of two vowel letters together, each of which is pronounced with a "gliding" sound (**oy** in **boy**, **ou** in **house**). See *Vowel combination*.

Discrimination. See *Auditory discrimination* and *Visual discrimination*.

Ear training. See *Auditory training*.

Encoding. The process of converting ideas, information, or dictated words into written form (a code). Spelling is encoding. Speaking also is an encoding process, in which the speaker transmits thoughts and messages through a verbal code.

Homophone. A word having the same sound as another word but differing in spelling, meaning, and origin (**son**, **sun**). (This term is often confused with *homonym*, which is a word that has the same spelling and same sound as another word but differs in meaning, as in the various meanings of **fair**, **pool**, **course**. The term *homonym* is not used in the *WORDS* program.)

Irregular spelling pattern. A non-phonetic spelling containing a distinguishable pattern that appears in a limited number of words (**ight** in **night**, **right**, **light**, **sight**, etc.; **ould** in **would**, **could**, **should**).

Key word. A word in which a specific letter or letter combination is used as a recall device to help individuals remember a certain spelling pattern. (For example, **boat** is a key word for the **oa** vowel combination.)

Kinesthetic. Refers to the sensory messages that inform the brain of the movements and positions of body parts through nerve endings in the muscles, tendons, and joints. The kinesthetic channel is important in speaking and writing (the sensations of muscle movement when using the mouth to speak and the hand to write).

Language skills. The skills necessary to communicate through words—their pronunciation, and the methods of combining them for speech, reading, spelling, and writing.

Letter-sound relationships (also referred to as *sound-symbol correspondence*). Refers to the variant speech sounds that are assigned to alphabetical letters or letter combinations.

Maverick. By definition, a maverick is one who refuses to conform to the dictates of a group or abide by general rules. (In the *WORDS* program, the term is applied to sight words, which are non-phonetic and do not conform to the general rules of English spelling.) See *Sight word*.

Memory. The ability to store selective information and to retrieve that information from storage (the brain) whenever needed. Two types of memory are short-term memory (recently learned but not yet stabilized) and long-term memory (remembered over a long period of time). See *Auditory memory* and *Visual memory*.

Multisensory. Refers to stimulating several pathways to the brain at the same time. The multisensory approach to teaching reading, spelling, and writing involves the main sensory pathways of language—visual, auditory, and tactile-kinesthetic.

Multi-syllable word. A word that contains three or more syllables. (The *WORDS* program uses the hyphenated form for easier reading.)

Phonetic word. A word that is spelled the way it sounds; that is, each letter or letter combination represents a predictable speech sound.

Phonics. A method of teaching reading and spelling that deals with relationships between speech sounds and letters of the alphabet. As an aid to word recognition and spelling, the method teaches students how to analyze ("break down") a word for decoding and synthesize ("build up") a word for encoding.

Root word. A base word to which prefixes and suffixes may be added. (In the word **enjoyment, joy** is the root.)

Schwa. The most common vowel sound in the English language. The schwa is heard in unaccented syllables and sounds like a weak / ŭ /. In some regions of the country, it is pronounced as a weak / ĭ /. The spelling for this sound can be **a**, **e**, **i**, **o** or **u** (**sofa, travel, pencil, ballot, campus**) or it can be vowel combinations such as **ai** (**mountain**) and **ou** (**famous**). The schwa is represented by a symbol that looks like an upside down **e**: ə.

Sight word. A non-phonetic word; that is, a word that is not spelled the way it sounds (**was, laugh, sign, ocean**).

Stem. The main part of a word to which affixes are added. A stem is not an English word by itself, but part of a word borrowed from another language. (For example, the stem **pel** is borrowed from the Latin word *pellere*, "to push, to drive." When the affix **ex** is added to the beginning of this stem, it becomes an English word, **expel**, meaning "to push out" or "to drive out.") A stem is considered a root word. See *Root word*.

Syllable. A word or part of a word. A syllable contains one vowel sound. (See *WORDS* Student Books Two and Three for complete explanations of the various types of syllables.)

Synonym. A word having the same or similar meaning as another word (**rich** is a synonym of **wealthy**).

Synthesis. The combining of separate parts to make a whole; the process of combining letters, letter combinations, or syllables and/or their sounds into a whole word. Compare *Analysis*.

Syntax. The way in which words are put together to form a sentence.

Tactile. Refers to the sense of touch. Tactile sensation is important to speaking and writing—the "feel" of the tongue and lips when forming a word, or the "feel" of holding a pencil or forming a word with the fingertips on a surface.

Tactile-kinesthetic. Refers to a combination of the sense of touch and the sense of muscle movement. Tactile-kinesthetic impulses follow a common route in the brainstem.

Visual. Refers to the sense of sight or information going into the brain through the eyes.

Visual discrimination. The ability to detect differences in letters, words, or numbers. Includes the discrimination of gross forms (pictures, geometric forms, etc.).

Visual memory. The ability to remember how letters and words "look" and to reproduce them from memory. Visual memory is particularly important to spelling. See *Memory*.

Vowel. The alphabetic letters **a**, **e**, **i**, **o**, or **u**. The letter **y** is a vowel if it is used in place of an **i** (**gym**, **cyclone**, **try**) or at the end of a two-syllable word for the sound of / ē / (**lady**). Vowels give "voice" to words. Every syllable is built around a vowel or vowel combination.

Vowel combination. A diphthong or a vowel digraph. The term *vowel combination* is used in the *WORDS* program to avoid the confusion that exists in distinguishing between "diphthong" and "digraph." See *Diphthong* and *Vowel digraph*.

Vowel digraph. A combination of two vowel letters together which are pronounced as a single sound (**haul**, **eat**, **field**, **boot**). See *Vowel combination*; compare *Diphthong* and *Consonant digraph*.

Appendix F: Sight Word (Nonphonetic) List

(Listed in Alphabetical, not Sequential, Order)

STUDENT BOOK ONE	STUDENT BOOK TWO	STUDENT BOOK THREE	STUDENT BOOK FOUR
a*	both	again	build
are	busy	against	built
buy	does	any	breakfast
come	eight	answer	friend
do	eighth	been	garage
done	four	broad	handkerchief
eye	fourth	business	heart
for	goes	danger	honest
from	knock	dangerous	honor
gone	license	doubt	laugh
guard	listen	every	lose
have	office	knee	mischief
her	people	kneel	ocean
here	shoe	many	sew
into	sugar	once	their
live	sure	only	vegetable
love	there	says	
money	they	straight	
move	thumb	through	
of	tongue	very	
often	truth	write	
one	where		
said	wrong		
sign			
some			
the			
to			
two			
was			
were			
what			
you			
your			

* The word **a** is listed as a sight word because of its pronunciation. In American speech, it is almost always pronounced as a weak short **u**: / ŭ /.

Appendix G: Scope and Sequence Chart

TOPIC	STUDENT BOOK	TOPIC	STUDENT BOOK
CONSONANTS		**MODIFIED VOWELS**	
b, d, f, h, j, k, l, m, n, p, q, r, t, v, w, x, y, z	1	**a** as in *ball*	1
s, sounds of	1	**a** as in *father, car*	1
plural	2	**u** as in *push*	1
s-form of the verb	2	Schwa, introduction of	1
c, sounds of	1	in two-syllable words	2, 3
g, sounds of	1	in multi-syllable words	4
		o as in *son* (The Scribal O)	3
CONSONANTS BLENDS		**ow, aw, ew**	4
Beginning blends: **bl, br, cl, cr, dr, dw, fl, fr, gl, gr, pl, pr, sc, sk, sl, sm, sn, sp, st, sw, tr, tw, scr, spl, spr, str**	1	**VOWEL COMBINATIONS** (Digraphs/Diphthongs)	
		ay, ai, ee, oa, ou	3
Ending blends: **ft, ld, lk, lp, lt, mp, nd, nt, sk, sp, st, xt**	1	**oo, oi, oy, ea, au, ui, ie, ei**	4
		R-CONTROLLED VOWELS	
CONSONANT DIGRAPHS		**ar** as in *car*	1
sh, ch, th, ~~th~~, wh, ph, ng, nk, ck	1	**or**	2
trigraph, **tch**	1	**er, ir, ur**	3
dge, compared with **ge**	2	**ar** as in *care, parent*	4
ch (Greek / k /)	4	**air** as in *hair*	4
ch (French / sh /)	4		
		IRREGULAR SPELLING PATTERNS	
VOWELS		**old, ild, ind, ost, olt**	1
Short vowels, one-syllable words (closed syllables)	1	**ight, igh, ought, ould**	3
		ch (/ k /), **ch** (/ sh /)	4
Short vowels, two-syllable words (closed syllables)	2	Silent consonants, **wr-, kn-, -mb**	4
Long vowels, one-syllable words ending in silent **e**	1	**AFFIXES** (Prefixes/Suffixes)	
		-ed, -ing, -y	1
Long vowels, two-syllable words (open syllables)	2	**-s**, plural	2
		s form of the verb	2

AFFIXES (Prefixes/Suffixes) – *cont.*

for-, a-, -ment, -er, -est, -less, -ful, -ly, re-, un-, -able, -ness	3
-hood, mis-, dis-, -en, -al, en-, em-, -ee, be-, -ous, -age, -ive -ion, -ate	4

SYLLABLE DIVISION

Dividing between two consonants	2
Dividing open and closed syllables	2
Dividing words ending in Consonant-**le**	2
Dividing compound words	2
Schwa-**a** as an open syllable	3
Dividing multi-syllable words	4

ACCENT (Stress)

Introduction of concept	2
The schwa in closed syllables	2
The schwa in open syllables	3

SPELLING RULES

The Silent **e** Rule	1
The Doubling Rule	2
The Consonant-**y** Rule	3
The Doubling Rule for Two-Syllable Words	4
Plurals, -**s** and -**es**	2

ABBREVIATIONS

Mr., Mrs., Ms., Dr., St., Ave., N., S., E., W., a.m., p.m.	2
Days of the week	3
lb., oz., hr., min., sec., m.p.h.	3
etc.	4

ALPHABETIZING

Introductory exercises	1
Practice exercises	2, 3

COMPREHENSION

(See *Format of the Student Books*, page 2 of this Guide.)

CONTRACTIONS

Introductory Exercises	2
Contractions with **would, could,** and **should**	3

DICTIONARY

Introductory Exercises	1
Practice Exercises	2, 3, 4

SENTENCE STRUCTURE

Nouns	
Discussion of	3
Plurals	
-s, -es forms	2
Irregular forms	
men, women, children	2
sheep, deer	3
feet, teeth, geese	4
Object of the Verb (Direct)	
Concept of (in *Sentence Focus* exercises)	1
Discussion of	3
Pronouns, discussion of	4
Subject of a sentence	
Concept of (in *Sentence Focus* exercises)	1
Compound subjects	3
Verbs	
Compound verbs	3
Concept of (in *Sentence Focus* exercises)	1
Discussion of	2
-ed, -ing forms	1
Helping verbs	
Concept of (in *Sentence Focus* exercises)	1
Discussion of	2
Irregular forms	
Concept of (in *Sentence Focus* exercises)	1
Discussion of	2
-en form (participle)	4
-s form	2

VOCABULARY

(See *Format of the Student Books*, page 2 of this Guide.)

Appendix H: Relevant Material for Further Reading

Adams, Marilyn J., *Beginning to Read: Thinking and Learning About Print (A Summary)*, University of Illinois at Urbana-Champaign, Reading, Research and Education Center, 1990.

Arnold, G.F., *Our Language: The King's English*, Coronado, CA, 1967.

Chall, Jeanne, *Learning to Read: The Great Debate*, New York, NY, McGraw-Hill Book Company, 1987.

Gardner, Howard, *Frames of Mind: The Theory of Multiple Intelligences*, New York, NY, Basic Books, 1983.

Gillingham, Ana, and Stillman, Bessie W., *Remedial Training for Children with Specific Disability in Reading, Spelling, and Penmanship*, Cambridge, MA, Educators Publishing Service, Inc., 1970.

Harmon, David, *Illiteracy: A National Dilemma*, New York, NY, The Cambridge Book Company, 1987.

Harris, Margaret, and Coltheart, Max, *Language Processing in Children and Adults: An Introduction*, London and New York, Routledge and Kegan Paul, 1986.

Johnson, Doris, and Myklebust, Helmer R., *Learning Disabilities: Educational Principles and Practices*, Austin, TX, Pro-Ed, Inc., 1971.

Levine, Mel, *Developmental Variations and Learning Disorders*, Cambridge, MA, Educators Publishing Service, Inc., 1987.

Levine, Mel, *Keeping a Head in School: A Student's Book about Learning Abilities and Learning Disorders*, Cambridge, MA, Educators Publishing Service, Inc., 1990.

McClelland, Lorraine, and Hale, Patricia A., *English Grammar Through Guided Writing: The Parts of Speech*, Englewood, NJ, Prentice Hall, Inc., 1978.

Myers, L.M., *The Roots of Modern English*, Boston, MA, Little, Brown and Company, 1966.

Phelps-Teraksaki, Diana, and Phelps, Trisha, *Teaching Written Expression: The Phelps Sentence Guide Program*, Novato, CA, Academic Therapy Publications, 1980.

Slingerland, Beth H., *A Multisensory Approach to Language Arts for Specific Language Disability Children*, Cambridge, MA, Educators Publishing Service, Inc., 1970.

Steere, Amy, et al., *Solving Language Difficulties: Remedial Routines*, Cambridge, MA, Educators Publishing Service, Inc., 1984.

What Works: Research about Teaching and Learning, Washington, D.C., U.S. Department of Education, 1986.

Wiig, Elizabeth H., and Semel, Eleanor, *Language Assessment and Intervention for the Learning Disabled*, Columbus, OH, Charles E. Merrill Publishing Co., 1984.

Answer Keys for Mastery Review Tests

The Mastery Reviews are informal assessments designed to be given at the end of each of the four parts of a Student Book. For example, Mastery Review 1, Student Book 1, Part 1, is intended to be given after learners have completed Lesson 4 in the first Student Book.

PURPOSE OF THE MASTERY REVIEWS

The aim of the Mastery Reviews is to evaluate learners' reading* subskills: Have they mastered the skills covered in a particular group of lessons? Have they retained the information acquired in previous lessons? Can they apply generalizations? In what area(s) do they need in-depth help? Are they ready to go on to the next section in the Student Book? Test performance should be analyzed as a guide to teaching.

SCORING THE MASTERY REVIEWS

Each review yields a raw score of 50 points, which is indicated at the top of the first page of the test. The teacher or tutor may choose to convert the raw scores into percents: A possible total of 50 points (2 points for each correct answer) would yield a score of 100%. Six incorrect answers, for example, would be 88%.

Most adult and older adolescent learners are knowledgeable about percent scores and "letter grades," so you may want to further convert the percents into letter grades. It is suggested that no grade lower than a "C" be given to a literacy student. If a learner has not achieved, simply write "Retake" on the top of the paper and allow him or her to review, then retake the test at a later time.

If you are converting raw scores into percent scores, and further, into letter grades, the following breakdown is suggested:

98%–100% : A+	88%–89% : B+	78%–79% : C+
93%–97% : A	83%–87% : B	73%–77% : C
90%–92% : A-	80%–82% : B-	70%–72% : C-

Students who score below 80% are probably experiencing difficulty in one or more of the language subskills. Review is indicated. A score of 70% or below is a signal that a learner may need in-depth training in specific skills before proceeding to the next section in the Student Book.

---

* Spelling dictation and sentence-writing skills are not included in the Mastery Reviews. Progress in these skills should be assessed separately and frequently.

ALLEVIATING TEST ANXIETY

The term *Review* is used because "test" may be a synonym for "failure" in the minds of many literacy students, and test-taking anxiety can sometimes reach phobic proportions.

Several steps can be taken to alleviate test anxiety:

- Avoid using the word "test," at least in the beginning. Learners understand soon enough that it is a test, but as you work to lessen their apprehension and as they begin to experience success, anxiety decreases.

- Have a "rehearsal" of an upcoming Review. Describe the format of a Review — how it is set up. Give examples from the workbook, or demonstrate on the board. Review the material with them. Let them ask questions about what will be on the Review and give them straightforward answers. Learners will perform much better if they know what to expect.

- During the test session, make sure the environment is relatively quiet.

- Stand by to read directions to the learners, if necessary, and be available to help them "discover" an answer.

- Set no time limits. Make it clear to the learners that they are allowed all the time they need to finish a Review. If they do not finish within a reasonable time, or if signs of stress begin to appear, stop the testing and assure them that they can finish during the next session.

Mastery Review 1

A.

1. Write the alphabet. _a, b, c, d, e, f, g, h, i, j, k, l, m, n, o, p, q, r,_

_s, t, u, v, w, x, y, z_____ *(26 points)*

2. Write the vowel letters. _a, e, i, o, u_____ *(5 points)*

3. What letter can be a vowel or a consonant? ___y_____ *(1 point)*

B.

One word in each row is a SIGHT WORD. Circle it. *(2 points)*

1. pill   rot   (of)   fun

2. safe   (have)   pie   robe

C.

Write **L** if the vowel within the word is LONG. Write **S** if the vowel is SHORT. *(10 points)*

Example: hat __S__   dime __L__

1. tap __S__   **6.** wine __L__

2. tape __L__   **7.** mess __S__

3. rod __S__   **8.** robe __L__

4. fizz __S__   **9.** tune __L__

5. hum __S__   **10.** pet __S__

D.

Listen, then circle the word that the teacher says. *(6 points)*

(TEACHER'S CHOICE)

1. hat   hot   hit   hut

2. rod   rode   rude   rid

3. mule   mile   mole   male

4. pin   pane   pan   pine

5. nut   net   note   not

6. dome   dime   dim   dame

A.

Fill in the blanks to complete the rule about the sound of the letter **c**.
(3 points)

> The letter **c** will sound like / s / if the
>
> letter __e__ , __i__ , or __y__ comes after the **c**.

B.

Write **S** if the **c** letter sounds like / s /. Write **K** if the **c** letter sounds like / k /. *(6 points)*

Example: cot ___K___   city ___S___

1. cape ___K___   **4.** cove ___K___
2. cite ___S___   **5.** ice ___S___
3. cub ___K___   **6.** cell ___S___

C.

Write **S** if the **s** letter sounds like / s /. Write **Z** if the **z** letter sounds like / z /. *(6 points)*

Example: sun ___S___   nose ___Z___

1. fuss ___S___   **4.** save ___S___
2. fuse ___Z___   **5.** wise ___Z___
3. us ___S___   **6.** kiss ___S___

D.

One word in each row is a SIGHT WORD. Circle it. *(2 points)*

1.   yes   yet   yell   (you)
2.   cope   cone   (come)   cove

E.

Fill in the blanks to complete the rule about the sound of the letter **g**.
(3 points)

> The letter **g** will sound like / j / if the
>
> letter _e_ , _i_ , or _y_ comes after the **g**.

F.

Write **G** if the **g** letter sounds like / g /. Write **J** if the **g** letter sounds like / j /. *(6 points)*

Example: gem ___J___   gum ___G___

1. got ___G___   4. hug ___G___

2. gym ___J___   5. huge ___J___

3. age ___J___   6. gate ___G___

G.

Write CONSONANT if the **y** letter is a consonant. Write VOWEL if the **y** letter is a VOWEL. *(6 points)*

Example: yell _consonant_   lady _vowel_

1. yet   _consonant_

2. type   _vowel_

3. happy   _vowel_

4. you   _consonant_

5. gym   _vowel_

6. my   _vowel_

H.

Fill in the blanks to make each sentence complete. Use the words from the list below. *(5 points)*

box   fix   tax   quit   quite

1. Sue _____quit_____ her job at the mill.

2. Did you _____fix_____ the hole in the fence yet?

3. Max will buy a _____box_____ of candy for his girl.

4. The bus ride made the man _____quite_____ ill.

5. Will the _____tax_____ rate go up in June?

I.

Write the KEY WORDS for the short vowel sounds that the teacher will say. *(5 points)*

1. / ă /   at   4. / ŏ /   ox
2. / ĕ /   Ed   5. / ŭ /   up
3. / ĭ /   if

J.

Listen, then circle the word that the teacher says. *(8 points)*

(TEACHER'S CHOICE)

1.	rig	rag	rage	rug
2.	fun	fan	fin	fine
3.	robe	rob	rub	rib
4.	cap	cop	cup	cope
5.	quote	quake	quite	quit
6.	came	cam	can	cane
7.	got	gut	gate	get
8.	cube	cub	cut	cute

Name _____Key_____

A.

Match each word in Column A with its definition in Column B. Write the letter of your answer on the line next to the number. *(8 points)*

Column A   **Column B**

__d__   **1.** damp   **a.** cut

__c__   **2.** swift   **b.** not tame

__a__   **3.** snip   **c.** fast

__g__   **4.** grin   **d.** wet

__f__   **5.** dwell   **e.** stop

__h__   **6.** blaze   **f.** live

__b__   **7.** wild   **g.** smile

__e__   **8.** halt   **h.** fire

B.

One word in each row is a SIGHT WORD. Circle it. *(2 points)*

1.   size   (sign)   side   site
2.   twist   twice   twin   (two)

C.

Draw a line from each word in the left column to a word that means the OPPOSITE in the right column. *(5 points)*

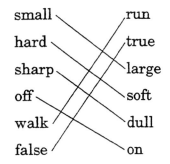

D.

Fill in each blank with the correct word. *(8 points)*

1. A glass lamp fell from the _____desk_____ and broke.
   disk   desk

2. The baby in the sandpile had a _____grin_____ on his face.
   grim   grin

3. Next time, I can cut the grass _____myself_____ .
   yourself   myself

4. The guard had a large red _____scar_____ on his arm.
   scarf   scar

5. Is the water in the tub still _____warm_____ ?
   warn   warm

6. A cop drove to the crime lab in a _____squad_____ car.
   squad   squat

7. The small child held a bug in the _____palm_____ of her hand.
   palm   part

8. Mark _____went_____ to get some gas for the car.
   want   went

E.

Divide these compound words. *(5 points)*

1. himself   =   _____him_____   +   _____self_____

2. sidewalk   =   _____side_____   +   _____walk_____

3. classmate   =   _____class_____   +   _____mate_____

4. wildlife   =   _____wild_____   +   _____life_____

5. lifeguard   =   _____life_____   +   _____guard_____

F.

Follow the directions. *(11 points)*

1. Write the word **slim**. _____slim_____
2. Change the *m* to *p*. _____slip_____
3. Change the *i* to *a*. _____slap_____
4. Change the *s* to *f*. _____flap_____
5. Change the *a* to *o*. _____flop_____
6. Change the *o* to *i*. _____flip_____
7. Change the *f* to *c*. _____clip_____
8. Change the *i* to *a*. _____clap_____
9. Change the *p* to *m*. _____clam_____
10. Change the *c* to *s*. _____slam_____
11. Change the *a* to *i*. _____slim_____

G.

The teacher will pronounce six words. Write the LETTER of the short vowel that you hear in each word. *(6 points)*

(TEACHER'S CHOICE)

1. _____   2. _____   3. _____

4. _____   5. _____   6. _____

H.

Listen, then circle the word the teacher says. *(5 points)*

(TEACHER'S CHOICE)

1.	sign	sin	sun	sane
2.	mast	most	must	mist
3.	stall	stale	style	still
4.	band	bond	bend	bind
5.	bake	bark	brake	broke

Name ___Key___ | Mastery Review 4 |

Student Book 1
Part 4
(50 points)

A.

Join each root word and its affix. *(5 points)*

1. use + ing = ___using___

2. haze + y = ___hazy___

3. file + ed = ___filed___

4. fill + ed = ___filled___

5. ice + y = ___icy___

B.

Fill in each blank with the correct word. *(5 points)*

1. The root word of **hoping** is ___hope___ .

2. The root word of **fussy** is ___fuss___ .

3. The root word of **named** is ___name___ .

4. The root word of **dining** is ___dine___ .

5. The root word of **baby** is ___babe___ .

C.

Separate each root word from its affix. *(5 points)*

1. ___bake___ + ___ing___ = baking

2. ___nose___ + ___y___ = nosy

3. ___cross___ + ___ed___ = crossed

4. ___type___ + ___ing___ = typing

5. ___cure___ + ___ed___ = cured

D.

Draw a line from each word in the left column to a word that means the OPPOSITE in the right column. *(5 points)*

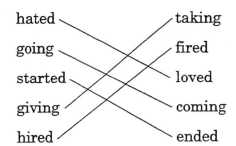

hated — loved
going — coming
started — ended
giving — taking
hired — fired

E.

One word in each row is a sight word. Circle it. *(2 points)*

1. send   sand   (said)   side

2. (are)   arm   art   ark

F.

Follow the directions. *(6 points)*

1. Write the word **rent.** _____rent_____

2. Change the *e* to *a.* _____rant_____

3. Take away the *n.* _____rat_____

4. Change the *a* to *u.* _____rut_____

5. Add *n* after the *u.* _____runt_____

6. Change the *u* to *e.* _____rent_____

G.

Fill in the blank to complete the Silent **e** Spelling Rule. *(1 point)*

> If a word ends with a silent **e**, drop the **e** before
>
> adding an affix that starts with a _____vowel_____ .

H.

Put these words in ALPHABETICAL ORDER. *(10 points)*

1. job   _grasp_   2. quit   _old_

     haze   _hope_   scar   _plan_

     file   _job_   old   _quit_

     fill   _kite_   smart   _scar_

     ice   _lost_   plan   _smart_

I.

Fill in each blank with a word from the word list. *(7 points)*

1. The sun is _____rising_____ .

2. Will the plane be _____landing_____ at 7:30?

3. My boss is _____hiring_____ more men for the job.

4. His old car was _____costing_____ him a lot of money.

5. I am _____sending_____ a postcard to my father.

6. We were _____lifting_____ the large box into the cart.

7. Fog was _____drifting_____ in from the lake.

WORD LIST

costing
drifting
hiring
landing
lifting
rising
sending

J.

Listen, then circle the word that the teacher says. *(4 points)*

(TEACHER'S CHOICE)

1. side   said   sad   sod

2. faced   fast   fussed   fist

3. boss   bass   base   bus

4. mile   mill   mall   male

A.

Divide these words into syllables. (8 points)

		First syllable	Second syllable
1.	submit	sub	mit
2.	ambush	am	bush
3.	helmet	hel	met
4.	costume	cos	tume
5.	tonsil	ton	sil
6.	system	sys	tem
7.	ignore	ig	nore
8.	seldom	sel	dom

B.

Put these words in alphabetical order. (6 points)

brass	bass
bass	batch
batch	boss
boss	brace
brace	brass
bus	bus

C.

ch or **tch**? Complete each word by filling in the blank with **ch** or **tch**. (5 points)

1. pin _ch_   3. ca _tch_   5. di _tch_

2. mar _ch_   4. bun _ch_

D.

Join each root word and its affix. *(5 points)*

1. chase + ed = _____ chased _____

2. shine + y = _____ shiny _____

3. shave + ing = _____ shaving _____

4. stretch + ed = _____ stretched _____

5. itch + y = _____ itchy _____

E.

The teacher will say words that end with **tch**. Write the vowel that you hear. *(5 points)*

(TEACHER'S CHOICE)

1. _____ 2. _____ 3. _____ 4. _____ 5. _____

F.

Listen, then circle the word that the teacher says. *(6 points)*

(TEACHER'S CHOICE)

1.	cast	cost	catch	cash
2.	must	musk	mush	much
3.	champ	chomp	jump	chump
4.	since	cinch	chintz	chance
5.	jest	gist	chest	chess
6.	lost	last	lash	latch

G.

The teacher will pronounce these words with you.
    If **ed** sounds like / əd /, write **əd** on the line.
    If **ed** sounds like / t /, write **t** on the line.
    If **ed** sounds like / d /, write **d** on the line. *(5 points)*

1. crashed __t__   3. pitched __t__   5. shaved __d__

2. shifted __əd__   4. charged __d__

H.

One word in each row has a schwa sound in the SECOND syllable.
Circle that word. *(3 points)*

1. (legal)   hotel   ambush
2. until   plastic   (kitchen)
3. combat   (seldom) sandwich

I.

In the words below, mark the vowels long (ˉ) or short (ˇ). <u>Do</u> <u>not</u> mark
the silent **e**. *(5 points)*

Example: ĭnvīte

1. shĭp   2. chāse   3. mătch   4. shīne   5. clŭtch

J.

There are two SIGHT WORDS in the list below. Circle them. *(2 points)*

napkin   contest   mascot   (listen)   traffic

umpire   motel   immune   dispute

locate   (office)   costume

Name ___Key___

A.

Write OPEN if the syllable ends with a vowel.
Write CLOSED if the syllable ends with a consonant.
Mark the vowels long (‾) or short (˘). *(12 points – 2 points each)*

Example: ŏp ___closed___   pō   ___open___

1. ĕc ___closed___   4. slū   ___open___

2. ĭb ___closed___   5. twī   ___open___

3. rā ___open___   6. brŏm   ___closed___

B.

Divide these words into syllables. *(6 points)*

	1st syllable	*2nd syllable*			*1st syllable*	*2nd syllable*
1. hotel	ho	tel	**4.** ugly	ug	ly
2. cabin	cab	in	**5.** photo	pho	to
3. lemon	lem	on	**6.** virus	vi	rus

C.

In one of the words below, the letter **y** at the end has the sound of / ī /.
Circle that word. *(1 point)*

(supply)   happy   duty   lady

D.

One word in each row below is a SIGHT WORD. Circle that word.
(3 points)

1. (thumb)   bathtub   sixth   lunch

2. throb   athlete   math   (eight)

3. whale   whiplash   (where)   white

E.

Match each word in Column A with its definition in Column B. Write the letter of your answer on the line next to the number. *(8 points)*

		Column A	Column B
f	1.	final	a. a flying insect
e	2.	crazy	b. entire; to add up
d	3.	pardon	c. a drive-in hotel
a	4.	moth	d. excuse
c	5.	motel	e. insane; mad
g	6.	timid	f. last; the end
b	7.	total	g. shy; bashful
h	8.	throb	h. to pulsate; to vibrate

F.

Use a word from the list to complete each sentence. *(5 points)*

    excuse   income   program   trophy   truth

1. When is your _____income_____ tax due?

2. Which _____program_____ are you going to watch on TV?

3. Did Eve win a _____trophy_____ for coming in first?

4. What _____excuse_____ did Phil give for being late?

5. Are you sure that witness was telling the _____truth_____ ?

G.

Join each word and its ending affix. *(5 points)*

1. rescue + ing   =   <u>rescuing</u>

2. bathe   + ed   =   <u>bathed</u>

3. phone   + ed   =   <u>phoned</u>

4. clothe + ing   =   <u>clothing</u>

5. filth   + y   =   <u>filthy</u>

H.

Draw a line from each word in the left column to a word that means the OPPOSITE in the right column. *(6 points)*

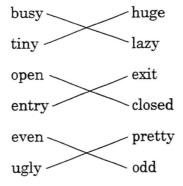

busy — lazy
tiny — huge
open — closed
entry — exit
even — odd
ugly — pretty

I.

Listen, then circle the word that the teacher says. *(4 points)*

(TEACHER'S CHOICE)

1.	broth	both	bath
2.	thin	then	them
3.	clot	cloth	clothe
4.	math	moth	myth

A.

Fill in each blank with a word from the list below. *(8 points)*

check   drank   jacket   neck
padlock   song   Thanksgiving   truck

1. Why did Mr. Ridler put a _____padlock_____ on the gate?

2. Where did you hang my _____jacket_____ ?

3. When is the landlady going to cash her _____check_____ ?

4. Which _____song_____ do they want to sing next?

5. Who _____drank_____ all of the Shasta cola?

6. What is that thing on the back of your _____neck_____ ?

7. Whose black pickup _____truck_____ is this?

8. Whom are you bringing for _____Thanksgiving_____ dinner?

B.

ge or **dge**? Complete each word by filling in the blank with **ge** or **dge**.
(5 points)

1. char_ge____   3.   ju_dge____   5.   hin_ge____

2. bri_dge____   4.   ba_dge____

C.

Draw a line from each word in the left column to a word that means the
OPPOSITE in the right column. *(4 points)*

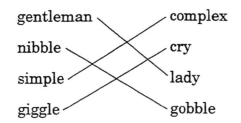

gentleman   complex
nibble   cry
simple   lady
giggle   gobble

D.

Divide these words into syllables. Mark the vowel in the FIRST syllable long (⁻) or short (˘). *(8 points)*

	1st syllable	2nd syllable			1st syllable	2nd syllable
1. sizzle	sĭz	zle	**5.** gable	gā	ble
2. title	tī	tle	**6.** humble	hŭm	ble
3. settle	sĕt	tle	**7.** bugle	bū	gle
4. gabble	găb	ble	**8.** wimple	wĭm	ple

E.

Match each word in Column A with its definition in Column B. Write the letter of your answer on the line next to the number. *(5 points)*

	Column A	Column B
c	**1.** tremble	**a.** a small bite
d	**2.** maple	**b.** soft; mild; tame
b	**3.** gentle	**c.** to shake; to vibrate
a	**4.** nibble	**d.** a tree; a kind of syrup
e	**5.** topple	**e.** to fall; to collapse

F.

The teacher will say words that end with **dge**. Write the VOWEL that you hear. *(5 points)*

(TEACHER'S CHOICE)

1. _____   **2.** _____   **3.** _____   **4.** _____   **5.** _____

G.

Listen, then circle the word that the teacher says. *(5 points)*

(TEACHER'S CHOICE)

1.	sign	sing	singe	sin
2.	riffle	raffle	rifle	ruffle
3.	unit	unite	untie	until
4.	batch	badge	bash	bask
5.	theme	them	then	thin

H.

Separate each root word from its affix. *(5 points)*

Example: ___pledge___ + ___ed___ = pledged

1. ___settle___ + ___ed___ = settled

2. ___judge___ + ___ing___ = judging

3. ___simple___ + ___y___ = simply

4. ___buckle___ + ___ed___ = buckled

5. ___struggle___ + ___ing___ = struggling

I.

One word in each row is a SIGHT WORD. Circle it. *(2 points)*

1. sample   apple   fumble   (people)   tremble
2. quick   pickle   (knock)   bucket   nickname

J.

Divide these compound words with a slash (/). *(3 points)*

1. timeclock   ___time / clock___

2. snakebite   ___snake / bite___

3. thumbtack   ___thumb / tack___

Name ___Key___ | Mastery Review 4

A.

Write the plural form of each word. *(8 points)*

Example: badge ___badges___

1. tax ___taxes___   **5.** ash ___ashes___

2. wage ___wages___   **6.** boss ___bosses___

3. bulb ___bulbs___   **7.** child ___children___

4. woman ___women___   **8.** bench ___benches___

B.

Divide these words into syllables. Mark the vowel in the FIRST syllable
long (¯) or short (˘). *(5 points)*

	First syllable	*Second syllable*
1. infants	ĭn	fants
2. students	stū	dents
3. robots	rō	bots
4. kettles	kĕt	tles
5. plastics	plăs	tics

C.

Choose a word from the list below to complete each sentence. You must add **s** or **es** to each word as you write it in the blank. *(5 points)*

buy   do   go   sell   push

1. That little old lady _____pushes_____ her shopping cart all the way home from the store.

2. He _____does_____ a fine job pitching for the Atlanta Braves.

3. His father _____goes_____ to all of the home games.

4. This market _____sells_____ a lot of fresh produce.

5. Ms. Clark _____buys_____ all of her clothes at the Hodgepodge Clothing Shop.

D.

Match each word in Column A with its definition in Column B. Write the letter of your answer on the line next to the number. *(6 points)*

	Column A	Column B
_f_	1. skids	a. takes a long walk
_e_	2. travels	b. saves
_d_	3. stops	c. washes the body
_c_	4. bathes	d. comes to a halt
_a_	5. hikes	e. goes on a trip
_b_	6. rescues	f. slides to one side

E.

Join each root word and its affix. *(9 points)*

1. swim + ing = _____swimming_____
2. age + ing = _____aging_____
3. fog + y = _____foggy_____
4. grin + ed = _____grinned_____
5. fib + ed = _____fibbed_____
6. star + y = _____starry_____
7. take + ing = _____taking_____
8. tack + ing = _____tacking_____
9. tax + ing = _____taxing_____

F.

Fill in each blank. *(5 points)*

1. The root word of **trapped** is _____trap_____ .
2. The root word of **riding** is _____ride_____ .
3. The root word of **snappy** is _____snap_____ .
4. The root word of **shiny** is _____shine_____ .
5. The root word of **wedding** is _____wed_____ .

G.

Separate each root word from its affix. *(4 points)*

1. _____nose_____ + __y__ = nosy
2. _____beg_____ + __ed__ = begged
3. _____dine_____ + __ing__ = dining
4. _____jam_____ + __ed__ = jammed

H.

Listen, then circle the word that the teacher says. *(6 points)*

(TEACHER'S CHOICE)

1. filling   filing
2. hoping   hopping
3. shiny   shinny
4. slopped   sloped
5. taped   tapped
6. mopping   moping

I.

One word in each row has a schwa sound in the SECOND syllable. Circle that word. *(2 points)*

1. insects   (benches)   plastics
2. (wages)   robots   desktops

Name ___Key___ | Mastery Review 1 |

A.

Write the contraction for each combination. *(11 points)*

1. it is   _____it's_____   7. we have   _____we've_____

2. I am   _____I'm_____   8. do not   _____don't_____

3. will not   _____won't_____   9. they are   _____they're_____

4. you will   _____you'll_____   10. Madam   _____Ma'am_____

5. are not   _____aren't_____   11. of the clock   _____o'clock_____

6. cannot   _____can't_____

B.

Match each word in Column A with its definition in Column B. Write the letter of your answer on the line next to the number. *(7 points)*

	Column A	Column B
_e_	1. aid	a. market
_d_	2. carve	b. map; graph
_b_	3. chart	c. to move from side to side
_g_	4. forgive	d. to cut up
_f_	5. trail	e. help
_a_	6. mart	f. path
_c_	7. sway	g. to excuse; to pardon

C.

Divide these words into syllables with a slash (/). *(4 points)*

1. complain _____com / plain_____   3. absorb _____ab / sorb_____

2. maintain _____main / tain_____   4. always _____al / ways_____

D.

Write the abbreviation for each day of the week. *(7 points)*

1. Sunday   _____Sun._____
5. Saturday   _____Sat._____

2. Friday   _____Fri._____
6. Thursday   _____Thur._____

3. Tuesday   _____Tues._____
7. Monday   _____Mon._____

4. Wednesday   _____Wed._____

E.

Draw a line from each word in the left column to its definition in the right column. *(4 points)*

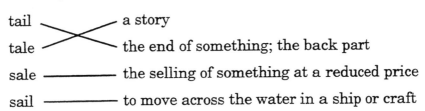

tail — a story

tale — the end of something; the back part

sale ——— the selling of something at a reduced price

sail ——— to move across the water in a ship or craft

F.

Join each word and its ending affix. *(5 points)*

1. raise   +   ing   =   _____raising_____

2. orange   +   s   =   _____oranges_____

3. crab   +   y   =   _____crabby_____

4. forgive   +   ing   =   _____forgiving_____

5. rain   +   y   =   _____rainy_____

G.

Read this paragraph:

    Does your <u>state</u> have a <u>sales</u> tax? This tax is the extra money you <u>pay</u> on the things you buy. A <u>sales</u> tax helps your <u>state</u> to <u>maintain</u> its budget.

In the paragraph above, underline the words that contain the long sound of the letter **a**. *(6 points)*

H.

Listen, then circle the word that the teacher says. *(4 points)*

(TEACHER'S CHOICE)

1.	rise	raise	rose	ruse
2.	bran	barn	brine	brain
3.	hill	he'll	who'll	hole
4.	messed	mast	most	must

I.

Circle the SIGHT WORD in each row. *(2 points)*

1.	pays	trays	displays	(says)
2.	strain	claim	(straight)	wail

Name _____Key_____

A.

Divide each word into syllables. Mark the vowel in the FIRST syllable as *long* (¯), *short* (˘), or *schwa* (ə). *(12 points – 2 points each)*

		First syllable	*Second syllable*
1.	adult	ə̱	dult
2.	bottom	bŏt	tom
3.	sofa	sō	fa
4.	amend	ə̱	mend
5.	tuna	tū	na
6.	sudden	sŭd	den

B.

Join each word and its ending affix. *(5 points)*

1.	amuse	+	ing	=	amusing
2.	settle	+	ment	=	settlement
3.	red	+	est	=	reddest
4.	amuse	+	ment	=	amusement
5.	settle	+	er	=	settler

C.

Fill in each blank. *(4 points)*

1. The root word of *taped* is _____tape_____ .

2. The root word of *furry* is _____fur_____ .

3. The root word of *gambler* is _____gamble_____ .

4. The root word of *widest* is _____wide_____ .

D.

Match each word in Column A with its definition in Column B. Write the letter of your answer on the line next to the number. *(10 points)*

Column A   Column B

  d   **1.** among   **a.** wide awake; watchful

  h   **2.** dozen   **b.** to chase; to go after

  j   **3.** nothing   **c.** maybe

  g   **4.** furnish   **d.** in the middle of

  a   **5.** alert   **e.** up-to-date; at the present time

  b   **6.** pursue   **f.** to rule

  f   **7.** govern   **g.** to supply; to provide; to equip

  i   **8.** urban   **h.** twelve

  c   **9.** perhaps   **i.** related to a city; having to do with a city

  e   **10.** current   **j.** not anything

E.

Read this paragraph:

    A (person) trained in (first) aid can help victims of snake bites, (burns), or choking. Most of the time, a victim must not be moved until medical help can be obtained. Victims who have been (hurt) also must be kept warm.

In the paragraph above, circle the words that contain the sound of / ûr /. *(4 points)*

F.

Choose the correct word and write it in the blank. *(4 points)*

1. The planet Mars is _____smaller_____ than Venus.
   smaller   smallest

2. Portland is the _____largest_____ city in Maine.
   larger   largest

3. Today is the _____hottest_____ day of the summer.
   hotter   hottest

4. Rachel can work _____quicker_____ than the other nurses.
   quicker   quickest

G.

Listen, then circle the word that the teacher says. *(5 points)*

(TEACHER'S CHOICE)

1.	cave	crave	carve	curve
2.	biker	bicker	backer	baker
3.	ton	tone	tune	tan
4.	dune	done	din	dine
5.	banned	bend	bond	boned

H.

Circle the two words that contain a Scribal O. *(2 points)*

(some)   hotel   broke   robot   job   (front)

I.

Read the sentence below. Add apostrophes and punctuation marks.
(4 points)

Doesn't Mr. Miller go to work at seven o'clock?

Student Book 3
Part 3
(50 points)

A.

Read this paragraph:

(I) was (flying) home. The plane dipped as it began to come in for a landing. From (high) above, (I) could see the (bright)(lights) of the city blinking in the (night.) (I) (smiled) to (myself.) The (lights) seemed to be saying, "Welcome home!".

In the paragraph above, circle the words that contain the long **i** sound. *(11 points)*

B.

Fill in each blank with the correct word. *(4 points)*

1. Do you _____think_____ that your boss will give me a job?
   think   thought

2. She _____bought_____ four tickets for the concert on Friday night.
   buy   bought

3. The night watchman _____brought_____ his dog to guard the front gate.
   bring   brought

4. Two boxers will _____fight_____ at the Athletic Club next week.
   fight   fought

C.

Divide these words into syllables with a slash (/). *(6 points)*

1. needle _____nee / dle_____   4. coastline _____coast / line_____

2. nighttime _____night / time_____   5. lightning _____light / ning_____

3. freedom _____free / dom_____   6. asleep _____a / sleep_____

D.

Write the contraction for each combination. *(4 points)*

1. I would   I'd

2. should have   should've

3. they would   would've

4. could not   couldn't

E.

Join each word and its ending affix. *(7 points)*

1. study   +   ed   =   studied

2. happy   +   ly   =   happily

3. pity   +   ful =   pitiful

4. hurry   +   ing =   hurrying

5. pretty   +   est =   prettiest

6. attorney +   s   =   attorneys

7. story   +   s   =   stories

F.

Use a word in the parentheses to fill in the blank. *(4 points)*

1. *(hopeful, hopeless)*   The doctors are ___hopeful___ that she will fully recover by next month.

2. *(painful, painless)*   The nurse gave me a ___painless___ shot in the arm. It didn't hurt at all!

3. *(harmful, harmless)*   A lot of sun may be ___harmful___ to your skin.

4. *(restful, restless)*   At 5:00 p.m., I became ___restless___ .

G.

Match each word in Column A with its definition in Column B. *(6 points)*

	Column A	Column B
_d_	**1.** steel	**a.** the upper part of the leg
_e_	**2.** slept	**b.** a gentle wind
_a_	**3.** thigh	**c.** past tense of *bleed*
_f_	**4.** oath	**d.** a strong metal
_b_	**5.** breeze	**e.** past tense of *sleep*
_c_	**6.** bled	**f.** a sworn statement to tell the truth; a pledge

H.

Draw a line from each word in the left column to its definition in the
right column. *(4 points)*

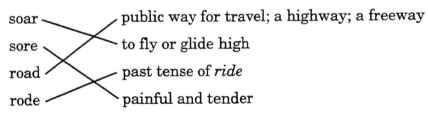

soar — to fly or glide high
sore — painful and tender
road — public way for travel; a highway; a freeway
rode — past tense of *ride*

I.

Listen, then circle the word that the teacher says. *(3 points)*

(TEACHER'S CHOICE)

1.	boat	bought	but	bat	bait
2.	ought	oat	oath	ate	at
3.	sleep	slip	slap	slop	slope

J.

One word below is NOT a sight word. Circle that word. *(1 point)*

write   many   been   (roast)   knee   broad

A.

Write the plural (more than one) of each word. *(7 points)*

1. tour ___tours___
2. couch ___couches___
3. country ___countries___
4. blouse ___blouses___
5. mountain ___mountains___
6. mouse ___mice___
7. county ___counties___

B.

Fill in each blank with a word from the list below. *(6 points)*

courses	courthouse	cousin	hour	our	soup

1. Wiley is taking a couple of ___courses___ at the local college.
2. The file clerk was one ___hour___ late getting to work.
3. My attorney will meet the judge at the county ___courthouse___ .
4. She almost always has ___soup___ and salad for lunch.
5. On Thursday, we're taking ___our___ son to the clinic for his shots.
6. His young ___cousin___ got a ticket for running a red light.

C.

Read the sentence below. Add capital letters, an apostrophe, and punctuation marks. The entire sentence must be correct for credit. *(1 point)*

D R   F
dr. roberts couldn't remove the stitches on friday.

D.

Write the abbreviation for each word below. *(7 points)*

1. second _____sec._____
2. minute _____min._____
3. hour _____hr._____
4. ounce _____oz._____

5. pound _____lb._____
6. mile _____mi._____
7. miles per hour _____mph *(or)* m.p.h._____

E.

Match each word in Column A with its definition in Column B. Write the letter of your answer on the line. *(6 points)*

Column A

__e__ 1. detour

__a__ 2. young

__f__ 3. couple

__c__ 4. scour

__b__ 5. sour

__d__ 6. thousand

Column B

a. not old

b. having a sharp, strong taste, like a lemon

c. to scrub; to rub hard

d. 10 × 100

e. a roundabout route that takes the place of the main route

f. two

F.

Divide these words into syllables. Mark the vowels in each syllable *long* (¯), *short* (˘), or *schwa* (ə). *(6 points)*

		First syllable	Second syllable
1.	panic	păn	ĭc
2.	lotto	lŏt	tō
3.	item	ī	tĕm
4.	extra	ĕx	trȧ
5.	comet	cŏm	ĕt
6.	adapt	ȧ	dăpt

G.

Read this paragraph:

Do you like (ghost) (stories)? If you do, you're not (alone). (Most) of us love creepy tales about monsters, demons, and vampires. Many times, these (stories) take place in a graveyard on a foggy night or during a thunderstorm on a (lonely) (road). We wait for the (moment) when something spine-chilling will happen.

Read the paragraph again and circle all the words that contain the sound of long **o**. *(8 points)*

H.

Fill in each blank with the correct word. *(4 points)*

1. The root word of *happiness* is _____happy_____ .

2. The root word of *unwashable* is _____wash_____ .

3. The root word of *rehired* is _____hire_____ .

4. The root word of *unsnapping* is _____snap_____ .

I.

In each row, circle the SIGHT WORD. *(2 points)*

1. about   mouth   (doubt)   cloud   pouch
2. restless   sleepiness   darkness   (business)   sadness

J.

Listen, then circle the word that the teacher says. *(3 points)*

(TEACHER'S CHOICE)

1. house   hose   whose
2. shut   shot   shout
3. bought   bout   boat

Name _____Key_____

A.

Join each root word and its affix or affixes. (8 points)

1. fate + al = _____fatal_____

2. noise + y = _____noisy_____

3. try + al = _____trial_____

4. mis + use + ing = _____misusing_____

5. en + joy + able = _____enjoyable_____

6. mis + spell + ed = _____misspelled_____

7. re + move + al = _____removal_____

8. for + give + en = _____forgiven_____

B.

The word **except** means "leaving out." All of the words in the list below are compound words except two. Circle the words that are not compounds. (2 points)

doorway   noontime   (shampoo)   bathroom
ballpoint   cookbook   waterproof   (rooster)

C.

Divide these words into syllables with a slash (/). (8 points)

1. noodle _____noo / dle_____

2. avoid _____a / void_____

3. cartoon _____car / toon_____

4. boycott _____boy / cott_____

5. sarcastic _____sar / cas / tic_____

6. October _____Oc / to / ber_____

7. example _____ex / am / ple_____

8. stepladder _____step / lad / der_____

D.

Draw a line from each word in the left column to a word that means the OPPOSITE in the right column. *(4 points)*

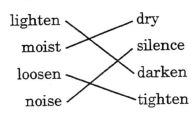

lighten   dry

moist   silence

loosen   darken

noise   tighten

E.

Fill in each blank with a word from the list below. *(5 points)*

hood	mood	roof	too	two

1. Fans at the football game were in a cheerful _____mood_____ .

2. Woody raised the _____hood_____ of the pickup and checked the oil.

3. Those _____two_____ young boys were asked not to loiter in front of the store.

4. "It's going to rain," he said, looking at the darkening sky. "I'd better fix that hole in the _____roof_____ ."

5. "It's _____too_____ warm in this classroom," complained the student.

F.

These sentences are "scrambled." On the line below each scrambled sentence, write it in correct order. *(2 points)*

1. restrooms is the Smoking in prohibited

   Smoking is prohibited in the restrooms.

2. you are for good Vegetables

   Vegetables are good for you.

G.

Below is a list of words. Write the correct word on the line after its definition. *(7 points)*

choose	currency	loose	poison	prohibit	stood	took

1. Cash; money   _____currency_____

2. The past tense of *take*   _____took_____

3. Not tight   _____loose_____

4. To forbid; to prevent   _____prohibit_____

5. To pick out; to select   _____choose_____

6. The past tense of *stand*   _____stood_____

7. A substance that can injure or kill   _____poison_____

H.

Correct this sentence. Add capital letters and punctuation marks. *(1 point)*

   I   M   M   B   K   C   N
i visited mr. and mrs. boyden in kansas city last november.

I.

Complete each sentence with a word that has the same meaning as the words under the line. (The new word must begin with the affix **dis-**.) *(3 points)*

1. Why did the judge _____disagree_____ with the jury?
                    (not agree)

2. The witness was _____dishonest_____ about what he told in court.
                  (not honest)

3. Did the court _____discontinue_____ that case?
             (not continue)

J.

Read this paragraph:

Many large cities in the (United) States have an (employment) development office. This office is a branch, or (department), of the state (government). If you are (unemployed), this (agency) can help you find a job. Also, there are programs that provide job training and job placement.

In the paragraph above, circle all three-syllable words. *(6 points)*

K.

Listen, then circle the word that the teacher says. *(3 points)*

(TEACHER'S CHOICE)

1.	muss	mouse	moss	moose
2.	all	oil	ail	ill
3.	shoot	shout	shot	shut

A.

Read these sentences. Circle all NOUNS. *(5 points)*

1. That (author) wrote five (books).

2. A (mechanic) fixes the (brakes) on my (car).

B.

Fill in each blank with a word from the list below. *(6 points)*

ache	daughter	Earth	health	heavy	plead

1. Spicy food gives me a stomach ____ache____ .

2. ____Earth____ is the fifth largest planet in our solar system.

3. Did the defendant ____plead____ "not guilty"?

4. His ____daughter____ is a member of the city council.

5. Smoking is dangerous to your ____health____ .

6. A "bulldozer" is a big, ____heavy____ , earth-moving machine.

C.

If **ch** sounds like / ch /, write CH on the line.
If **ch** sounds like / k /, write K on the line.
If **ch** sounds like / sh /, write SH on the line. *(5 points)*

1. sandwich ___CH___

2. mechanic ___K___

3. chilly ___CH___

4. chrome ___K___

5. parachute ___SH___

D.

In Row 1, circle the word that follows **real**. In Row 2, circle the word that is followed by **juice**. *(2 points)*

1.   seat   cream   real   (heart)   peaceful

2.   fruit   suit   (build)   juice   recruit

E.

Divide these words into syllables with a slash (/). *(6 points)*

1. wriggle   ___wrig / gle___   4. season   ___sea / son___

2. applause   ___ap / plause___   5. heatstroke ___heat / stroke___

3. headache   ___head / ache___   6. because   ___be / cause___

F.

Read this paragraph: *(5 points)*

Heatstroke is caused by extreme sweating and the loss of body salt. The skin becomes hot, dry, and red. The heart beats rapidly. A victim of heatstroke may become dizzy and faint. A cold bath is one good treatment for heatstroke. If a bath is not available, the victim should be rubbed with cold water or alcohol. Heatstroke can be prevented. During very hot weather, people should drink lots of liquid and eat salted food.

1. Name three things that are likely to happen if a person gets heatstroke.

   ___The skin becomes hot, dry, and red.___

   ___The heart beats rapidly.___

   ___A victim may become dizzy and faint.___

2. A good treatment for heatstroke is ___a cold bath.___

3. In hot weather, heatstroke can be prevented by ___drinking lots of___

   ___liquid and eating salted food.___

G.

Below is a list of homophones. Write the correct word on the line after its definition. *(6 points)*

| meet | meat | steel | steal | week | weak |

1. The flesh of animals used as food   __meat__

2. To be introduced; to come together; to encounter   __meet__

3. A strong metal   __steel__

4. To rob; to take by theft   __steal__

5. Not strong   __weak__

6. Seven days   __week__

H.

On the line next to each word, write the SOUND of the **ea** combination. *(6 points)*

Example: eat __ē__   head __ĕ__   great __ā__

    1. team __ē__   4. break __ā__

    2. dead __ĕ__   5. heaven __ĕ__

    3. each __ē__   6. reason __ē__

I.

All but two of the words in the list below contain SILENT CONSONANTS. Circle those two consonants. *(2 points)*

wrong   often   knife   limb   (blimp)

knuckle   comb   (remark)   wreck   listen   knob

1.

Read this paragraph:

(Tombstone) is a small city in (Arizona) that is a popular tourist center. (Over) one hundred years (ago), (gold) and silver were mined here. Large-scale mining ended by 1890 because water flooded the mines. Today, people visit "Boot Hill" to see the graves of the Earp brothers and then Clanton gang. These men killed one another in a rip-(roaring), (Old) West gun battle.

In the paragraph above, circle the words that contain the long **o** sound. *(7 points)*

A.

Join each root word and its affix or affixes. *(6 points)*

1. friend   +   ly   +   ness   =   _____friendliness_____

2. dawdle   +   ing   =   _____dawdling_____

3. grow   +   en   =   _____grown_____

4. weird   +   est   =   _____weirdest_____

5. achieve   +   ment   =   _____achievement_____

6. draw   +   en   =   _____drawn_____

B.

Correct these sentences. Add capital letters and punctuation marks.
(3 points)

1. H̶ow much weight have you lost since A̶ugust?

2. I̶n the downtown district of N̶ew Y̶ork C̶ity the traffic is awful.

3. W̶hy didn't M̶r. S̶awyer call me yesterday?

C.

Fill in each blank with a word from the list below. *(6 points)*

allow	either	known	receipt	shown	yield

1. When turning onto Main Street, all vehicles must _____yield_____
    the right-of-way.

2. You may have _____either_____ clam chowder or oyster stew for supper.

3. During the summer months, reruns are _____shown_____ on TV.

4. Did the cashier give you a _____receipt_____ ?

5. My neighbor doesn't _____allow_____ his dogs to run loose.

6. How long have you _____known_____ that lawyer?

D.

PRONOUNS are substitutes for nouns. Rewrite the paragraph on the lines below. Substitute the correct pronoun for the words that are underlined. *(3 points)*

Many stories have been written about Billy the Kid, who was an out-law in the old Southwest. His real name was William H. Bonney. During his brief lifetime, <u>Billy the Kid</u> shot and killed twenty-one men. <u>Billy the Kid</u> killed his first victim in Fort Grant, New Mexico, in 1878. Billy the Kid was only twenty-two years old when <u>Billy the Kid</u> was shot to death by a sheriff in 1881.

Many stories have been written about Billy the Kid, who was an outlaw in the old Southwest. His real name was William H. Bonney. During his brief lifetime, he shot and killed twenty-one men. He killed his first victim in Fort Grant, New Mexico, in 1878. Billy the Kid was only twenty-two years old when he was shot to death by a sheriff in 1881.

E.

In Row 1, circle the word that precedes **owl**.
In Row 2, circle the word that follows **shower**.
In Row 3, circle the word that is followed by **owl**.
In Row 4, circle the word that is preceded by **towel**. *(4 points)*

1.	towel	(shower)	owl	downtown
2.	towel	shower	(owl)	downtown
3.	towel	(shower)	owl	downtown
4.	towel	(shower)	owl	downtown

F.

Divide these words into syllables with a slash (/). *(6 points)*

1. believe   __be / lieve__   4. protein   __pro / tein__

2. shadow   __shad / ow__   5. curfew   __cur / few__

3. achieve   __a / chieve__   6. lawyer   __law / yer__

G.

Complete these analogies. *(4 points)*

1. *Night* is to *day* as *dusk* is to __dawn__ .

2. *Grasshopper* is to *insect* as *hawk* is to __bird__ .

3. *Louse* is to *lice* as *mouse* is to __mice__ .

4. *Doctor* is to *hospital* as *lawyer* is to __court(house)__ .

H.

Below is a list of homophones. Choose one of the homophones to fill each blank. *(4 points)*

eight	know	their	weigh
ate	no	there	way

1. They each __ate__ two pieces of pie with vanilla ice cream.

2. Do you __know__ the answer to this math problem?

3. Put that small table over __there__ in the corner.

4. How much do you __weigh__ ?

I.

On the line next to each word, write the vowel sound for the **ei** combination. *(6 points)*

Example: receipt __$\bar{e}$__   eight __$\bar{a}$__

1. neighbor __$\bar{a}$__   4. vein __$\bar{a}$__

2. either __$\bar{e}$__   5. ceiling __$\bar{e}$__

3. weigh __$\bar{a}$__   6. receive __$\bar{e}$__

I.

Read this paragraph: *(4 points)*

Caffein is a bitter-tasting substance that is found in coffee, tea, choco-late, and most cola soft drinks. Caffein can produce harmful side effects in some people. For example, it may cause a person to breathe faster. It may cause the heart to beat more rapidly. Some people say that caffein prevents them from sleeping. For these reasons, caffein-free products now are being sold in most supermarkets across the country. Many coffee drinkers have switched to "decaf."

1. Name two possible side effects of caffein.

   Faster breathing / Rapid heartbeat / Inability to sleep

   (Answers may vary.)

2. Does caffein keep all people awake at night? ___No___

3. One of these words is the ANTONYM for bitter. Circle it.

   salty　　(sweet)　　harmful　　soft

4. The paragraph above has these five words that contain the ea combination:

   tea　　breathe　　(heart)　　beat　　reasons

   One word is a SIGHT WORD. Circle it.

K.

Listen, then circle the word that the teacher says. *(4 points)*

(TEACHER'S CHOICE)

1. filled　　filed　　field　　failed　　fooled
2. nice　　niece　　noise　　nose　　noose
3. priced　　pressed　　priest　　praised　　prized
4. hook　　hock　　hawk　　hack　　hike

A.

Fill in each blank with a word from the list below. *(6 points)*

addictive chairperson damage directions military primary

1. Ms. Clary is the __chairperson__ of the committee.

2. For the right dosage, always read the __directions__ on the label of a bottle of aspirin.

3. How much __damage__ did the earthquake cause?

4. The Red Cross helps members of the __military__ and their families.

5. A child's education is a __primary__ concern of parents.

6. Drugs can be __addictive__ .

B.

Follow the directions. *(3 points)*

1. In the list below, circle the month that precedes **July**.

2. Underline the month that is followed by **March**.

3. Cross out the month that is preceded by **October**.

January   <u>February</u>   March   April   May   (June)

July   August   September   October   ~~November~~   December

C.

In each row of words, circle *two* words that have the SAME meaning. *(3 points)*

1. sorrow   (love)   hate   (affection)

2. (conversation)   protect   silence   (talk)

3. unemployment   (profession)   (career)   style

D.

This paragraph contains 3 sentences. Add the missing capital letters and punctuation. *(6 points)*

    L̸arry is a construction worker. H̸e works on high-rise buildings, and his job is sometimes very dangerous. H̸is wife wants him to find another occupation.

E.

Join each word and its ending affix. *(10 points)*

1.	forgot	+	en	=	forgotten
2.	bag	+	age	=	baggage
3.	refer	+	ed	=	referred
4.	fury	+	ous	=	furious
5.	operate	+	ion	=	operation
6.	marry	+	age	=	marriage
7.	suffer	+	ing	=	suffering
8.	fame	+	ous	=	famous
9.	omit	+	ed	=	omitted
10.	vary	+	ous	=	various

F.

Read this paragraph. (Circle) all nouns. Underline all pronouns. *(7 points)*

    (Clare) started working at the (library) in (February). *(3 nouns)* She works part-time. *(1 pronoun)* After (July) she will begin working full-time as a (secretary). *(2 nouns and 1 pronoun)*